Weston Park

The Marble Staircase at Weston Park. (Paul Highnam/Trustees of the Weston Park Foundation.)

Weston Park

The House, the Families and the Influence

Gareth Williams

THE BOYDELL PRESS

WESTON PARK

First published 2022
The Boydell Press, Woodbridge

ISBN 978 1 78327 612 7

The Boydell Press is an imprint of Boydell & Brewer Ltd
PO Box 9, Woodbridge, Suffolk IP12 3DF, UK
and of Boydell & Brewer Inc.
668 Mt Hope Avenue, Rochester, NY 14620–2731, USA
website: www.boydellandbrewer.com

A CIP catalogue record for this book is available
from the British Library

The publisher has no responsibility for the continued existence or accuracy of URLs for
external or third-party internet websites referred to in this book, and does not guarantee
that any content on such websites is, or will remain, accurate or appropriate

This publication is printed on acid-free paper

To the Creators of Weston Park, to its Guardians
and in Memory of
Rose Paterson,
Trustee of the Weston Park Foundation and its Chairman 2014–2019

Contents

Illustrations

CHAPTER FOUR   *The Early Bridgemans*

CHAPTER FIVE *Georgian Weston*

CHAPTER SIX   *The Early Nineteenth Century*

CHAPTER SEVEN   *A Changing World*

CHAPTER EIGHT *The Reign of Victoria*

CHAPTER NINE *Edwardian Weston*

CHAPTER TEN *The Reality of the Twentieth Century*

CHAPTER ELEVEN   *The Weston Park Foundation*

The author and publisher are grateful to all the institutions and individuals listed for permission to reproduce the materials in which they hold copyright. Every effort has been made to trace the copyright holders; apologies are offered for any omission, and the publisher will be pleased to add any necessary acknowledgement in subsequent editions.

KENSINGTON PALACE
LONDON W8 4PU

We are fortunate in this country that so much that was created by previous generations is still with us, whether Castles or Cathedrals, and we can visit them and appreciate what impressed in centuries past.

Many of the finest houses were built in the centre of rural estates, where the owners were leaders of the communities and were traditionally the custodians of law and order.

Weston Park is just such an example of a splendid building set in a well nurtured park and filled with the treasures that appealed to the owners as taste evolved from century to century.

This book explains how the great house came to exist and what succeeding generations brought to its splendour. Inevitably my interest is focused on the extensive collections of family portraits, as my mother's mother was brought up at Weston, together with my many Bridgeman cousins.

The popularity of 'Downton Abbey' has shown how a great house reacts to good times and bad, and Weston too had its ups and downs with the many different characters who controlled its destiny.

I hope all who read the book will find the story reveals more than just the history of bricks and mortar.

Acknowledgements

A book about Weston Park, its collections, supporting estates and family would not have been possible without the interest and assistance from the descendants of the 'founders of the feast'. I would, therefore, particularly like to thank the present Earl of Bradford, Viscount Newport, the Hon. Charles Bridgeman, John Bridgeman, Mark Bridgeman and Constantine Bridgeman for their help in many ways and for their interest throughout my protracted researches for this book. It is a sadness that other relations of the family are no longer with us to see the emergence of the publication, notably Mary Kenyon-Slaney (née Bridgeman) whose recollections of the house and of her grandmother, the 4th Earl's Countess, brought life and added interest to written accounts. Her late husband Simon – himself a descendant of the 3rd Earl and Countess – was likewise a source of helpful fact and anecdote.

The Weston Park Foundation, the house's owner and guardian, has been a great supporter of this work and its former chairmen William Montgomery and also the late Rose Paterson have been especially encouraging. Without Rose this book would never have been written. The current chairman Christina Kenyon-Slaney and chief executive Colin Sweeney have continued to champion the need for the publication and have enabled its necessary resources, for which I am particularly grateful.

In terms of research on Weston Park and its associated histories, a great debt is owed to the team at Staffordshire Records Office, where much of the Bradford collection is lodged. There, I would thank Thea Randall, and her successor Joanna Terry, as county archivists, and Rebecca Jackson, archivist responsible for the Bradford MS. Rebecca's knowledge of the collection and her dexterity in coordinating its cataloguing is, frankly, breath-taking. Work on the papers and an ongoing interest in Weston and its people has been tirelessly undertaken over many years by June Ellis, and it has now also been taken up by Joy Pownall; June and Joy's transcriptions and knowledge of the sources have underpinned this book and every reader owes them an incalculable debt of gratitude. Dorothy Lloyd has shared her researches into the Bridgeman family and the First World War. Philip and Marianne van Dael have generously made accessible their journals of Lady Charlotte Bridgeman, transcribing them and those of the University of Birmingham. They have made them available to all online and have now gifted the original journals to Staffordshire Archives. Gareth Glover has also been kind in assisting with information about the Hon. Orlando Bridgeman, ADC to Lord Hill, whose letters he has transcribed and published.

I have been appreciative of the assistance of Mary MacKenzie and of Sarah Davies and the team at Shropshire Archives. I am also grateful for assistance in research to: Dr Dianne Barre, Catherine, Lady Forester, Thomas Galifot, Amanda Bock, Roger and the late Wendy Taylor. The late Julia Ionides and Peter Howell's Dog Rose Georgians' Bradford Study Weekend, held in 2009, did much to stimulate interest in the multidisciplinary study of the Bradford family across a number of sites in Shropshire and Staffordshire and – post mortem – I pay deep tribute to Julia's brilliance and never-failing humour in doing this.

My most recent predecessors as curator at Weston Park – the late Michael Tebbutt and Keith Verrell – generously shared their infectious interest and enthusiasm for the house, helping to induct me in the importance of the place and its collection. Keith's meticulous record-keeping and distinctive handwritten notes remain a stellar guide. Katherine Dowd, Julieanne McMahon, Chris Madeley, Alison Poole, Claire Cumming and Andrea Webster have also, in various ways, provided collegiate assistance over the last few years. I have also been deeply appreciative of the assistance of Gill Gardiner, for her help with editing and dealing with matters which at times must have been extremely tiresome. She and all of the volunteer team at Weston Park have all been strong in their encouragement. The Balfours team, who manage Weston Park have been particularly helpful; Michael Evans was agent from the Foundation's inception and his information about that period has been invaluable. I am grateful to current custodians Rory Galliers, James Trant and Tabitha Denny-Northover. Vicky Kershaw at Balfours has kindly produced the map of the park.

At Walsall I have been assisted by Mike Glasson; at Bolton by the late Elizabeth Tatman, Ray Jefferson and the Bolton Documentary Photography team; at Wigan by Pat Roscoe, Phil Clarke, the late Anthony Grimshaw, Rev. Canon Ray Hutchinson, former Rector of Wigan and now Rev. Will Gibbons, and Kenneth Talbot. At Chester Cathedral, Canon Jeremy Dussek kindly permitted me to see the portrait of Bishop John Bridgeman.

Where the picture collection is concerned, I would extend my thanks to a number of specialists, not least to Ann Massing, Dr Mary Kempski, Dr Christine Kimbriel and the director Rupert Featherstone at the Hamilton Kerr Institute, whose long-term care of the Weston Park collection has enabled a far greater understanding of the works. Dr Mary Beal's rediscovery of the Lely portrait of Richard Symonds was supported by Diana Dethloff whilst the collection as a whole has benefitted from information supplied by the delegates of the National Portrait Gallery's Understanding British Portraits Network, who visited the house and made a number of helpful observations in 2017. The understanding of what still remains at Weston Park of the great Newport collection owes greatly to the scholarly researches of Sally Goodsir. Sally dedicated many weeks to establishing – from the vaguest of eighteenth-century inventory descriptions – as to what was still in the house and, indeed, what could now be found globally in other collections, and she has continued to make discoveries since her initial work.

A number of architectural historians have made valuable contributions to the understanding of Weston Park's complex architectural evolution, but none more so than Richard Hewlings, whose elucidation of the development of the house began when he was evaluating the house for English Heritage (as then was) and the National Heritage Memorial Fund (NHMF) in 1984 and he has continued to take an active interest. John Goodall, too, engaged his interest for an article written by Richard in *Country Life* and has helped question the development of house and St Andrew's church in a learned way. Other specialists have been generous in their information for the house and its collections and I should especially like to thank: Andrew Arrol, Chris Pickford, Dr David Wilson, James Lomax, Adam Bowett, Judith Wensley, Miranda Goodby, Gaye Blake-Roberts, Dr Ian West, Professor Marilyn Palmer, Dr Diana Davis, Dr Martin Perkins, Margaret Pritchard, Laura Pass Barry, Professor Kenneth Quickenden, Christopher Rowell, Geoffrey Fisher, Dame Rosalind Savill and Dr Malcolm Dick.

The understanding of the park and garden landscape has been aided by Todd Longstaffe-Gowan, Patrick James, Dr Paul Stamper, the late Fiona Grant, Dr Tim Mowl, Advolly Richmond, Dr Elaine Mitchell, Steffie Shields, John Phibbs, and Ceryl Evans, whose leadership of CB300 unlocked many doors.

The interior decorators who have worked on Weston Park in recent years have been courteous and helpful in sharing their schemes and thought processes. I would particularly thank: Caroline Lawson of Chelsea Decorators; Janie Money of Sibyl Colefax & John Fowler and her colleague Trudi Ballard; Shirley Guy; John Fullick; Rita Konig; Lucinda Griffith. I am grateful to Catherine Hassall for her paint analysis in a number of rooms in 2010 and also to Camilla Evans for the work that she undertook in 2009–10 in determining the various incarnations of the drawing room and entrance hall at Weston Park.

In terms of the images in this book, I am particularly grateful to Paul Highnam, to Luke Unsworth, to Toby Neal of the *Shropshire Star*, and to Chris Burton at Richmond Arts Service. The image research has been superbly undertaken by Martina Phillips-Turner of the Weston Park Foundation and I am enormously grateful to her for her tenacity. Lee Cordery of Badger Print has helpfully produced a brilliantly streamlined pedigree and also the map of associated properties. A number of helpful comments were made about the initial draft and I am especially grateful to John Gregory for his perceptive observations.

I am also grateful to Dr Richard Barber and the team at Boydell & Brewer for their support and interest in the work. Rohais Landon's pre-press expertise has been especially helpful and efficient.

All of the residential cultural tour groups that visit Weston Park and many of their leaders have made observations about the house and its collections and they have aided me in seeing Weston Park from a different perspective. One is naturally proud of what one cherishes but sometimes it takes an outsider to make one truly understand the significance. Of those who have done this I would particularly thank Curt DiCamillo, Barry Greenlaw, Tom Savage, Richard Wendorf, Susan Guillia and Anthony Worcester.

Last, but by no means least, my thanks to Stacey for tolerating prolonged periods of research, writing and editing, and for making sure that the dogs were not forgotten.

Abbreviations

BA	Bolton Archives
BL	British Library
NA	National Archives
PROB	Public Records Office
SHA	Shropshire Archives
SA	Staffordshire Archives
TSANHS	*Transactions of the Shropshire Archaeological and Natural History Society*
WLHC	Walsall Local History Centre
WRO	Warwickshire Records Office

Map of Weston Park

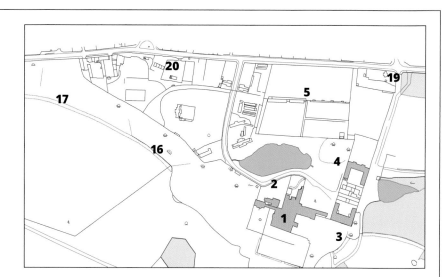

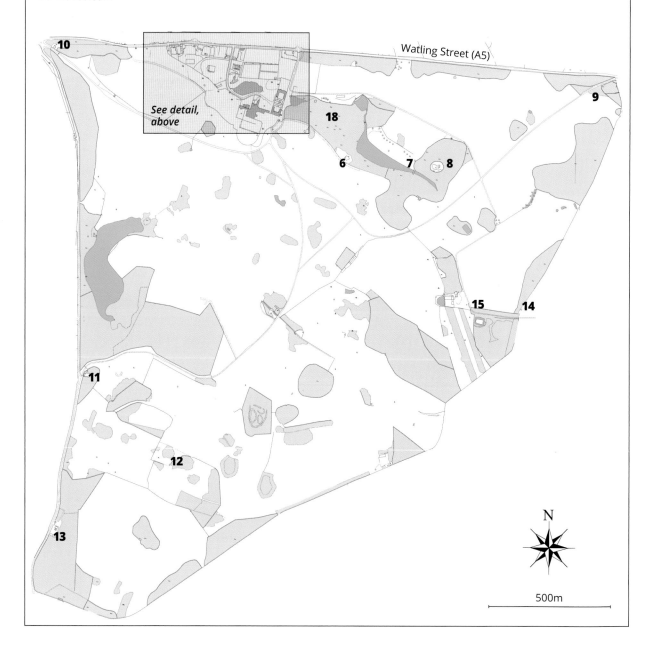

See detail, above

Watling Street (A5)

N

500m

Properties in the United Kingdom with a historical association to Weston Park and its owning families

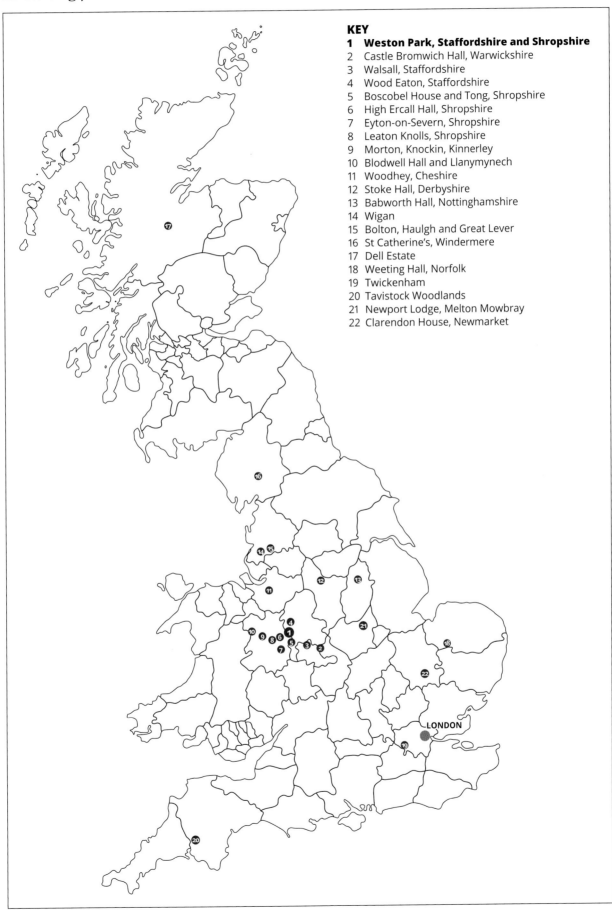

KEY
1 Weston Park, Staffordshire and Shropshire
2   Castle Bromwich Hall, Warwickshire
3   Walsall, Staffordshire
4   Wood Eaton, Staffordshire
5   Boscobel House and Tong, Shropshire
6   High Ercall Hall, Shropshire
7   Eyton-on-Severn, Shropshire
8   Leaton Knolls, Shropshire
9   Morton, Knockin, Kinnerley
10 Blodwell Hall and Llanymynech
11 Woodhey, Cheshire
12 Stoke Hall, Derbyshire
13 Babworth Hall, Nottinghamshire
14 Wigan
15 Bolton, Haulgh and Great Lever
16 St Catherine's, Windermere
17 Dell Estate
18 Weeting Hall, Norfolk
19 Twickenham
20 Tavistock Woodlands
21 Newport Lodge, Melton Mowbray
22 Clarendon House, Newmarket

LONDON

The Earls of Bradford and their ancestors

Owners of Weston Park indicated in bold

Newport family of High Ercall, Shropshire

JOHN BRIDGEMAN,
Bishop of Chester (1577–1652)
Eldest son of Thomas Bridgeman of
Greenways, Devon and Alice Jones.
Married Elizabeth Helyar (d.1636), daughter
of Rev. William Helyar

SIR ORLANDO BRIDGEMAN,
1st Bt (1608–1674) Son of Bishop
John Bridgeman. Created baronet 1660.
Married (1) in 1627/8 Judith Kynaston, daughter
of John Kynaston and heiress of Morton and
Kinnerley. Married (2) Dorothy Saunders, daughter
of John Saunders and widow of George Cradock
of Caverswall Castle, Staffs.

SIR JOHN BRIDGEMAN,
2nd Bt (1631–1710)
Son of the first baronet. Married Mary
(d.1713), daughter of George Cradock of
Caverswall Castle, Staffs

SIR JOHN BRIDGEMAN,
3rd Bt (1667–1747)
Son of the second baronet. Married in
1694 Ursula (d.1719/20), daughter and heir of
Roger Matthews of Blodwell Hall, Shropshire

LADY ANNE NEWPORT
(1690–1752)
Daughter of the 2nd Earl

═

SIR ORLANDO BRIDGEMAN,
4th Bt (1695–1764)
Eldest son of the third baronet.
Married in 1719 Lady Anne Newport

EDWARD MITTON/ MYTTON (d.1638)
Descendant, via the female line, of the
de Weston family of Weston.
Married Cicely Skeffington (d.1649).

ELIZABETH MITTON/ MYTTON,
later Lady Wilbraham (1631–1705)
Daughter of Edward Mitton.
Married 1650 Sir Thomas Wilbraham,
3rd Baronet (1630–1692)

THOMAS NEWPORT,
4th & last Earl of Bradford
of first creation
(c.1696–1762)
Third son of 2nd Earl.
Died unmarried

RICHARD NEWPORT,
1st Baron Newport (1570–1650)
Created 1st Baron Newport 1642.
Married pre 1615 Rachel Leveson, daughter
of Sir John Leveson (1555–1615)

FRANCIS NEWPORT,
2nd Baron Bradford & later 1st Earl of
Bradford (1619–1708) Eldest son of the
1st Baron. Created 1st Viscount Newport
1675, created 1st Earl of Bradford 1694.
Married in 1642 Lady Diana Russell,
daughter of the 4th Earl of Bedford

RICHARD NEWPORT,
2nd Earl of Bradford
(1644–1723)
Eldest son of the 1st Earl.
Married in 1681 **Mary Wilbraham**
(1661–1737)

HENRY NEWPORT,
3rd Earl of Bradford (1683–1734)
Eldest son of 2nd Earl. His relationship with
Anne Smyth produced an illegitimate son,
John Harrison (later Newport) to whom
he left the Newport estates, including
High Ercall & Eyton-on-Severn

SIR HENRY BRIDGEMAN, 5th Bt, later 1st Baron Bradford (1725–1800)

Son of the fourth baronet. Created 1st Baron Bradford in 1794.

Married in 1755 Elizabeth (1735–1806), daughter and heir of the
Rev. John Simpson of Stoke Hall, Derbyshire

ORLANDO BRIDGEMAN, 2nd Baron Bradford & later 1st Earl of Bradford (1762–1825)

Son of the 1st Baron. Created 1st Earl of Bradford of the second creation 1815.

Married 1788 the Hon. Lucy Byng (1766–1844), daughter of 4th Viscount Torrington

GEORGE BRIDGEMAN, 2nd Earl of Bradford (1789–1865)

Eldest son of 1st Earl. Married (1) in 1818 Georgina (1790–1842), daughter of Sir Thomas Moncreiffe of Moncreiffe Bt.

Married (2) in 1849 Helen (d.1869), daughter of Thomas Æneas Mackay of Scotston

ORLANDO BRIDGEMAN, 3rd Earl of Bradford (1819–1898)

Eldest son of 2nd Earl. Married in 1844 the Hon. Selina Forester (1819–1894), daughter of
1st Baron Forester of Willey Park, Shropshire

GEORGE BRIDGEMAN, 4th Earl of Bradford (1845–1915)

Eldest son of 3rd Earl. Married in 1869 Lady Ida Lumley (1848–1936),
daughter of 9th Earl of Scarbrough

ORLANDO BRIDGEMAN, 5th Earl of Bradford (1873–1957)

Eldest son of 4th Earl. Married in 1904 The Hon. Margaret Cecilia Bruce (1882–1949),
daughter of 2nd Baron Aberdare

GERALD BRIDGEMAN, 6th Earl of Bradford (1911–1981)

Eldest son of 5th Earl. Married in 1946 Mary Willoughby Montgomery (1918–1986)

RICHARD BRIDGEMAN, 7th Earl of Bradford (b.1947)

Eldest son of 6th Earl. Married (1) in 1979 Joanne Elizabeth Miller.

Married (2) in 2008 Dr Penelope Anne Law.

Gifted Weston Park to the Weston Park Foundation via the NHMF in 1986

Introduction

Weston Park is many things to many people. It was the ancestral home of one family, the Bridgeman Earls of Bradford, and their forebears prior to its gifting to the nation and its custodianship by the Weston Park Foundation since 1986. To the visitors who come to see the house and collection and to walk the thousand acres of its parklands and gardens, it is a place of enjoyment and recreation owned and cared for by a progressive independent charity. To the children and students who visit, it is a place of learning and inspiration. For couples who marry, it is a place of cherished memories, whilst to governments and to companies, it is a place of retreat, for focused meetings away from the noise of the modern world within an incomparable setting. In the instance of the thousands who attend large-scale events in the park, it is a place to see favourite bands, or to shop for local foods or, perhaps, to see either rally driving or horse trials. For each and every person that visits – whether they are aware of the significance of the place or not – it is a place of great beauty, of outstanding quality in its collections and with a history which, if explored, fans out through human engagement at every level into national and global history, and to a surprisingly wide range of geographical locations elsewhere in Britain.

In spite of being open to the public since 1964, Weston Park remains a beguiling and perhaps unexpected place. It was largely ignored by the seventeenth-century Staffordshire historian Robert Plot and also in 1793 by the Hon. John Byng who, when in Weston-under-Lizard, did not think that the house would have anything to show him. Even in 1945, Christopher Hussey noted that the house had been seen by very few people. It still remains hidden from view, behind its great park wall, but in reality, is as welcoming as it can be private.

Weston Park has a complicated and geographically widespread history that is as rich and as intricate in its evolution as the collections that the house contains. Today, ostensibly, when seen from the east, the house is not enormous; a comely three-storied stone-dressed brick building of nine by eleven bays, enveloped by a wooded parkland setting. It is no vast palace, and is unable to rival the likes of Blenheim or Castle Howard in a showy demonstration of scale proclaimed across miles of landscape by proud avenues. Yet with ten main ground-floor rooms and twenty-eight bedrooms – in addition to service areas and seven staff flats – it is still a sizeable country house. As it now stands, the house presents a complex architectural evolution. It did not dart impressively onto the architectural stage like, say, Derbyshire's Kedleston where Robert Adam's controlling influence created a neoclassical masterpiece that, in its architecture and decorations, is one sensational set-piece.

Weston, instead, still shields evidence of its medieval origins within its cellars, where a pair of stone arches suggest the site of a great hall above. The Restoration period witnessed the building of the house's south and east ranges with their engagingly different fronts, and its attendant eastern stable block – both structures seemingly designed by the London architect William Taylor within the careful patronage of Lady Wilbraham. The rebuilding of the parish church of St Andrew's, which nestles besides the house to the north-west – also benefitted from her patronage and attentive cost control, following shortly after a reworking of the family's Cheshire seat, Woodhey, near Nantwich. Lady Wilbraham's dynastic awareness included the rearrangement of the chancel of the church as an extraordinarily historicist assemblage of chancel window and a series of monuments which seek to demonstrate her ancestry and proud lineage. The marble monuments were, in part, the work of Sir William Wilson (1641–1710) who probably also designed the church itself. For successive generations, her work was held in high respect; early twentieth-century family members hailed her, without evidence, as an the 'architect' of the house, whilst from the opening of Weston Park to the public in the 1960s, the house was regarded as a great Restoration mansion rather than a house of any other era.

Such marketing claims, though, have failed to acknowledge the efforts of previous and later generations who have made the house what it is today. It is, in fact, a house that relies on successive generations of hereditary owners – Westons, Peshales, Myttons, Wilbrahams, Newports and Bridgemans – for all that it represents today. Whilst the facades of the Wilbraham era have remained largely intact, a late eighteenth-century renaissance of house and estate was effected by Sir Henry Bridgeman. He, moving to Weston from the Bridgeman's Warwickshire (now Birmingham) seat of Castle Bromwich, with his large and eminently sociable family, set about the transformation of the house and its setting. A man of his time, Sir Henry was aided by his capable land agent Henry Bowman, who worked in tandem for the Dukes of Devonshire. In addition to achievements at Weston, he was swift to recognise the increased industrial mineral potential of the family's estates from coal at Great Lever in Lancashire and limestone at Llanymynech in Shropshire. Together with road and canal projects, which might widen the markets of the estate's resources, and an inward investment in agricultural improvement, Sir Henry also made outward financial input towards ground-breaking technology in being a subscriber for Abraham Darby III's Iron Bridge across the River Severn and had links to several members of the Lunar Society.

At Weston, Sir Henry reinvented the house's interiors under the aegis of the architect James Paine, sweeping away the east wing's top-floor long gallery to create more bedrooms. Paine also produced designs for the multi-purpose Temple of Diana, for the Roman Bridge, and also probably for the model Palladian Home Farm (now Granary building), plus the model Roman barn and farm at Woodlands. The house's setting was transformed by Lancelot 'Capability' Brown, whose two contracts and recently rediscovered map make clear the importance of his work. This included the rare proposition of two pleasure grounds for morning and evening amenity – Shrewsbury Walk to the west and Temple Wood to the east – and an immense kitchen garden, which still survives, with its classical pinery pavilions.

Just as Lady Wilbraham's imperious Lely portrait still presides from the drawing room wall, Sir Henry's jovial countenance appears throughout the house, his clubby character brought out in no fewer than five portraits at Weston. With house guests who included the Ladies of Llangollen, Anna Seward – the so-called Swan of Lichfield – and the Edgeworth family, Sir Henry and his family also entertained at their own theatre in the park and he endowed the house with some of its greatest treasures from pre-eminent English and French makers. The house already contained a significant portion of one of the great London art collections that had been formed by Sir Henry's great-grandfather Francis Newport, 1st Earl of Bradford of the first creation and by his great-great uncle Thomas Newport, 1st and last Baron Torrington. In spite of being composed of notable works by van Dyck, Holbein, Bassano and other old masters, the collection's rustication at Weston Park has allowed its origins and former significance to become forgotten to all but a few.

Sir Henry's son, Orlando – the eventual 1st Earl of Bradford of the second creation – and each of his successors, continued to embellish and alter the house to make it suited to the lifestyle of their generation and for receiving honoured guests. From this first Earl's associations with the Prince Regent and Mrs Fitzherbert, numerous succeeding generations had notable links to their reigning monarch, including the 3rd Earl's service to Queen Victoria in a number of roles, whilst the 4th Earl's wife Lady Ida Lumley devotedly served Queen Mary as a Lady of the Bedchamber for much of her married life, and this led to the house becoming a foil for grand entertaining. For Lady Ida and her son Orlando, the 5th Earl, this included Weston Park hosting the early part of the honeymoon of HRH Princess Mary the Princess Royal and her husband, Viscount Lascelles (later 6th Earl of Harewood).

All later owners were respectful of the Wilbraham era's external elevations, which remained largely intact and gave a cue to the style of additions throughout the house's various incarnations. Only an icing of stucco was cast over the house's exterior by the 1st Earl in the first decade of the nineteenth century – removed by the 5th Earl and Countess in circa 1930 – distracting from the vermilion brick and locally quarried stone of the seventeenth-century works. Although the nineteenth-century possessors of Weston made sweeping changes to accommodate the additional guests and servants of house parties that the advent of the railways allowed, all were accommodated within the house's walls. Only the easterly Victorian wing, which extends to greet the visitor arriving to the present front door, and an arched-windowed orangery on the west, provided any significant visible extension of the house. On the north side, the lime-washed service quarters extended at slight angles to the main house, maintaining the dynamic momentum of the household within and providing employment in the third quarter of the nineteenth century for up to forty servants at a time.

The conservatism of the house's external elevations does not mean that Weston Park has ever stood still. It is no Calke Abbey, a house that time forgot, where generation followed generation by closing the door on their predecessors' rooms to start afresh elsewhere and leaving an antiquated house as a result. Until the early twentieth century, as a result of its large and varied estate interests, Weston Park always had funds and always looked to the future, reinventing itself along the way. This has always made the house feel a part of its own significant heritage and yet relevant for the present generation, a mantra which continues to be the case to this day.

As with all country houses, Weston Park was built for hospitality: a place for house parties, for eating and drinking and for celebrations. It was a show place and a backdrop to gatherings, where its collections could be seen to advantage. It was never intended to be simply an art gallery or repository of the arts set in a rural location, but has always been a vital part of a wider world that has, historically, grown up around it as a result of the direct drive and ambition of its owners. Yet, since 1986, the house has ceased to be owned by the Earls of Bradford, having – with its collections and park of a thousand acres – been gifted to the nation with assistance from the National Heritage Memorial Fund following the death of the 6th Earl of Bradford in 1981. At that point it became separated from its historic landed estate which had left a topographical footprint in Shropshire, Staffordshire, Warwickshire, Lancashire, Cumbria and Devonshire. The estate had, however, defined the house and vice versa. Objects in the house to this day make reference to the connections between these various different places and the people. Some are to be expected, like illuminated addresses that were gifted on the occasions of marriages or attainment of majorities. Others, though, are more individual and pay testimony to a close bond between Weston Park's owning family and their tenants or employees.

Whilst many houses reflect their supporting surrounding estates, Weston Park is unusual for its web of connections that link the house to more distant and diverse localities within Britain. Like so many country houses, its parklands were enveloped by a broad agricultural acreage, that ebbed and flowed with the generations, and, as one might expect for aristocratic owners, there were London townhouses too. What makes Weston more unusual are the number of distant urban communities that its landholdings contained and which, in turn, were created from steady accumulations by inheritance, as other families came to unite with the owners of Weston Park by marriage. In addition to Walsall – located in the same historic county as Weston Park – the owners had strong connections and influence with the Lancashire towns of Bolton and Wigan. At Bolton, the association came by purchase in the seventeenth century, at a time when the town's minerals and inklings of industrial expansion made the town a useful economic asset for the Bridgeman family. In the case of Wigan, the association came through the purchase of the Rectory in the seventeenth century, which brought the unusual benefits of manorial lands and rights – of what was historically an exceptionally rich rectory with control over the town itself – into the hands of the family and their appointed rectors. For the Bridgemans, these assets were not simply there to be ruthlessly exploited, but the individual towns themselves gained benefits from careful stewardship under several generations of skilled agents. Improved transport links, model town planning, churches, schools, hospitals, parks and beneficial supportive societies formed a part of the social flux in each of the towns, with benefits finding their way back to Weston Park. These riches were not simply financial, but included architects and other professionals who brought their skills to bear on the home estate.

Even before the gifting of Weston Park to the nation in 1986, twentieth-century taxation had already severed many of the house's links to its supporting urban estates, with sales of freeholds and a focus on the core estate. The ties were not wholly cut, though, and for the Weston Park Foundation there yet remain connections with each of the distant estates which have been maintained and have been periodically celebrated by lectures, exhibitions and educational activities.

The Foundation, which today offers daily free access to part of Weston Park via the Granary Art Gallery and Brasserie, which it developed from 2009 with National Lottery Heritage Fund and regional development agency assistance, is in many ways unusual in being a self-contained conservation and educational charity. It preserves Weston Park through the strategic development of commercial activities that take place within Weston's park wall and which, in turn, drive the place forward as a result of their income and public engagement. The range of these activities bring ever-changing scenes to Weston Park and ever more diverse audiences. As the clock marches forwards, this means that Weston Park's history, its interpretation and its contemporary connections have never been more important to its future success.

CHAPTER ONE

Dramatis Personae

Weston Park's setting is an ancient landscape of many layers, just as complicated and rich in its make-up as is the pedigree of those who have lived there. The King and Queen Oak of the southern part of the park – ancient, gnarled stag-headed trees that appear almost suspended between immortality and sudden death – have their seeding some five hundred years or more back in history. The visible signs of an earlier age, beyond the seventeenth-century reinvention of the house and the late eighteenth-century landscaping of the park, are not so obvious, having been absorbed into later owners' Arcadian

FIGURE 1 The King Oak in Weston Park in a photograph of 1893. This veteran tree still stands, with another known as the Queen Oak, in the southern part of the current park. Accession number 117.0075. (Copyright Trustees of the Weston Park Foundation.)

visions for which land-moving on a massive scale, enclosure of heathland and the rerouting of roads were, to later generations, apparently easily accomplished. Yet, the evidence of the last thousand years is there and is sometimes in plain sight, accounting for how the place existed and how its occupants came to live and thrive at Weston.

The most obvious of the early evidence is Watling Street, the Roman road which later came to be defined as the A5, and which originally connected Dover to Wroxeter – the Roman Viroconium – in Shropshire. Wroxeter is just twenty miles from Weston and it later came to be a possession of the Newport family who, in the late seventeenth century, were to be associated with Weston and remained its owners until the second half of the eighteenth century. Yet of Weston in the Roman times little is known. Was there a pagan shrine at the site of the present Church of St Andrew? Did the place even have any occupants, or was it yet another swathe of dense woodland of the Brewood Forest on a road through the heart of England? At present neither the archaeological nor the documentary evidence is forthcoming of an answer.[1]

A greater enlightenment can be found in documentary resources of the medieval era, when Weston – the 'western town' – gave its name to the chief family that lived there. The place came to bear the distinctive additional descriptive of 'Weston-under-Lizard' from the village's position close to the long, low hill known as The Lizard, which distinguished this particular Weston from the numerous other villages of that name across England. The eponymous family of Weston laid the genealogical foundations of the dynasty that ultimately descended through the female line to the Peshall family, and then to the Myttons, the Wilbrahams, the Newports (Earls of Bradford of the first creation), and most recently to the Bridgemans (Earls of Bradford of the second creation). Of the surviving landscape features and built heritage of this epoch, little can now be found, although the remnants of ridge and furrow fields, in the park to the south of the present house, which can be seen in raking early morning light, might be survivors of the subsistence of the open-field farming of the medieval occupiers.

Sir Hamo de Weston was recorded at Weston in circa 1176, and it has been suggested that he was descended from the Domesday owner of the property, Rainald de Bagiole or Bailleul.[2] The evidence for this is disputed, though, and

FIGURE 2 The view to the long low hill, known as The Lizard, from Tong Knoll, the highest point in the present Weston Park. (Photo: Dr Paul Stamper.)

FIGURE 4 The medieval tower of the parish church of St Andrew at Weston-under-Lizard. Still the parish church, the manor
house site is immediately adjacent. (Paul Highnam/Copyright Trustees of the Weston Park Foundation.)

it seems more likely that Hamo was in fact a tenant or a mesne lord under the Fitz Alan family.[3] He is referenced as one of four knights who were summoned to elect a jury at Lichfield in 1199, in the reign of King John, and, again, was summoned to elect a jury in 1212.[4] By 1214, though, Hamo had died and John de Weston was involved in a law suit with Agnes, Hamo's widow, over her dower.

Hamo's oaken effigy reclines now against the south wall of the chancel of St Andrew's church.[5] The effigy has been restored and probably repositioned from an apse on the northern side of the nave as a part of Lady Wilbraham's late seventeenth- and early eighteenth-century reorganisation of the church's chancel to assert her own dynastic right to the estate, when she evidently had the sculpture repainted.[6] The inscription on a tablet that now accompanies the monument suggests his lineage as her ladyship wished it to be known: 'Sir Hamo de Weston, Knight of the Order of Templars, father of Robert and Osbert, grandfather to John, great grandfather to Sir Hugh, Knight, departed this life about the year mclxxxviij.'

There is uncertainty about the exact succession at Weston, although opposite Sir Hamo in the church chancel rests another oaken effigy which is said to commemorate Sir Hugh de Weston, the grandson – or perhaps great-grandson – of Sir Hamo. Sir Hugh died prior to 1305 and at this time the manor of Weston and the vill of Newton were recorded as including the house, garden, dovecot, and also two fish ponds.[7]

Sir Hugh's son John was twenty-eight years old in 1305 and was knighted in the following year by the Prince of Wales (the eventual King Edward II).[8] He is known to have served in France in 1340. He married twice: first to Isabella Bromley (d.1317), and second to Isolda, daughter of William de Newton, and he had progeny by both wives. The children of the second marriage became distinct family lines of Westons from Rugeley and Lichfield.

Sir John died in 1349, and he was followed to the grave in the following year by his son Sir Thomas, Sir Thomas's son Robert, and also by a younger son John de Weston. These deaths brought about an end to the male de Weston line and it seems likely that the Black Death may have been the cause. Certainly, female members of the medieval household would have been less exposed to contact with others and the risk of plague and so, in 1349, the property was divided into five equal parts between the five daughters of Sir John de Weston and Isabella Bromley. Eventually the manor of Weston was reunited by Adam de Peshale or Peshall (d.1419) who had married in circa 1362, as his first wife, Elizabeth de Weston (d.c.1366), one of Sir John and Lady de Weston's daughters.[9] Elizabeth had been previously married to Sir John de Whyston and, during his time, a deed of 1358 implies that, whilst the manor of Weston had a deer park and fishing pools, the manor house itself was in disrepair.[10] Sir John had evidently brought together by purchase some of the five parts of the manor as is evidenced by a deed of 1380, although this refers to the 'site of the manor', suggesting that the manor house might have been demolished.[11]

It might have been the de Weston daughters or Adam de Peshall and his wife specifically who commissioned the stained glass donor figures of Elizabeth's parents, Sir John de Weston and his first wife Isobel or Isabella Bromley, which still remain in the east window of St Andrew's church at Weston. Although much restored, the figures now kneel at the foot of a figure of St Andrew, the church's patron saint.[12] Whether the creation of the window was a part of works which extended to a rebuilding of the manor house itself is uncertain.

The Peshalls were a family that appear to have descended from the de Swynnerton family and so had emanated from the Eccleshall area, to the north of Weston. Adam Peshall's generation had made a series of advantageous marriages to Shropshire heiresses, with his elder brother Sir Richard marrying Joan, the granddaughter and heir of Sir John Chetwynd of Chetwynd near Newport, whilst another brother, Sir Hamo, married, as his first wife, Alice the daughter and heir of Sir Robert de Harley of Harley and of Willey.

Adam de Peshall was knighted in 1379 and he served as Sheriff of Shropshire in 1398 and, later, as Sheriff of Staffordshire, in 1418. After Elizabeth de Weston's death, following what might have been just four years of marriage, he married a second time, to Elizabeth (died circa 1384), the daughter and co-heir of Sir Philip ap Rees and widow of Sir Henry Mortimer of Chelmarsh. Although the marriage further enriched de Peshall's possessions, it did not

FIGURE 6 The effigy said to represent Sir Hugh de Weston, of 1304, set into an arched recess on the south wall of the chancel of St Andrew's church. (Paul Highnam/Copyright Trustees of the Weston Park Foundation.)

produce an heir. By his third wife, though, Sir Adam had two daughters and heiresses. Their mother was Joyce or Jocosa (d.1420), the daughter and eventual co-heir of Sir John de Bottetort, a knight from Weoley in Herefordshire, whom Adam married in 1388. Both Joyce and Adam Peshall appear to have been commemorated by alabaster monuments in St Andrew's church at Weston – she with a gravestone in the chancel engraved with her portrait and he with a tomb on the south side of the chancel that depicted a man in armour with the arms of Peshall. These were recorded by Sir William Dugdale in notes of the 22 September 1663 but have long since disappeared.[13]

The couple's two daughters were Joan and Margaret. Joan married Sir William de Birmingham (d.1426), who had inherited the estates of his cousin Sir John de Birmingham at Birmingham, and these were further enriched by Joan's inheritance of Tamhorn and properties at Rugeley and Handsacre. Weston-under-Lizard, together with Blymhill, Newton and Bobbington, was to pass to Margaret (c.1393–1420), who succeeded her father by just a year. She had married to Sir Richard Mytton (d.1418), by whom she had a son William (b.1415) who grew up to inherit her family's estates.

William served Staffordshire as Sheriff in 1443, 1458 and 1463 and was also Member of Parliament for Staffordshire in 1446–7. He married Margaret, the daughter of Thomas Corbet of Leigh, to the south-west of Shrewsbury in

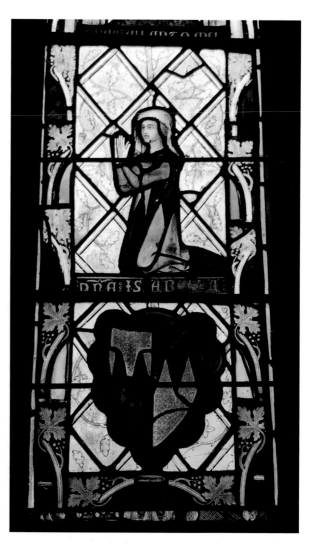

FIGURE 7 Stained glass donor figures in the east window of St Andrew's church, Weston-under-Lizard. To the left is the figure of Sir John de Weston, whilst to the right is the kneeling image of his wife Isabella Bromley. (Photos: courtesy of the author.)

Shropshire, and appears to have been longer lived than his forebears in being recorded as still alive in 1489. The couple had four daughters and two sons, of whom the eldest John (d.1499/1500) succeeded his father into the estates and was also Sheriff of Staffordshire in 1495–6. The exact origins of the Mytton family are uncertain; although nineteenth-century pedigrees continued to assert that the Weston-under-Lizard family were of the same stock as the Shropshire line seated at Halston in north Shropshire, this is not firmly established. The heraldry of a double-headed eagle – used by the Halston branch – was, however, certainly used in the late seventeenth century on the Weston line's armorial achievements.

In the sixteenth century Edward (fl.1583), son of John Harpesfield of London, inherited through the will of his maternal grandfather John Mytton (d.1532) – supposedly the son of John Mytton (d.1499/1500) – and he took the Mytton name upon succession. The adherence to the Mytton name was not, however, to last for many generations, since Edward's grandson and namesake, Edward Mytton (c.1575–1638), had but a single surviving daughter Elizabeth as the heir to the Mytton family estates at Weston-under-Lizard. During Edward's ownership, the family's antiquity was delineated in 1632 in an illuminated pedigree by Henry Lilly, then *rouge croix*, which was certified by Sir William Segar, Garter King of Arms. This sought to establish a genealogical link between Richard Weston, 1st Earl of Portland (1577–1634/1635) and the Westons of Weston and other branches of the family. Although the validity of some of the pedigree's genealogical claims has been questioned, it did provide a record of Edward Mytton's coat of arms and also of the recumbent de Weston knight monuments, plus the stained glass donor figures that were in St Andrew's church prior to its rebuilding by Edward's daughter Elizabeth almost seventy years later.[14]

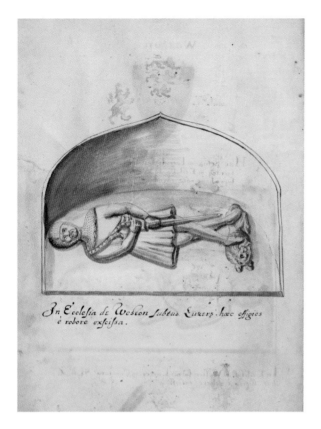

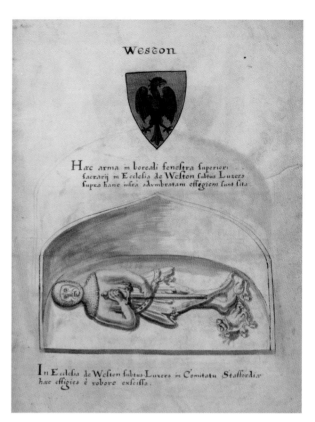

FIGURE 9 Drawing of the effigy of Hamo de Weston of 1188, by William Sedgwick, circa 1632, and included in the illuminated genealogy of the family of Weston. (© The British Library Board – Add MS 74251, f.31r.)

FIGURE 10 Drawing of the effigy of Sir Hugh de Weston of 1304, by William Sedgwick, circa 1632, and included in the illuminated genealogy of the family of Weston. (© The British Library Board – Add MS 74251, f.31v.)

FIGURE 11 The coat of arms of Edward Mitton/Mytton, drawn by William Sedgwick, circa 1632, and included in the illuminated genealogy of the family of Weston. (© The British Library Board – Add MS 74251, f.12r.)

Elizabeth Mytton (1632–1705) was to be ever conscious of her family's ancestry, as her work at Weston and in particular in the Church of St Andrew reveals. At her marriage on 29 July 1651, she was, in accepting Sir Thomas Wilbraham, 3rd Bt of Woodhey in Cheshire to be her husband, to renounce her maiden name. In doing so, the Mytton name would no longer in future be associated with her ancestral home at Weston, although the commemorative work that she would later undertake, following the rebuilding of the church, would serve as an architectural and sculptural commemoration of those that had come before her.

The estate, seven years after her marriage, was recorded in a survey map. This helpful document records the sizable house as what appears to be a multi-gabled structure, set to the east of a pool within gardens and orchards. To its west stands the parish church, with the parsonage to the east, and northwards a pool on the site of the present Church Pool's location. Various other buildings are shown, including a house on a site now occupied by the Curatage to the north-west of the Hall, whilst another building stands east of what is today known as the Church Drive. This latter building, given in 1658 as Edward Ilsleyes' tenement, appears to conform to the site of the present Garden House, a two-storied building which was tricked up with bargeboards and decorative chimneys in the early nineteenth century but within which – a restoration in 2012 revealed – is a vernacular oak timber frame. The map indicates two parks: an 'Upper Park' to the east, which is now outside of the park wall, and a 'Lower Park' lying to the south-east of the Hall. The Lower Park is now mostly contained within the current park boundary and still contains a rectangular moated site that is now a scheduled ancient monument. The moated area appears on the map with a building at its centre, perhaps a hunting lodge or pavilion for repast or rest during sport within the park.

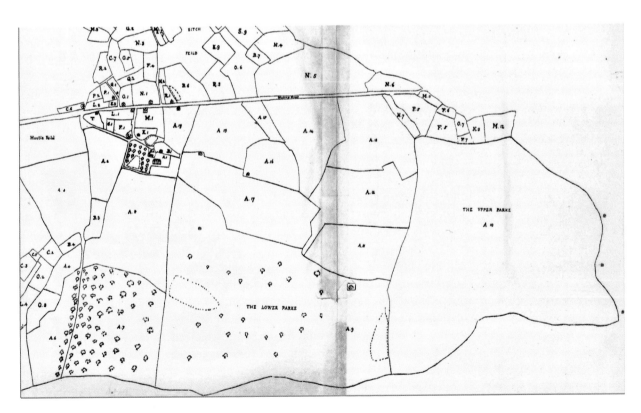

FIGURE 12 The house at Weston Park and its surroundings, from a map of 1658, copied in the late nineteenth century. The house, at that time, owned two parks which are clearly shown. The mansion itself is indistinctly represented but appears to have been a multi-gabled structure. (Copyright Trustees of the Weston Park Foundation.)

FIGURE 13 Stone escutcheon,
bearing initials assumed to
relate to Constance Mitton/
Mytton. The stone was
discovered at the rear of the
Morning Room chimney at
Weston Park during building
works in the late nineteenth
century and was re-set in its
current location in a service
passage, opposite the kitchen
door. (Photo: courtesy
of the author.)

It is frustrating that so little is known of the form or appearance of the
main house itself, although it was supposedly already a house of quadrangular
form before its late seventeenth-century rebuilding. Within the cellars the pair
of arches supported on columns – which stand below the present Marble Hall
– might be the undercroft of the original great hall, whilst the western external
walls of the kitchen are of a significant depth and are thought to represent
one of the earliest parts of the house. Outside the kitchen door is now to be
found an escutcheon carved with what appear to be the initials 'CM'. This was
found in 1899 in the wall behind the present Morning Room fireplace on what
had formerly been an external location and was reset in its present site at that
time. It is thought to refer to Constance Mytton (fl.1534), the great-great-great
grandmother of Elizabeth Mytton, Lady Wilbraham.[15]

Lady Wilbraham's role as the genealogical conduit for the inheritance of
Weston Park in its reinvented form would, firstly, enable the estate to pass
to her daughter Mary, wife of Richard Newport, 2nd Earl of Bradford of
the first creation. After Mary's death in 1737, Weston passed in trust for the
life of her son Thomas, 4th Earl of Bradford, until it was inherited by her
grandson. Mary Countess of Bradford's daughter Lady Anne Newport, having
married Sir Orlando Bridgeman, had produced a son – the eventual Sir Henry
Bridgeman, 5th Bt and later 1st Baron Bradford – and he was to receive his
grandmother's family home.

Weston Park had, therefore, within but a few generations in the seventeenth
and eighteenth centuries, passed from Mytton to Wilbraham to Newport and
then to Bridgeman. With each family's succession, further territorial associations became connected to the owners of Weston Park. The Wilbrahams
had lands around Nantwich and brought a first connection to Walsall.
The Newports also had links to High Ercall, Eyton-on-Severn and Shrewsbury,
in addition to London and to Twickenham. The Bridgemans, besides their
north Shropshire and Warwickshire estates, brought connections in the north
of England, especially at Bolton and Wigan. It was, not least for Weston Park
itself, a complicated succession but one in which the role of the heiresses was
of the greatest importance. Each heiress has left their mark to posterity, and
they remain just as important within the pedigree as any male members of the
family. Of them all, Lady Wilbraham especially left nothing to chance; during
her tenure at Weston Park she was to define the future of the property in more
ways than simply its ownership.

CHAPTER TWO

Powerful Patronage in the Provinces
Lady Wilbraham and Architectural Ambition

When Dr Robert Plot, the first keeper of Oxford's Ashmolean Museum, published his magisterial *The Natural History of Staffordshire* in 1686, he dedicated a plate showing early antiquities to Sir Thomas Wilbraham (1630–1692), but of his house at Weston – which had recently been rebuilt – he noted with resignation:

> There are as fine buildings not represented in sculpture [i.e. engraved for illustration] as any that are; such as the seat of the right worshipful Sr. Thomas Wilbraham at Weston-under-Lizard, the Front whereof I could have gladly engraven, but that forbidden by the Proprietor … whether out of modesty or any other private respects, I pretend not to know.[1]

Modesty was most likely the ready reason, for its owners were Presbyterian in their religious beliefs and for whom shows of display would, seemingly, have been anathema. There was, though, an element of pride in their stewardship of the estate and their building work. These architectural works at Weston included the rebuilding of the house's south and east wings, the building of the stables, and of the body of St Andrew's church. There was also a rebuilding of the old Wilbraham seat at Woodhey, near Nantwich in Cheshire, in around 1690, although the true extent of the Cheshire works is now unclear due to the demolition of that house in the early eighteenth century. What is unusual in Plot's reference to Weston is that he wrote only of Sir Thomas, and neglected to mention his Lady – who was clearly one of the main drivers of the works.

Weston had been the family home of Elizabeth Mytton (1632–1705), Lady Wilbraham, and a property in which she determined to define its destiny. She was born the daughter of Edward Mytton of Weston and his second wife Cecily (d.1649), the daughter of Sir William Skeffington, 1st Bt of Fisherwick, Staffordshire, and his wife Elizabeth Dering. Edward's first wife Elizabeth, the daughter of James Weston of Lichfield, had died without bearing children just a few years into their marriage. His second wife, however, on 4 February 1632, bore him Elizabeth – an only daughter to survive as the heir to Weston. Edward died when his daughter was just six years old, in 1638, and his widow went on to remarry to a Cheshire landowner Sir William Brereton (1604–1661) of Handforth Hall, who became a guardian to Elizabeth. With her mother, he had

two daughters, Cecily – who grew up to marry the 4th Earl of Meath[2] – and
Mary, stepsisters to the young ward. A strict Puritan who is now best known to
posterity as a Parliamentary general during the English Civil Wars, Sir William
had travelled extensively in France, the Netherlands, Ireland and Scotland in the
period 1634–5.[3] Amongst the places that he visited in the Low Countries in 1634
were the Prince of Orange's Huis ten Bosch, which he admiringly described
at length and also noted the prince's now-lost Huis Honselaarsdijk. He made
purchases of works of art whilst in Amsterdam, also acquiring Delft tiles –
'painted stones' – the subject matter of which he noted. His journals reveal a
keen sense of observation of both the human state and of the world around
him and it is likely that this heightened worldly awareness was something that
he instilled into his stepdaughter.

Elizabeth's mother died when she was seventeen, but two years later, on
29 June 1651, she was married at Weston to Thomas Wilbraham (1630–1692),
the son and heir of Sir Thomas Wilbraham, 2nd Bt (c.1601–1660) of Woodhey
near Nantwich, Cheshire. The Wilbrahams were an ancient Cheshire family
who had been seated at Woodhey since the early fifteenth century when the
estate had come to them through the marriage of Margaret, daughter and heir

of John de Golborne with Thomas de Wiberham (or Wylbram). During the
intervening generations, the family had made a series of high-status marriages
within Cheshire, so that Warburtons, Cholmondeleys, Savages, Dones,
Egertons, Davenports and Grosvenors were kinsmen of Thomas's generation.
His aunt Elizabeth had married Sir Humphrey Briggs, 2nd Bt of Haughton,
an estate located just six miles from Weston Park, and so it is possible that this
had a bearing on the Wilbraham–Mytton union.

For Weston Park, not only did the marriage make a connection between the
house and the Woodhey estate in Cheshire, but it also brought a connection
within Staffordshire. The Wilbrahams – in addition to their Cheshire estates
– had been Lords of the Manor of Walsall in Staffordshire since 1553 when
Thomas's great-great-great-grandfather Richard Wilbraham (d.1558), Master
of the Jewel House and of Revels to Queen Mary, had taken a lease from the
Crown.[4]

Thomas and Elizabeth Wilbraham produced four daughters: Elizabeth
(1653–1675); Grace (1656–1719); Mary (1661–1737) and Cecilia (1667–1669)
of whom the surviving two – Grace and Mary – would ultimately become the
heiresses of the estates. With the death of his father in 1660, Thomas succeeded

to the baronetcy and his wife gained the title of Lady Wilbraham, yet throughout Lady Wilbraham's married life she appears to have cherished a sense of her own family's importance and a sense of responsibility for further elevating the family in its succession. It is perhaps notable that when the parish church of Acton, on her husband's Cheshire estate, was presented with a flagon, it was inscribed: 'The gift of the Honble. Lady Wilbraham of Weston in Staffordshire to the Church of Acton in Cheshire' with reference to neither her husband nor her association with his estates.[5] As the last of her family's line, she clearly saw her responsibility as being to perpetuate the glory of her family and its association with the Weston estate.

In recent years, her role at Weston, and specifically her importance as a patron, has been unhelpfully given distraction by unfounded assertions of Lady Wilbraham having been an architect. These claims have been embroidered with unsubstantiated suggestions: there is, for example, no documentary evidence to suggest that the Wilbrahams had an architecturally focused honeymoon or that Lady Wilbraham met the Dutch architect Pieter Post as one commentator has suggested. The notion of Lady Wilbraham as architect appears to have been sprung from twentieth-century family tradition, fuelled with pride, which was based upon a misreading of fourteen pages of notes that she inscribed into the front and rear pages of a copy of Godfrey Richards' translation of Palladio's *First Book of Architecture* (1663) which remains in the collection at Weston Park.[6] The scholarly late nineteenth-century historians Rev. Ernest R.O. Bridgeman and Charles G.O. Bridgeman – working from the manuscripts of the Hon. and Rev. G.T.O. Bridgeman – in 1899 kept to the known facts, referencing the Palladio annotations but doing so solely to note the various building works that had taken place under Elizabeth Wilbraham's rule. As a patron though, her role and attention to detail should not be treated lightly. It should also be considered alongside other examples of female seventeenth-century architectural patronage, such as that of Lady Bridgeman at Castle Bromwich (see Chapter 4), and also Lady Wrottesley at Wrottesley Hall who is referenced in Lady Wilbraham's Palladio annotations.

The Palladio notes are random in their nature, almost akin to a personal memorandum, for recalling the prices and providers of essential materials and services relating to building projects. The projects, though, are not referenced sequentially, with many of the notes relating to the rebuilding of the house at the Wilbraham's Cheshire estate at Woodhey, which took place in circa 1690–2, followed by notes relating to the rebuilding of the church at Weston in 1699, and then latterly, and evidently retrospectively, 'For Building Weston house 1671'. The fact that the notes are known to be by Elizabeth Wilbraham herself is borne out by a comparison of handwriting with signed letters and also by her note suggesting an arbitration of the rate for installing 'the old wanscote [wainscot] formerly in the best Hale' at Woodhey by two persons, one of whom was 'me E.W.'

Fragmented and abstract as the notes are, they do give a sense of the quality of the works at Weston, Woodhey and in the church at Weston, and also of the working practices of the building projects, with Lady Wilbraham evidently taking advice from neighbours engaged on building projects, together with that of her own family. Of the neighbours, she mentions 'Mr Peirponds Joyner [who] offers March 1701 to wainscote the church att [sic] Weston'. 'Mr Peirpond' would presumably have been Gervase Pierrepont (1649–1715) of Tong Castle who, in the same year was raised to the peerage as Baron Pierrepont. His mother Elizabeth Harries, the Hon. Mrs William Pierrepont, had been the heiress of the neighbouring estate of Tong Castle which her father, the successful lawyer Sir Thomas Harries, 1st Bt (1550–1628), had purchased. Although the family

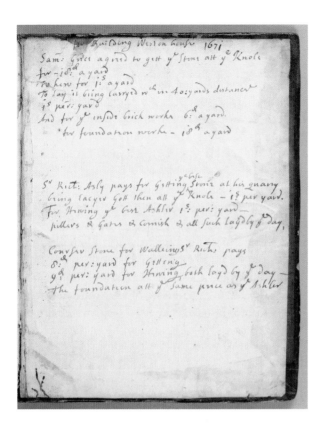

FIGURE 16 End papers of Lady Wilbraham's copy of Godfrey Richard's first English translation of Palladio's *First Book of Architecture* (1663), annotated in her hand. This page contains apparently retrospective details headed 'For Building Weston house 1671' including the costs of the acquisition and carriage of stone. The lower part of the text makes comparisons of cost between Sir Richard Astley (1625–1688), 1st Bt of Patshull's stone quarry and that from the Knoll, to the south of Weston. Accession no. 118.0539. (Copyright Trustees of the Weston Park Foundation.)

were probably considered as incomers by Lady Wilbraham, they were never-theless well connected. Elizabeth Pierrepont's husband the Hon. William (1608–1679) was the son of Robert, 1st Earl of Kingston-Upon-Hull (1584–1643) and his elder brother Henry (1606–1680) went on to succeed as 2nd Earl and was created 1st Marquess of Dorchester. In 1670 Lord Dorchester rebuilt his seat at Thoresby in Nottinghamshire, an estate which at his death passed, with the Kingston earldom, to the children of Gervase Pierrepont's elder brother Robert (c.1634–1669).

Robert who, like Gervase, had been brought up at Tong Castle, had married the heiress Elizabeth Evelyn of West Dean, an estate to the east of Salisbury in Wiltshire.[7] Her family, who were wealthy from government gunpowder manufacturing monopolies, rebuilt West Dean with a giant segmental pediment on its south front, whilst the mortuary chapel – formerly a part of a demolished parish church – contains a series of monuments that Elizabeth Pierrepont (née Evelyn) erected to her husband and parents – the former being a dramatic classical set piece with a central figurative sculpture of Robert Pierrepont that is attributed to the sculptor John Bushnell.

Gervase Pierrepont's sisters, meanwhile, also made grand marriages; Frances married Henry Cavendish, 2nd Duke of Newcastle; Grace married Gilbert Holles, 3rd Earl of Clare; whilst Gertrude married to Sir George Savile, 1st Marquess of Halifax. Tong and the broad family network associated with its Pierrepont-owning family at that time was certainly grander than that at Weston. The house at Tong encapsulated a medieval castle which had been rebuilt in brick by Sir Henry Vernon in the sixteenth century and – if the Buck brothers' engraving of the castle as it stood in the early eighteenth century is to be believed – it also had one of the very earliest of English classical porticos superimposed on its frontage – a giant Ionic tetrastyle portico, supporting a triangular pediment.

Of the other families referenced in the Palladio notes, one finds Mr Cotes of Woodcote, six miles to the north, and also the owners of Wrottesley Hall a house located nine miles south of Weston, and of Patshull eleven miles to the south. The former Eleanor Archer, Lady Wrottesley (c.1660–1693), was the daughter of Sir John Archer of Coopersale, Essex, and his second wife Eleanor Curzon of Kedleston in Derbyshire. She had married in 1678 to Sir Walter Wrottesley, 3rd Bt (1659–1712) and was evidently actively involved in the rebuilding of Wrottesley as a tall three-storied H-plan mansion in 1694–7 with William and Richard Smith acting as builders. Celia Fiennes had sought out the house on her progress, describing how it 'stands very finely on a hill and woods by it look very stately'.[8] Patshull, the other house, was noted by Fiennes as 'old and low' and yet its gardens, with sculptures and water works, ranked as the 'finest and best kept',[9] having been created by Sir Richard Astley, 1st Bt (c.1625–1688) who was known to the Wilbrahams.

Weston, even prior to the Wilbraham rebuilding, was not a small house and it was assessed for hearth tax on the large number of twenty-five hearths in 1666. The house was probably quadrangular in plan, judging by its later evolution, with an estate map of 1658 having a vignette of the south elevation as a gabled frontage, suggesting what might have been a timber-framed house. It was the south front, which faced towards Tong, and also the east range that became the subjects of a rebuilding effected by the Wilbrahams, and which appears to have commenced in 1671, with the attendant stable block, built on a U-plan to the east, following and being completed in 1688 according to the date on the lead rainwater hoppers. The extent of the house rebuilding is uncertain although there are factors that would indicate that it was largely a re-fronting. Timber-framed wall construction can still to be found at first-floor level on the east side, whilst the outer west wall of the Morning Room below was found to contain a stone escutcheon of uncertain early date during alterations in the late nineteenth century. Further south, the Tapestry Room was found to have Tudor floor elements when works to remedy dry rot were undertaken in the early twentieth century, whilst the cellars of the Marble Hall – the room behind the central bays of the Wilbrahams' east front – have a pair of early arches that are suggestive of having been the undercroft of a great hall above.

The rebuilding of each wing appears to have been of a single room's depth on each elevation, with enfilades of rooms that opened from one to the next. The notable space within the east wing, on its second floor, was a long gallery. This space of parade and show survived, in its entirety, until the late eighteenth century when James Paine divided its length to create a series of bedrooms.

Externally, the east wing is of nine bays which are divided into three individually symmetrical elements. The roof balustrading is later nineteenth century, but at the centre is a giant triangular pediment that is set with a stone escutcheon of the Wilbraham arms. The pediment extends over three slightly projecting bays and below it the outer windows of ground and first floor have arched heads. The centre bay on these floors, though, has a rusticated stone centre, with a shouldered, tablet-centred moulded window surround at the first floor and a bolection-moulded doorcase below. The rustication is distinctive and also appeared at a now-demolished Cheshire house, Aston Hall, Aston-by-Sutton, that may have been known to the Wilbrahams. More poignantly, though, it is a feature used on the west and south doorways of the Church of the Holy Trinity at Minsterley, Shropshire of 1683. This church, which had been built for the 1st Viscount Weymouth, had been designed by William Taylor, an architect who had also made alterations at Lord Weymouth's Wiltshire house, Longleat.

A 'Mr Taler' is referenced by Lady Wilbraham in her Palladio notes and, tellingly, William Taylor wrote to another of his clients on 1 August 1674 from 'Weston in Stafford sheer', suggesting his involvement at the house.[10] Although

FIGURE 17 The east front of Weston Park. This elevation remains largely as built in 1671, although the sills of the ground floor windows were lowered in the first decade of the nineteenth century and the parapet balustrading is post-1866. (Copyright Trustees of the Weston Park Foundation.)

his name was not generally recognised as an architect as recently as 1963, recent research that has largely been published in the *Georgian Group Journal* has established him as a significant London figure, with notable buildings ascribed to him in the West Country and in the Welsh Marches.[11] He was a member of the Carpenters' Company in London and had been actively involved in the rebuilding of the city in the aftermath of the Great Fire of 1666, steadily building up an important client base that included the bankers Sir Robert Clayton and John Morris. For Morris, he had produced designs for a house at Rossall to the west of Shrewsbury, some twenty-seven miles from Weston.

Taylor is also associated with works at Chirk Castle, where the accounts reference payments between June and October 1675 to 'mr Taylor, the contriver',[12] for works which included the surviving long gallery in the castle's east range. The client at Chirk was the Dowager Lady Myddelton, acting for her grandson Sir Thomas Myddelton, 2nd Bt (1651–1683). Sir Thomas married the Wilbrahams' daughter Elizabeth on 6 February 1673, two months after coming of age, and the Chirk accounts show links between the building operations at both properties including the shared use of the sculptor Nicholas Needham, his assistant Thomas Dugdale, and possibly also Jonathan Hooke. Although the young Lady Myddelton was to die tragically in childbirth in 1675 – when her portrait was taken from Weston for John Bushnell to sculpt the moving monument to her which remains in the parish church at Chirk – a connection was maintained with Weston Park in the building operations. This is indicated in the Chirk accounts which record on 28 July 1677 one Evan of the Nant making a 'journey to Weston, for my lady Wilbraham's direccons about the wainscot in the greate roome in the bell Tower'.[13] Since he was not apparently a carver, this might have been instructions for painting of the wainscot, which was evidently an interest of Lady Wilbraham's since she records details in her Palladio of the costs of painters for paint effects in emulation of different wood types.

At Chirk, within the courtyard on the east end of the south wall, remains a segmental pediment carved with a weathered winged putti, above a door to the chapel, which recalls similar details on Weston Park's south front. This elevation of Weston, seemingly also of the 1671 build, is the real bravura façade. Here, the eleven bays are divided 2:3:1:3:2, with the ends and centre projecting slightly, defined by alternating stone angle quoins and with the centre bay faced in ashlar. The stone detailing of the centre includes putti heads and garlands sunk in panels similar to those used also at Minsterley Church which might also have been the work of Needham and Dugdale. Axial to this bay, within the house, is a staircase giving access to the roof which still retains its seventeenth-century flat-balusters. Its position suggests that there might originally have been a cupola of some form which would have further enlivened the southern elevation of the house. What defines this front still, though, is the memorable pair of giant two-bay segmental open pediments, resting on rich acanthus-carved cornice-ends, which are each centred with an *oeil-de-boeuf* window. They are handsome and unusual features which, for a London architect like Taylor, might readily have been inspired by the pair of segmental pediments on the main gateway of the contemporary Royal Exchange in London that had been designed by Edward Jerman (c.1605–1668).[14]

With the exception of the staircase to the roof noted above, very little survives of the seventeenth-century interiors, although their quality is hinted at by references made by Lady Wilbraham in her Palladio notes. These include 'Corinthyan [*sic*] Capitalls … as upon ye best stear head att Weston', and a 'marble Harth [*sic*] for ye drawing room att Weston [having] Cost five shillings'.

FIGURE 18 The south front of Weston Park in winter. The façade survives largely as designed by William Taylor. (Copyright Trustees of the Weston Park Foundation.)

FIGURE 19 The Church of the Holy Trinity, Minsterley, Shropshire. Designed and built by William Taylor in 1688–9 for the patron Lord Weymouth of Longleat, Wiltshire, the church's giant segmental pediment and rusticated stone detailing has an echo of Weston Park's south front. (Photo: courtesy of the author.)

One notable feature, now hidden away in the service area of the house and in a garden store, are some bolection moulded panels – since reinvented as cupboards – which were evidently sections of wainscot that must have been used in many of the main rooms and which might have been the work of Needham and Dugdale. Some of these panels might have been used to line the long gallery, a room of similar scale to that surviving at Chirk and which until James Paine's work at Weston in the 1760s occupied the entire floor space of the east wing's top floor. This was a space which Taylor was also to create in other houses including both Halifax House, St James' Square for the 1st Marquess of Halifax and his Pierrepont Marchioness, and also at their country house of Rufford Abbey, Nottinghamshire.[15] The house's interiors at Weston may indeed, have remained largely as they were rebuilt until the 1760s Paine alterations and certainly a 1762 inventory[16] contains evocative references to rooms such as the 'Pedlers Hall', Prayer Hall, Gilt Leather Passage and Mohair Room which convey both the contrasting earnest religious aspirations and the socially aspirant fashionable decorative mediums of Lady Wilbraham's age.

Taylor might also have been responsible for the stable block, which stands to the east of Weston, a two-storied block with giant pediment presiding over three bays on its southern elevation and enveloping a sundial within its stone mouldings. The lower central doorcase, with shouldered-surround set upon a rusticated foil, has an unusual flat-ended pediment cresting which may also be found at Minsterley Church and also at Aldenham Park, Shropshire, where Taylor was at work for Sir Edward Acton, 3rd Bt (1649–1716) in the 1680s. At Aldenham, the staff-rod moulding, which can be seen at the angles of Weston's stable window apertures, is also used on the south front windows. Both the stables' south front and the east pediment of the house contain handsome carved stone escutcheons of the Wilbraham arms. It is perhaps pertinent to note that these do not have a quartering of the Mytton arms in spite of Lady Wilbraham's pride in her family's own property and in her ancestry.

FIGURE 20 Bolection moulded wooden panels, which would have formed a part of the joinery in the main rooms of the late seventeenth-century house at Weston Park, that have since been repurposed as cupboards in the kitchens of the house. (Photo: courtesy of the author.)

FIGURE 21 The staircase from the upper floor to the lead-flats of the roof, at the centre of the south front of Weston Park. This simple oak staircase, with handrail carried on silhouette balusters, is the only remaining piece of joinery in situ within the house. (Photo: courtesy of the author.)

FIGURE 22 Plan of the upper floor of Weston Park (south to top), attributed to James Paine (1717–1789) and thought to show the room layout prior to alterations for Sir Henry and Lady Bridgeman in the late 1760s. The seventeenth-century gallery can be seen, with its two fireplaces, occupying the whole of the east wing on the left of the plan. (Photo: Staffordshire Archives D1287/8/6 (M/657 A and B).)

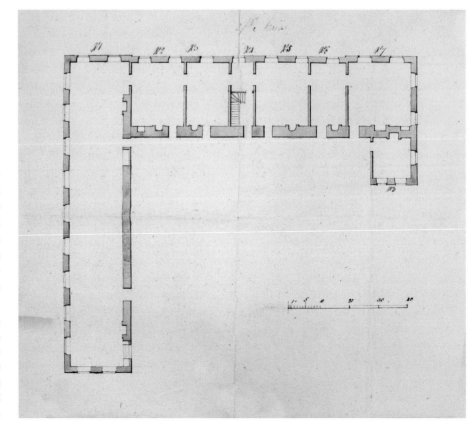

FIGURE 23 The gallery at Rufford Abbey, Nottinghamshire photographed prior to demolition in 1956. Although the strap-work decorated ceiling is of nineteenth-century date, the gallery itself is attributed to William Taylor and was created for George Savile, the 1st Marquess of Halifax (1633–1695), whose second wife Gertrude Pierrepont – married in 1672 – was a member of the family then seated at Tong, neighbouring the Weston property of Lady Wilbraham. The room's proportions are similar to what would have existed at Weston Park. (AA51_00076 Historic England.)

FIGURE 24 The stables at Weston Park, seen from the south. (Photo: courtesy of the author.)

FIGURE 25 *Grace Wilbraham, Countess of Dysart* (1656–1740), painted by John Michael Wright (1617–1694), oil on canvas, 125 x 97.8 cm. Accession number 101.0043. (Copyright Trustees of the Weston Park Foundation.)

FIGURE 26 *Mary Wilbraham, Countess of Bradford* (1661–1737), painted by John Michael Wright (1617–1694), oil on canvas, 125 x 97.8 cm. Accession number 101.0042. (Copyright Trustees of the Weston Park Foundation.)

With the Wilbrahams' daughter Elizabeth, Lady Myddelton, having died in childbirth in 1675, their two surviving daughters, Grace and Mary, became the heiresses of the Woodhey and the Weston estates respectively. There had been a thought, on the part of Sir Thomas, to arrange a marriage for one of the daughters to the 2nd Viscount Mordaunt (1658–1735, later 3rd Earl of Peterborough) in 1678,[17] but in the event this did not come to pass and other suitors were found.

An indenture settling the estates was made on 20 May 1686,[18] whilst the Wilbraham daughters' betrothal portraits were both painted by John Michael Wright and remain at Weston Park, hanging as pendants to one another. Their original frames, which Lady Wilbraham 'caused … to bee made broader and richer'[19] were regrettably replaced in the early nineteenth century.

Their suitors were subjected to close and prolonged scrutiny by Lady Wilbraham; indeed Mary's future husband – then Mr Newport or 'Mr N' – clearly found his inspection a little too much to tolerate as Lady Wilbraham related in a letter to an unknown recipient, when she wrote: 'I have had an Eye upon Mr N. severall years (however he unseasonably mistooke the object).'[20]

Lord Huntingtower – later 3rd Earl of Dysart – who was to wed Grace, Lady Wilbraham went so far as to commission agents to examine his estates, which delayed the nuptials:

But that the other Mach is not fully resolved because we have som agents privately in Suffolke inquiering the Condissions of the person and his Estate and till they returne we defer matters wch otherwise might I thinke be esily agreed, our Agents were all the Last weeke examining his Estate in

Northamptonshire, and from thence give us a very good account both of ye qualitys of the Gentleman & ye vallue of his Estate.[21]

The enquiries proved sound, and the young nobleman also eventually inherited Ham House, Surrey from his mother the Duchess of Lauderdale, albeit that his family's estates were heavily encumbered.[22] He married Grace in 1680 and ultimately inherited the 20,000-acre Cheshire estate at Woodhey. His portrait, by Lely, remains in the collection at Weston, showing him in an unusually informal slumped pose.

Lord Huntingtower appears to have enjoyed cordial relations with his in-laws – portraits of both of them remain in the collection at Ham House – and Lady Wilbraham's Palladio notes imply that he, prior to his accession to the Dysart earldom in 1698, was actively involved in the rebuilding of the Wilbraham's Cheshire seat of Woodhey. In the first page of notes relating to Woodhey she recorded:

ffeb '97 My Lord H gives Patten ye joyner 4s for Each Window frame & 3d a light for ye sashes.

The Woodhey building works were apparently undertaken in circa 1689–97, with Sir Thomas dying in 1692. His grandfather Sir Richard (1579–1643) may, in fact, have intended to rebuild the family's seat, since his will – written in the course of the Civil War, when he was at Shrewsbury in 1642 – stipulates leaving his son 'all my bricke & stone at Woodhey & Shotwicke wch I intended to build withal'.[23] The Wilbrahams had been compounded for the sum of £2,500 for

FIGURE 27 *Lionel Tollemache, 3rd Earl of Dysart*, painted by Sir Peter Lely (1618–1680), oil on canvas, 104.2 x 87.6 cm. Accession number 101.0248. (Copyright Trustees of the Weston Park Foundation.)

FIGURE 28 *Richard Newport, 2nd Earl of Bradford of the first creation* (1644–1723), painted by Sir Peter Lely (1618–1680), oil on canvas, 125.7 x 100.4 cm. Accession number 101.0112. (Copyright Trustees of the Weston Park Foundation.)

their loyalty to the Royalist cause[24] and so any major works to the house had needed to wait until after the Restoration of the monarchy.

The extent of the works at Woodhey is not clear, since the house was demolished by the Dysarts' heir in circa 1740, leaving only the chapel, an earlier service building and gate piers which are now at the entrance to the present farmhouse that occupies its site. The majority of the notes in Lady Wilbraham's Palladio, however, appear to relate to the Cheshire estate as being an active concern of building activity. Here, reference in 1690 to the costs of brickwork compares the costs of 'Mr Webdalle' (probably the Alexander Webdalle, a carpenter and builder that she references elsewhere in the Palladio as working on Woodhey), 'the Londoners', and 'Mr Web' who is considered to be probably Thomas Webb (d.1699) of Middlewich, the builder of Erddig, Denbighshire. She also refers, in the past tense, to charges by 'Mr Taler [perhaps William Taylor]... Mr Russell ... Wm. Smith [William Smith of Tettenhall]', suggesting that she or her friends had used these men. By November 1691 the Palladio notes show comparison of costs for painters who could offer wood-graining and marbling, with quotes from London, Derby and Nantwich painters, suggesting that works in Cheshire were drawing to a close. Whilst the house no longer stands, drawings do survive to show two of the house's elevations, suggesting a very different house to that which she and Taylor created at Weston. Woodhey, with its recessed front door, panelled parapet and rusticated plinth set with *oeil-de-boeuf* windows, lacked the decoration of Weston's south front and presented a much more restrained, well-proportioned frontage.[25] Only the segmental pedimented doorcase really stands out as offering relief from the sober regularity of the sashes and the brickwork.

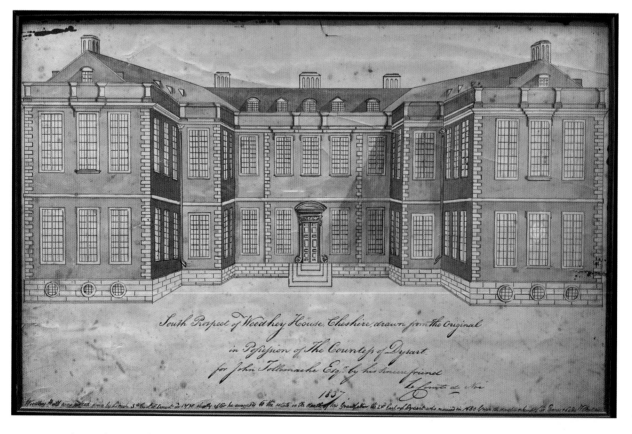

FIGURE 29 The south view of the house at Woodhey, Cheshire. An 1837 copy by Amédée Charles Henri, Comte de Noé (1819–1879), of a drawing then in the collection of the Countess Dysart. The house itself was demolished in circa 1730. (Photo: Helmingham Hall, Suffolk.)

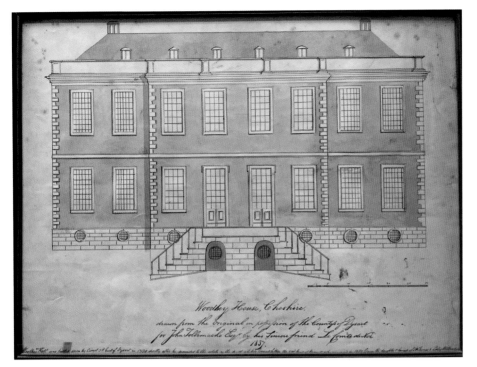

FIGURE 30 The east view
of the house at Woodhey,
Cheshire. An 1837 copy
by Amédée Charles Henri,
Comte de Noé (1819–1879),
of a drawing then in the
collection of the Countess
Dysart. (Photo: Helmingham
Hall, Suffolk.)

The chapel at Woodhey followed the main house, with its construction recorded as taking place between 1697 and 1699. A chapel had been recorded at Woodhey in William Wilbraham's will of 1534 and so what now stands was probably a rebuilding of an earlier structure. It stands to the east of the house site, attached to an earlier tripartite loggia which links what was probably an elevated bowling green with the family's balcony pew within the chapel. With three arched-headed windows and an *oeil-de-boeuf* above an arched door, the plain elevations are matched with a striking Netherlandish interior. Pews are ranged to each side, facing each other, as in a college chapel, their supports of scrolled Florentine form. A pulpit and tester stand before a segmental-pedimented declaration of the Ten Commandments, its floor still retaining original black and white marble square flags, whilst the rest of the floor has yielded to nineteenth-century replacements. There is no altar – the building serving its low-church family and their dependants as a preaching box.

With both daughters married to the heirs to earldoms, the widowed Lady Wilbraham at the age of sixty-five turned her attentions to the parish church at Weston. She undertook a rebuilding of the church of St Andrew from 1699, with the completed building reopened on St Andrew's Day in 1702.[26] The works seemingly left only the medieval tower and reused the east window, both of which now stand out, somewhat incongruously, on what is otherwise a baroque building. Before the church was rebuilt, a plan was drawn of its current state, showing the pew-holders, arches on the north wall of the nave that might have contained the medieval tomb effigies, and with a north porch. This, and another plan showing the rebuilt form of the church, have been claimed to have been the work of Lady Wilbraham and yet a cursory comparison of the script with that in her Palladio reveals completely different hands. That of the church as it stood might have been annotated by the rector, whilst the other drawing could have been the work of an architect or mason – neither, though, appear to have been the draughtsmanship of the patron.[27]

Following its rebuilding, the nave re-emerged as a pilaster-punctuated three-bay rectangular structure. The nave body was built of a red sandstone that was apparently quarried from Tong Knoll, whilst the classical detailing

FIGURE 31 The surviving chapel at Woodhey
Hall, Cheshire, seen from the north-west in
2021. (Photo: courtesy of the author.)

FIGURE 32 The interior of
the chapel at Woodhey Hall,
Cheshire, looking east, in 2021.
(Photo: courtesy of the author.)

of frieze, Tuscan pilasters and arched window-surrounds are in a contrasting white stone that gives the building added visual depth. A sense of movement is achieved by the cushion frieze, by the great shaped Dutch gable of the east ends which descends to tight scrolls at the wall-plate, whilst in 1858 the building also had *oeil-de-boeuf* windows above the remaining arched-headed windows at its west end. The nave's exterior design with pilasters and cushion frieze recalls the Chapel of the Ascension at Hall Green, Birmingham which was built for Job Marston and is attributed to Sir William Wilson (1641–1710).[28] Wilson is also said to have designed Four Oaks Hall in Warwickshire, where scrolled gables ornamented the main elevation of that house when it was rebuilt after 1696. These similarities suggest that Wilson might have had a hand in the church's design, although its execution probably went to others as a means of economy on the part of Lady Wilbraham; the window surrounds have no moulding, unlike those at Hall Green and, indeed, at the Wilbraham's surviving chapel at Woodhey, which strikes as a mean detail for Weston's parish church.

Wilson is certainly named in Lady Wilbraham's Palladio as the contracted supplier of a series of monuments within: 'I bargan^d: wth S^r W^m: Wilson to sett up 4 Monum^ts:'. These, evidently supplied after Wilson's knighthood of 1682, form a part of the chancel which was reinvented as a carefully choreographed celebration of Lady Wilbraham's ancestry, with a rearrangement of

FIGURE 33 St Andrew's church, Weston-under-Lizard, seen from the north-west in 1858, painted by Miss Theodosia Hinckes and Mrs Rebecca Moore. The view shows an *oeil-de-boeuf* window at the west end, which has since disappeared, and the nave of the church as it appeared prior to Victorian restorations. (Copyright Lichfield Cathedral.)

the medieval effigies into arched recesses, conveniently to north and south of the altar. Each has a white marble-framed oval escutcheon of black marble with gilt lettering above it, identifying the monuments in script, and with polychrome armorial escutcheons to the sides and above them. They are given as, respectively, Hamo and Hugh de Weston. Above, on each wall, are three smaller classical monuments to other members of the family; the uppermost has a shield of arms above a fruiting garland framing, whilst the lower pair each have heraldic escutcheons set upon a segmental pediment.

The east wall holds the stained glass of the main window, with depictions of St Andrew and the lower donor figures of Sir John and Isabella de Weston. To each side of the window are a pair of dramatic classical tabernacles of contrasting white and black marble, giving maximum visual impact. Originally, they appear to have flanked a central segmental-pediment crested panel – probably inscribed with the Ten Commandments as at Woodhey – which is shown in an 1858 watercolour of the interior. That to the left of the altar commemorates Sir Thomas and Lady Wilbraham, whilst on the right is a monument to her parents. Both have open segmental pediments – recalling in their basic form those of the house's south front – set with central escutcheons of arms. The plinths, columns and pilaster shafts and the frieze is in black marble, contrasting spectacularly with the white of pediments, Corinthian capitals, and, especially, on the long rectangular inscription tablets of each monument and drawing the eye to the patroness's own name.[29] Even the later small Newport monuments, that now sit above the pair of architectural set

FIGURE 34 The interior of St Andrew's church, Weston-under-Lizard, looking east in 1858 painted by Miss Theodosia Hinckes and Mrs Rebecca Moore. The segmental-pedimented tablet below the chancel's east window – replaced by the current reredos in the late nineteenth century – might have contained the Ten Commandments, as at Woodhey. (Copyright Lichfield Cathedral.)

FIGURE 35 The pulpit in St Andrew's church, Weston-under-Lizard, which was a gift from Lady Wilbraham to the church. (Photo: Paul Highnam/Copyright Trustees of the Weston Park Foundation.)

FIGURE 36 St Andrew's church, Weston-under-Lizard, seen from the north in 2021. The projection from the nave, dating from the late nineteenth century, contains a chapel and vestry which disrupts the original white sandstone architectural detailing highlighted against the red sandstone wall body. (Photo: Paul Highnam/Copyright Trustees of the Weston Park Foundation.)

pieces, do not diminish the dominance that they hold at the very altar of the church. Frustratingly, this re-presentation of the family's descent seems to have led to the disappearance of other earlier monuments that had been recorded by Sir William Dugdale in 1663. Gone now are the alabaster monuments presumed to be to Sir Adam de Peshale and his wife Joyce (or Jocosa), along with the brass figuratively inlaid stone to John Mytton (d.1499/1500), his wives Anne (or Agnes) and Joan and their children, and a brass inlaid stone to John Mytton (d.1532–3) and his wife Constance Beaumont, that were all formerly to be found in the chancel.

The pulpit was a gift from Lady Wilbraham and it remains to preside over the church from below its contemporary tester. If, as a patron, she made manifest with the architectural works of the house and the stables at Weston, plus the rebuilt house and chapel at Woodhey, then surely her soul and further evidences of her earthly dynastic ambition can be found in the interior of the church that she also caused to be rebuilt.

FIGURE 37 The east wall of the chancel of St Andrew's church, Weston-under-Lizard. The upper monuments to left and right of the window are later additions to the composition, whilst the pair of segmental pediment-surmounted monuments, and three wall tablets on both the north and south walls, to left and right, above the recumbent knight figures, form a part of Lady Wilbraham's demonstration of her ancestry. (Photo: Paul Highnam/Copyright Trustees of the Weston Park Foundation.)

CHAPTER THREE

Civil War and Restoration

The Creation of a Collection

During the period in which Elizabeth Mytton of Weston had grown up, married into the Wilbrahams and commenced the development of Weston and Woodhey, within twenty miles of Weston another family, the Newports, endured a very different Civil War and Restoration experience. Although, as Royalists, they initially suffered for their allegiance to the monarchy, they emerged at the Restoration with position, greater honours and with an important collection of paintings. The collection that they created was to make its way to Weston Park in 1735 as a result of the marriage of the elder son of one of its creators with the Wilbraham heiress of Weston.

The Newports were an ancient Shropshire family who had derived their patronymic from the market town that lies eight miles to the north of Weston-under-Lizard. They had been lords of the manor of High Ercall, a village between Shrewsbury and Newport, since the fifteenth century. In the sixteenth century, Thomas Newport had been a beneficiary of the inheritance of Sir John Burgh, which brought further lands to the family, located in Shropshire, Warwickshire and Kent. Thomas had married Alice Corbet of Moreton Corbet, Shropshire and the couple's son Richard made a further advantageous marriage.

FIGURE 38
High Ercall Hall as it appeared in circa 1906.
(Photo: courtesy of the author.)

Richard Herbert of blacke
Halls wife, being Daughter
of Lord Newport of High A...

Sir Richard Newport, as he became, married Margaret Bromley, the daughter and heiress of Sir Thomas Bromley (d.1555) and his wife Isabel Lyster. Bromley had enjoyed preferment under King Henry VIII and eventually became Lord Chief Justice under Queen Mary I, having acquired the estate of Eyton-on-Severn, to the south-west of Shrewsbury, which had been a possession of Shrewsbury Abbey until its dissolution. After Bromley's death and his commemoration with a sumptuous tomb in St Andrew's Church at Wroxeter, the Newport family came to inherit Eyton-on-Severn.

Sir Richard and Lady Margaret Newport were the parents of four sons and four daughters. Their youngest daughter was Magdalen (1561–1627), who married Richard Herbert (d.1597) as her first husband, and who was mother of both 1st Lord Herbert of Cherbury (1583–1648) – who was born at Eyton – and of the metaphysical poet George Herbert (1593–1633). Her portrait hangs in the Morning Room at Weston Park, being the earliest of the Newport family portraits, and it shows the enigmatic face of the woman who, following the death of her Herbert husband, 'erected a fair Monument for him in Montgomery Church, brought up her children carefully, and put them in good courses for making their fortunes …'[1] Her elder brother Sir Francis Newport (c.1555–1623)

FIGURE 40 Joan Carlile (c.1606–1679), *Lady Diana Russell arming Francis Newport (later 1st Earl of Bradford) in preparation for the Civil War*, oil on panel (from the Woburn Abbey Collection).

aided her in gaining wardship of her children following her husband's death. Sir Francis, who had married Beatrix Lacon, and succeeded to the estates at High Ercall and Eyton, was the father of Sir Richard Newport (1587–1651), who in turn became head of the family.

Richard made a beneficial marriage to Rachel Leveson, the daughter of Sir John and Lady Leveson of Whornes Place in Kent and whose elder brother Richard Leveson came to inherit the Trentham, Staffordshire and Lilleshall, Shropshire estates of his kinsman Vice-Admiral Richard Leveson (d.1605). Lilleshall was located close to High Ercall and the families of both properties came to be staunch Royalists during the English Civil Wars. Richard Newport had been knighted by King Charles I in 1615 and, on the eve of the Battle of Edgehill in 1642, he advanced his monarch £6,000 in return for a peerage, being ennobled as the 1st Baron Newport.

His son Francis Newport (1620–1708) in 1642 married Lady Diana Russell, a daughter of the 4th Earl of Bedford and his Countess the Hon. Catherine Brydges, from Woburn Abbey in Bedfordshire. The Bedfords were a highly cultured and well-connected family of advanced tastes, with the earl acting as patron to Inigo Jones. He employed him for the development of his Covent Garden estate, resulting in some of the earliest classical town planning in London, and in the creation of the square, piazza and church of St Paul at Covent Garden.

Francis shared his family's Royalist sympathies and, during the onset of the wars, he was captured fighting for the king at the Battle of Oswestry on 1 July

1644. He was thereafter subjected to two terms of imprisonment, including one spent at the Tower of London. In the meantime, his wife Lady Diana Newport remained steadfastly at High Ercall Hall. The house was garrisoned for the king and subjected to three sieges between 1644 and 1646 before it was finally taken by Parliamentary forces.

During one of the sieges, just three years after the couple's marriage and with a young son in her charge, Diana Newport received an urgent letter from her mother Lady Bedford:

> Never was there a sadder heart of mother than I have for you, and do know not which way to give you comfort … All I can devise to do is to beg this favour of Sir Sam. Luke … Certainly they did not give you good advice to tarry there. For God's sake come away and have a care of your little boy, and little love, which I fear you will lose.[2]

Many people lost their lives in the memorable action, as was evidenced even in the early eighteenth century when the north Shropshire historian Richard Gough of Myddle, when writing of the Civil War, described how two of the sons of William Preece of Myddle 'were killed at High Ercall'.[3]

For the family, the siege proved a disastrous failure. High Ercall Hall was significantly slighted and the family's property seized, whilst eventually Richard, Lord Newport sought sanctuary overseas on the grounds of his health, eventually dying at Moulins-en-Tonnerrois in 1651. In 1648 his wife, with Francis Newport's support, had been able to retrieve the family's estates for payment of a fine of £10,000, but Richard's will, written in that same year, emphasises his despair at the damage to his family and house and that his 'howsholdstuffe and stocke [had been] sold'.[4] Francis and his younger brother

FIGURE 41 Sir Godfrey Kneller (1643–1723), *Francis Newport, 2nd Baron Newport, later 1st Viscount Newport and eventually 1st Earl of Bradford of the first creation,* oil on canvas, 73.6 x 62.2 cm. Accession number 101.0143. (Copyright Trustees of the Weston Park Foundation.)

FIGURE 42 Simon Pietersz Verelst (1644–1721?), *Lady Diana Russell, later Viscountess Newport,* oil on canvas, 61 x 71.1 cm. Accession number 101.0017. (Copyright Trustees of the Weston Park Foundation.)

Andrew meanwhile remained committed royalists and, in 1655, Francis was arrested on suspicion of treason at the time of Colonel John Penruddock's uprising.

Following the Restoration, when King Charles II took the throne in 1660, Francis Newport was able to gain royal favour, leading to a restoration of the Newport family's own fortunes. He was appointed Lord Lieutenant of Shropshire on 26 July and was also granted a gift of Shrewsbury Castle in the same year. Two years later he was given a court position as Comptroller of the Household from 1668, and was also sworn a member of the Privy Council. His royal office entailed residence at Whitehall Palace and his residence there was adjacent to that of the architect Hugh May (1621–1684). In the year that he took office, he found himself short of space, and so sought to take on an adjacent property that had been His Majesty's Confectioner's.[5] It took until 1672 for this to become his and in the year following he gained permission to:

> erect and build a new building … to bee erected on the backside of the Lodgings belonging to the Esquires of the body and to bee ioyned [sic] to His Ldpps Lodgings, and … after such manner and modell as the Lord Newport shall direct.[6]

His own direct involvement, rather than that of a named architect, seems to have been suggested.

In 1672, Francis became Treasurer of the Household and in his roles would have had active involvement in many of the royal building, refurbishment and collecting works that were undertaken in the late seventeenth century. Although the accession of King James II put him out of favour – when he had to relinquish not only his role as Treasurer but also his position as Lord Lieutenant of Shropshire in 1686/7 – he was restored to royal favour at the Glorious Revolution when William III and Queen Mary took the throne in 1689. He was reinstated as Treasurer of the Household and also made Cofferer of the Household, an office that he retained until King William's death in 1702. His court positions were also reflected in the honours that he himself received: King Charles II had raised him within the peerage as Viscount Newport in 1675,

FIGURE 43 Newport House, situated on Dogpole, Shrewsbury, built by Francis Newport, Earl of Bradford in 1696. The house is dramatically sited on a ridge above the River Severn and faces, axially, to those making progress up Dogpole. (Photo: courtesy of the author.)

but then, under King William, in May 1694, he was advanced to an earldom, as 1st Earl of Bradford.

The Bradford title was not a reference to the West Yorkshire town but was derived from the Bradford Hundred of Shropshire, the largest of the county's administrative hundreds, which took its name from the 'broad ford' on the River Roden, which is first mentioned in the 1140s.[7] In Shropshire, his status was proclaimed by the building of a new house in the county town of Shrewsbury in 1696. Located on Dogpole, one of the main medieval thoroughfares at the highest point in the town where it might be seen from the English Bridge across the River Severn below, the house was artfully sited. Shrewsbury at that time would have been almost wholly architecturally dominated by timber-framed buildings, with the only notable exceptions being the stone churches of St Chad, St Alkmund, St Julian and St Mary and some surviving medieval stone houses. A timber-framed house already stood upon the site selected by Francis for the new residence and this was taken down, its frame utilised to create a new house at the approach to the family's property of Shrewsbury Castle on Castle Gates. On Dogpole, the new house was a near-cube of brick with stone quoins and string course, confrontationally sited on an axis with the road as it rose into the town from the hill known as Wyle Cop. Of five bays and two stories, with a vertiginous hipped roof pierced by three dormer windows to the front, the house stands as a Dutch-inspired alien, contrasting strongly with the surviving timber-framed houses that it still has for neighbours. It is not only an accomplished piece of architecture but also an acknowledgement of loyalty to the Dutch-born king. The architect Hugh May's influence is apparent in the house's elevations, whilst the handsomely carved central doorcase – now hiding within an early nineteenth-century Greek Doric portico of cast iron[8] – proclaims the original owner's status with a centrally placed earl's coronet.

The king evidently had a high regard for Francis since, on 27 February 1700, 'knowing his abilities and great merit', he honoured him with attendance at a dinner in celebration of Francis's eightieth birthday. This was noted by John Macky who observed of Francis that: 'He hath a great deal of Wit, is a just Critic, a Judge and Lover of Poetry, Painting, and nice living; hath been a handsome man, but is now near eighty Years old, was always a great Libertine'.[9]

The interest in painting was also something that was shared by Francis's younger son Thomas Newport (c.1655–1719), who enjoyed a successful career as a barrister and politician. Thomas served as Member of Parliament for Ludlow in 1695–8 and 1699–1700, had a short spell as Member for Winchelsea in 1701, and was later MP for Wenlock in 1715–16. He served both King William III and Queen Anne as Commissioner of Customs, as his tomb at St Andrew's church, Wroxeter, proclaims, and he was later made Lord of the Treasury by George I. Having ended his Parliamentary career in 1716, he was ennobled as 1st Baron Torrington.

The collection of father and son was put together relatively quietly, even though paintings were acquired at some high-profile sales. Amongst these were the sales of the executors of the painter Sir Peter Lely (1618–1680) in April and May 1681 and in April 1682, at which Francis made a number of acquisitions. This sale included not only works by Lely – some of which had apparently been left in his studio by sitters who were unable to claim their likenesses – but also old master paintings that Lely himself had collected. Newport purchased fifteen paintings for a total in excess of £300 in his own name and may have purchased other works via the hands of third parties.[10] Amongst the acquisitions was a self-portrait of van Dyck for which he paid £34 but which was sold after his death in 1708 to Richard Graham.[11] He also purchased van Dyck's portrait of the dramatist and theatre owner Thomas Killigrew, for which he paid the

FIGURE 44 *The Hon. Thomas Newport (c.1655–1719), 1st Baron Torrington from 1716*. Mezzotint of 1720 by John Smith, after a portrait by Sir Godfrey Kneller, 36 x 25 cm. Accession number 102.0010.1. (Copyright Trustees of the Weston Park Foundation.)

high price of £83[12] and the same artist's portrait of Sir Walter Pye. The former remains in the collection at Weston Park, whilst the latter was sold on and is now in the collection of the Dukes of Norfolk at Arundel Castle.[13]

From the same sale, he also purchased a version of Lely's portrait of Dr William Harvey, the discoverer of the circulation of blood, for £4[14] and a head of 'Symonds' for £10. This latter has recently been re-identified within the collection – having, for many years been an 'unknown' man – and is a rare likeness of Richard Symonds (1617–1660), the Royalist diarist and antiquary.[15]

Further pictures were also apparently bought from the collection of Holland House,[16] whilst other works were evidently acquired privately and perhaps through somewhat dubious means. His Holbein the younger drawing, then said to be of Anne Boleyn, and with provenance from the 14th Earl of Arundel, had apparently been an unreturned loan from Jonathan Richardson senior (1665–1745). Richardson's copy drawing of 1728 now in the Ashmolean Museum, Oxford, has an accusative note attached to it, written by his son and namesake:

> when he [Francis Newport 1st Earl of Bradford] was Confin'd
> with the Gout, a little before his
> Death, He sent a request of my F.
> that he would lend him a Book of
> Drawings to Divert him, wich my
> F. comply'd with. The E. sent him
> back the Book in a few days, but
> without this Drawing. My F. went
> immediately to wait on him, &
> found the Drawing hanging by the

FIGURE 45 Sir Anthony van Dyck (1599–1641), *Self-portrait*, oil on canvas, 56 x 46 cm. Accession number NPG 6987. (© National Portrait Gallery, London.)

FIGURE 46 Sir Anthony van Dyck (1599–1641), *Thomas Killigrew* (1612–1683), oil on canvas, 100.5 x 83.8 cm, signed and dated 1638. Accession number 101.0106. (Copyright Trustees of the Weston Park Foundation.)

FIGURE 47 Sir Peter Lely (1618–1680), *Richard Symonds* (1617–1660), oil on canvas, 75.8 x 63 cm. Accession number 101.0148. (Copyright Trustees of the Weston Park Foundation.)

FIGURE 48 Hans Holbein the younger (1497/8–1543), *A Lady previously said to be Anne Boleyn*. After the work formerly in the Weston Park collection and which, following its sale in 1975, is now in the British Museum. (Photo: courtesy of the author.)

Bed side in which he lay, in a Frame
of Glass. There was other Company
in the Room, so my F. could not
claim it at that time; but look'd
several times at ye Drawing,
stedfastly, & look'd at my Ld. My Ld.
stood it, discoursing with him, quite
unconcern'd; & in two or three days
fairly Sneak'd out of the World, &
kept the Drawing. My F. could not
claim it afterwards of his Heir ...
with out accusing Bradford of a
most Infamous piece of villany [sic],
of which he had no witness[17]

The drawing left Weston Park in 1975 when it was sold to the British Museum,
whilst a work that left the Weston for the National Gallery in 1983 – Jacopo
Bassano's *Way to Calvary* – might have been acquired through coercion and the
exploitation of his royal office. This exceptional painting had formed a part of

FIGURE 49 Sir Anthony
van Dyck (1599–1641),
*Sir Thomas Hanmer,
2nd Bt* (1612–1678), oil on
canvas, 107.5 x 85.5 cm.
Accession number 101.0090.
(Copyright Trustees of the
Weston Park Foundation.)

FIGURE 50 Sir Anthony van Dyck (1599–1641), *Beatriz van Hemmema, Countess of Oxford*, oil on canvas, 112 x 92 cm. Accession number 101.0091. (Copyright Trustees of the Weston Park Foundation.)

the 'Dutch Gift' of the States of Holland to Charles II in 1660, which included a large part of the collections of the merchant brothers Gerrit and Jan Reyns of Amsterdam. When Charles II's widowed queen Catherine of Braganza returned to Portugal in 1692 the picture remained in England and found its way into the Newport collection, seemingly as a bribe by which the remaining pictures in the dowager queen's collection could leave the country.

When John Evelyn dined with Francis in London on 24 January 1685, he noted the quality of the collection, drawing attention to three particular works:

> I dined at Lord Newport's, who has some excellent pictures, especially that of Sir Thomas Hanmer by Vandyck, one of the best he ever painted; another of our English Dobson's painting; but above all, Christ in the Virgin's lap by Poussin, an admirable piece; with something of most other famous hands.[18]

Van Dyck was evidently especially admired by Francis, and in addition to Hanmer and the previously mentioned portraits, the collection included a number of other works by the artist including the portraits of *Celia Crofts Mrs Killigrew*, the *Countess of Carlisle*, the *Countess of Sunderland*, and the *Countess of Oxford* which now hang at Weston Park. Perhaps the most outstanding of the van Dyck portraits, though, was the full-length portrait

FIGURE 51 Sir Anthony van Dyck (1599–1641), *Queen Henrietta Maria with Sir Jeffrey Hudson*, oil on canvas, 219.1 x 134.8 cm. This pre-eminent work by van Dyck was in the Newport collection by the second decade of the eighteenth century and then passed by descent from Mary, Countess of Bradford to her daughter Lady Diana Newport, Countess of Mountrath, and ultimately descended to the Portarlington family. Accession number 1952.5.39 (by courtesy of the National Gallery of Art, Washington, DC).

of *Queen Henrietta Maria with Geoffrey Hudson*, which he had acquired by 1705, when it was hanging in his house in Twickenham,[19] and which is now in the collection of the National Gallery of Art in Washington.[20]

Other notable artists were represented within the collection. Of Rembrandt's work there were no fewer than two attributed self-portraits, of which one has now been identified as that in the collection of the Norton Simon Museum in Pasadena, California.[21] There was evidently also a fondness for the work of Adam Elsheimer. The Newport collection works included the *Martyrdom and Stoning of St Stephen* now in the National Gallery of Scotland, the *True Cross* pictures at the Staedel Museum, Frankfurt, plus also two paintings that are now in the Fitzwilliam Museum, Cambridge.[22] The surviving part of the collection that is now at Weston Park still includes a rich range of cabinet paintings of Dutch and Italian schools, including Leandro Bassano's (1557–1622) *Council of War*, Gerrit Dou's (1613–1675) *Old Lady with an Hour Glass*, and a jewel-like Johann Rottenhammer (1564–1625) of *Danae*. At Weston Park there are still no fewer than three paintings of *St Catherine of Alexandria*, doubtless a reflection

FIGURE 52 Mary Beale (1633–1699), After Domenichino, *St Catherine of Alexandria*, oil on canvas, 62.8 x 45.5 cm. Accession number 101.0333. (Copyright Trustees of the Weston Park Foundation.)

FIGURE 53 Leandro Bassano (1557–1622), *A Council of War*, oil on canvas, 114.3 x 114.3 cm. The painting was a part of the Newport collection from at least the second decade of the eighteenth century; in a pre-1714 inventory it is recorded as hanging in the parlour of the family's house at Surrey Street, Westminster. Accession number 101.0063. (Copyright Trustees of the Weston Park Foundation.)

of Charles II's Queen Catherine of Braganza's dedication to the saint, including one which has recently been conserved and recognised as a work by Mary Beale (1633–1699).

Many of the pictures found their way to Richmond House, a substantial villa overlooking Eel Pie Island on the north bank of the River Thames at Twickenham. Francis Newport bought the house in 1682 and then proceeded to rebuild it. In his voluminous will he noted 'it hath cost me in building and reparations since I bought it as much as purchase money at least'. Peter Tillemans included a view of the house, pedimented and of brick, in his painting of the Thames and the nearby villa of Alexander Pope of circa 1725. In 1797, when still recalled as having been the 1st Earl's house, it was described as having

FIGURE 54 Gerrit Dou (1613–1675), *An Old Lady with an Hour Glass*, oil on panel, 24 x 17.8 cm. This small cabinet picture was in the collection of the Newport family prior to 1714, figuring in their early inventory at their Surrey Street house when it hung in the 'New Room next Somerset Garden'. Accession number 101.0064. (Copyright Trustees of the Weston Park Foundation.)

'a pleasing garden, and extensive terrace, guarded by handsome iron rails. The other front is to the street, but hid by a high wall, at each end of which is a porter's lodge. Within is a good courtyard.'[23] The house passed to Francis's younger son Thomas, on condition that he lived there for two months in each year, and it remained a home of Thomas's third wife and widow Anne, Lady Torrington (1683–1735) until her death.

Richmond House became a repository of the collection, with a few works kept there in Francis's lifetime, whilst others remained at his Westminster house. Gradually, though, after Francis's death in 1708 and until the demise of his daughter-in-law Lady Torrington in 1735, the collection was almost entirely brought together under Richmond House's roof. It was here that the extent and quality of the collection came to the notice of the engraver George Vertue who, in 1714, observed: 'At my Ld. Bradfords at Twittenham there are several pictures of Vandyke. & of other good painters. Amongst the rest an original of the Ld Clarendon & Dr. Harvey Phisitian [*sic*]. Likewise several heads of Sr. Peter Lely. & a most Excellent picture a head. Painted by Vandyke. & many other pictures.'[24] The surviving 9 November 1719 inventory of the house, created after Francis's son Thomas's death, allows for an evocative glimpse at the interiors through the rooms' given-names and it also enables a reconstruction of both the collection and the aesthetics of its hang. The Little Parlour was noted as containing just three pictures, all of them portraits of Francis Lord Bradford when aged, respectively, fifty-six, seventy-seven and eighty-nine. Great and Little Greenhouses, which were presumably early eighteenth-century orangery-type rooms, with one wall devoted to a row of large windows, were used for the display of some of the collection. There was also a 'Blue Parlour', 'Parlour Next to Greenhouse', and the Hall wherein hung van Dyck's *Henrietta Maria*.

Especially interesting was the 'Beauty Room'. This followed a mainland European tradition in celebrating female beauty in portraiture and which had been a mode of display previously used in the 1660s hanging of Lely's six Maids

FIGURE 55 Peter Tillemans (1684–1734), *A View of the Thames at Twickenham*, oil on canvas, 65.5 x 135 cm. The picture shows the view looking west across the Thames and includes a number of villas, the most prominent of which is Alexander Pope's, with its lower flanking wings. Richmond House, the 1st Earl of Bradford's house, is to the right. It is of red brick, with a pediment on its roofline, and stands back above the river, just before the tree covered tip of Eel Pie Island. Accession number LDORL 00886 (by permission of the London Borough of Richmond upon Thames Borough Art Collection, Orleans House Gallery).

of Honour in the White Room at Windsor Castle, and more recently in Kneller's Beauty Room of 1692 at Hampton Court. At Richmond House, the chosen works were eight paintings attributed to Lely, Wissing, van Dyck and Kneller, including Lely's *Mrs Davis* and *Mrs Roberts* which are now at Weston Park.

At Francis's death in 1708, he was laid to rest at St Andrew's church, Wroxeter, the parish church for the family's Eyton-on-Severn estate. His monument stands against the south wall of the chancel, a grand crested wall tablet with an arched recess containing a marble urn upon a swept plinth that is flanked by sleeping winged putti heads. Below is a marble sarcophagus, whilst the cresting bears his arms and the Newport unicorn crest. The sarcophagus originally had weeper figures until at least the late nineteenth century although they have since disappeared. Its design is convincingly attributed to Grinling Gibbons, being notably similar to the Gibbons monument to Admiral George Churchill (1654–1710), brother of the 1st Duke of Marlborough, and also of Arabella Churchill who was married to one of Francis's legatees Colonel Charles Godfrey, which stands near the Choir Gate at Westminster Abbey.[25] For the monument, Francis had left instructions in his will for £200 to be spent and, specifically, for it to be erected besides that of his great-grandfather Sir Richard Newport.

During his lifetime, although he had not been able to rebuild High Ercall Hall as a seat for the family, he did make provision in the village for a range of alms houses to provide accommodation to six elderly people. Built in 1694, the U-plan brick building still stands in the centre of the village. This philanthropy was yet further shown by a bequest of £10 for the poor of the parish of St Mary the Virgin at Twickenham, wherein Richmond House stood.[26]

This benevolence was further developed by his daughter Lady Catherine (d.1716), the wife of Henry (d.1691), 4th Baron Herbert of Cherbury. Having no children and as a thanksgiving for having been rescued when she got lost in the Alps, she directed that her personal fortune of £6,000 was to be vested in four

trustees – one of whom was her brother Thomas, Lord Torrington – who were
to acquire land in Shropshire and to build an alms house for twelve poor women
and twelve poor girls, who would be appointed by her elder brother Richard,
2nd Earl of Bradford and his wife and then by their successors in title. The result
was the creation of Preston Hospital, at Preston upon the Weald Moors, and
the need for the alms houses was initially such that the numbers of occupants
soon increased to twenty. Lord Torrington's own £1,000 legacy, following his
death in 1719, enabled the building of the central hall, and the buildings were
further enlarged in the early nineteenth century following a bequest from the
7th Earl of Mountrath.[27] The grouping of older and younger residents together
was not only an act of charity but also an interesting social experiment, which
lent experience to the training of the girls – many of whom found careers in
domestic service – and who provided labour, in a number of cases, to Weston
Park. The hospital's purpose has since been transferred to modern purpose-built
early twenty-first century premises in Newport, but the original buildings still
survive, converted to private residential use. It is a handsome group of provincial
baroque buildings in red brick with stone dressings that were perhaps the work
of the Smith family of architects, built in 1721–5 and entered via a courtyard

FIGURE 56 Sir Peter Lely
(1618–1680), *Mary Davis*
(1640–c.1721), oil on
canvas, 124.5 x 99 cm.
One of the paintings that
were hung in the beauty
room at Richmond House,
Twickenham, the portrait
depicts Mary – or
Moll – Davis, one of
Charles II's mistresses.
A talented musician, as
the painting shows, she
was described by the wife
of diarist Samuel Pepys
as 'the most impertinent
slut in all of the world'.
Accession number 101.0165.
(Copyright Trustees of the
Weston Park Foundation.)

FIGURE 57 *Newport Monuments at St Andrew's Church, Wroxeter*, shown in a watercolour of 1901 by the artist Thomas
Prytherch (1864–1926), 71.5 x 45 cm. This view of the church's chancel shows the Grinling Gibbons monument to Francis,
1st Earl of Bradford, in its original form complete with putti weepers. It is situated next to the monument to Francis's
great-grandfather, Sir Richard Newport, as his will had requested. Accession number 116.0027. (Copyright Trustees of the
Weston Park Foundation.)

FIGURE 58 St Andrew's church, Wroxeter, Shropshire. Francis Newport, 1st Earl of Bradford's monument as it now appears, without the weepers. (Photo: courtesy of the author.)

with an elegant wrought iron gate-screen by Robert Bakewell. Later wings and lodges were built in the early nineteenth century, designed in sympathy with the original by John Hiram Haycock and Edward Haycock.

The first Earl of Bradford was succeeded in his titles by his eldest son Richard (1644–1723), who had married Mary Wilbraham (1661–1737), the eventual heiress of Weston Park in 1681. Richard had not always been in favour with his father, as Francis's will indicates, leaving a detailed list of his silver which was to be placed in the care of trustees and treated as heirlooms, whilst Richard was left prohibited to 'intermeddle with more than the use and possession thereof'.[28] Some of this distrust might have stemmed from youthful excess and a somewhat cavalier character, which Samuel Pepys hinted at when he described Richard on 30 May 1668 as 'young Newport' who with his associates behaved 'as very rogues as any in the town … though full of wit who were ready to take hold of every woman that come by them'.[29]

The trusted son, who was to be executor of the will, was Francis' younger son and fellow connoisseur Thomas, Lord Torrington, to whom the picture collection was bequeathed. He appears to have followed the instruction of his father's will in sending specific paintings to hang at Eyton in the house's parlour.

FIGURE 59 *Preston Hospital, Preston upon the Weald Moors, Shropshire*, shown in a later nineteenth-century watercolour, 27 x 37 cm. The main hall was the gathering place for the old lady residents and for the young girls. The bell cote is an early nineteenth-century addition by the Shrewsbury architect Edward Haycock (1790–1870). Accession number 116.0079. (Copyright Trustees of the Weston Park Foundation.)

These were originally noted in a codicil of 1 April 1701 to be van Dyck's portraits of *Sir Thomas Hanmer*, *Sir Walter Pye*, *Sir William Killigrew* and *Sir Thomas Killigrew*, together with Francis's own portrait by Lely from Twickenham. Two years later, on 6 January 1703, Francis had changed his mind, instructing Sir William Killigrew's portrait to be replaced by that of Lord Chief Justice Sir Edward Littleton, 1st Baron Lyttleton (1589–1645). These works do not figure in later inventories of the collection – although Hanmer and Sir Thomas Killigrew survive at Weston Park – and so it appears that Thomas Newport honoured his father's wishes and enabled the creation of what would have been a somewhat remarkable homage to van Dyck and to his father's adherence to the Carolean court. Two works were bequeathed away from the family, with Colonel Charles Godfrey (1646–1714) able to make his own selection of a painting with the exceptions of the Eyton pictures and also of van Dyck's *Henrietta Maria*. The other bequest was to Lord George Howard, of a Lely full-length of his mother that Francis had acquired.

Lord Torrington moved the pictures that had been at his father's residence at Whitehall to his own house in Surrey Street, a road between the Strand and the River Thames, close to Somerset House, whilst others were kept at Richmond House. He was thrice married. His first wife had been Lucy Atkyns (d.1696) and, following her death, he married in 1700 to Penelope Bridgeman, the daughter of Sir Orlando Bridgeman, 1st Bt of Ridley (1649–1701, a second son of Sir Orlando Bridgeman, 1st Bt of Great Lever – see Chapter 4). When she died five years later, he married lastly in 1709 to Anne Pierrepont, daughter of Robert Pierrepont, a grandson of the 1st Earl of Kingston. Anne was a signatory to the Lady's Petition for the Establishment of a Foundling Hospital which Thomas Coram (1668–1751) presented to George II in 1735 and evidently had a firm interest in social welfare. The picture collection was catalogued following her husband's death in 1719, and the inventories of the houses at London and at Twickenham remain informative records of the placing and scope of the collection.

When Lady Torrington in turn died in 1735, Richmond House was sold and the picture collection was brought to Weston Park in June of that year by Francis's daughter-in-law Mary Wilbraham, Countess of Bradford. It took no fewer than thirty horse-drawn carts to bring the three hundred and twenty-five paintings to Weston Park.

A list detailing the paintings and the cases in which each one was packed still survives to show the care that had been applied to the task of logistics. It also provides evidence of how almost two-thirds of the original collection still remains at Weston Park. Lady Bradford only had two years in which to enjoy the collection at Weston and when she died her will directed that the collection should be divided into three equal parts for her children: Lady Diana, Countess of Mountrath; Lady Anne Bridgeman; and Thomas, 4th Earl of Bradford.

Thomas, Lord Bradford suffered from mental instability, and on his death in 1762 his portion of the collection was divided between the other two heirs. The van Dyck portrait of Henrietta Maria had been his and this passed to his sister Lady Diana Newport (1698/9–1766) who, in 1721, had married Algernon Coote, 6th Earl of Mountrath (d.1744). In the year prior to his death, the Irish peer had purchased Twickenham Park and here, Horace Walpole observed, Lady Mountrath passed her days in an increasingly intoxicated state, 'as rich and as tipsy as Cacofogo in the comedy. What a jumble of avarice, lewdness, dignity

FIGURE 60 *Anne Pierrepont, Lady Torrington* (d.1735). Mezzotint of 1720 by John Smith, after a portrait by Sir Godfrey Kneller, 36 x 25 cm. Accession number 102.0010.2. (Copyright Trustees of the Weston Park Foundation.)

– and claret!'[30] When she died, her will was also a jumble, and Twickenham Park was bequeathed to the Duchess of Newcastle, with a reversion to the Duke and Duchess of Montrose, and then to Lord Frederick Cavendish. Some of her share of the Newport paintings were left as heirlooms with the house,[31] whilst the remainder, with the contents of her house in Grosvenor Square, London, passed to Caroline, Lady Milton (1718–1775). Lady Mountrath's will went on to dictate that after Lady Milton's death the contents of the house were not to be inherited by any surviving husband, and so this portion of the collection passed ultimately, via Lady Milton's daughter Caroline, to the Earls of Portarlington. The Portarlingtons' late nineteenth- and early twentieth-century sales, partly from their Irish seat of Emo Court, Co. Laois, led to the fragmentation of this part of the Newport collection.

The other inheritor of a third of the collection from Lady Bradford was her other daughter, Lady Anne, who had married the eventual Sir Orlando Bridgeman, 4th Bt (1695–1764) in 1719. This section of the collection, with only minor losses, has remained at Weston Park ever since and has also come to include the portraits of Hanmer and Thomas Killigrew that had been sent to Eyton after the 1st Earl's death.

The collection, in spite of its division, remained well-known even after Bradford and Torrington's deaths, with Horace Walpole referencing the Robert Walker double portrait of *General Lambert and Oliver Cromwell* as being 'in Lord Bradford's collection' and recalling that Evelyn had commented upon the strength of Lambert's likeness in the work.[32] Walpole was also aware of a half-length portrait of *General Moncke*, that he attributed to Walker, which was then in the collection of the Countess of Mountrath at Twickenham Park and which had also a Newport provenance.[33] After Walpole's time, though, the significance of the collection was largely lost. In part this was due to its fragmentation but also since the major surviving elements of the collection had moved, so decisively, in 1735 from a metropolitan existence to a distinctly rural one. Without the collection's founders, Francis Newport, 1st Earl of Bradford and his son Lord Torrington, the meaning of the collection and, indeed, the attributions of artists and depictions of sitters became, in some cases, forgotten.

CHAPTER FOUR

The Early Bridgemans
A Bishop, a Baronetcy and the Birth of a Dynasty

The family which in 1762 inherited a share of the Newport art collection and Weston Park itself owed its rise through society to foundations that were laid in the seventeenth and early eighteenth century largely through the endeavours of one man. There can be few landowning families whose dynastic origins and foundations of their estates rest on the achievements of a man of God. Yet the Bridgeman family, who had previously prospered as small merchants in Exeter, Devon, owe a large debt to the diplomatic and administrative abilities of John Bridgeman (1577–1652), Bishop of Chester, whose preferment within the church and at court, coupled with a brilliant foresight in his acquisitions, provided the family with economic and social footings that were to enable the family's future wealth and elevation.

The son of Thomas Bridgeman of Greenway near Exeter, John Bridgeman studied at Oriel College, Oxford, before continuing to St Peter's College, Cambridge, and became a Fellow of Magdalene College, Cambridge in 1599. He was ordained a deacon and priest by Dr Thomas Dove (1655–1630), Bishop of Peterborough, at Walden two years later. Dove was evidently a mentor to Bridgeman – who named one of his younger sons after him – and had evident pride in his protégé when he wrote to Thomas Howard, 1st Earl of Suffolk (1561–1626) in 1604, describing the newly ordained Bridgeman as: 'an honest man, a good scholer [*sic*], and a rare preacher'.[1] With courtly friends, preferment soon came his way, and in 1605 Bridgeman, who had been presented to the rectory of Lezant, Cornwall, and to the vicarage of Alvington, Oxfordshire, became Chaplain in Ordinary to James I. In 1606 he married Elizabeth Helyar, the daughter of a prominent and influential landowning clergyman Rev. William Helyar (1559–1645) of Coker Court, Somerset, who served as Archdeacon of Barnstable and was a chaplain to Queen Elizabeth I.

In the following year, the vicarage of Heavitree followed for Bridgeman, and, whilst there, his second son, Orlando, was born in 1608/9 and christened at St George's, Exeter.[2]

In 1615/16, John Bridgeman was admitted as rector at Wigan in Lancashire. Wigan's rectory was remarkable as one of the few instances where a rector of the church held secular authority which amounted to feudal manorial rights. These included collecting tolls for markets and fairs, and mineral royalties within the glebe. The latter, of course, were extensive in what was a significant part of

FIGURES 61 & 62 *John Bridgeman, Bishop of Chester (1577–1652) and his wife, Elizabeth Helyar (d.1636)*, attributed to Cornelius Johnson. Oil on panel, respectively 58.5 x 40.6 cm and 57.1 x 42 cm. The pair of portraits appear to have been painted in 1616, when John Bridgeman noted in his account book: 'for my wife's picture drawing & my own 55s 11'. Accession numbers 101.0135 and 101.0130, respectively. (Copyright Trustees of the Weston Park Foundation.)

the Lancashire coalfield, providing its rectors with wealth as well as influence until 1861, when the town corporation purchased the rights.[3] Unsurprisingly, John Bridgeman sought to protect his rectorial assets, and having attended King James I/VI at Scotland in 1616, he began the process of recovering rents and manorial rights that were not being observed by the people of Wigan, petitioning the king to ensure that his case was taken up. His younger brother Edward Bridgeman (d.1645) had moved to Wigan with him and he, too, played an important part in governance, becoming MP for Wigan in 1625 and 1628, but being stood down in the year following when Charles I decided to rule without Parliament for eleven years.

To architecturally assert the importance of the rector, John Bridgeman made considerable additions to the old moated rectory, including the building of a plain private chapel, adding a dovecot above the gatehouse and also rebuilt the adjacent farm. The parish church of All Saints, as the focal point of Wigan parish, also benefitted from his attentions when he rebuilt the chancel in 1619–20.[4] The church also received a Mortlake tapestry, depicting the story of Ananias and Sapphira, which formerly served as a reredos, and he gave further tapestries to the Collegiate church of Manchester (now its cathedral), and to Chester cathedral.

There are three portraits of the bishop in the collection of Weston Park, but it is that attributed to Cornelius Johnson which perhaps captures his personality the best, depicting a shrewd and wise-looking man.[5] This also has the small painted device of the world in darkness and a light of heaven radiating above, with a Latin inscription 'Gratia dei Pons homini' (The bridge of the grace of God to man), a pun on the bishop's surname. Certainly, he had a head for business which was matched by his abilities as a politically aware cleric, demonstrated in the way in which he diplomatically ran the diocese and individual parishes that were within his care. Managing assets was a particular forte; he kept meticulous records of estate management in duplicated compendiums, their minute script capturing every detail of financial importance.[6]

With requisite skills and influence, he was destined for bishopric and was consecrated as Bishop of Chester in 1619. Although he retained the rectory of Wigan, he was active in Chester, where he altered the bishop's palace in 1620 and also gave a pulpit to the cathedral, which was once in the west end of the aisle and is now to be found in the consistory court, where it still bears Bridgeman's bishop's arms above an arcaded back. His diocesan duties, of course, took him away from Wigan but in 1628 he was able to appoint an able and trusted curate in the Lancashire town in the form of his brother-in-law Henry Helyar (c.1590–1634).[7]

When the bishop's parents died within six months of each other in 1627–8, he inherited the family properties in Devon and eventually sold them in 1630.[8] His own investment in property, from 1629, was in Lancashire. Here, he purchased the manor of Great Lever and also other lands nearby at Farnworth, Bolton and at Lady Hall and over time also bought further estates at Bromborough on the Wirral, at Wigland and at Wolvesacre in Flintshire.[9]

Great Lever had been sold to the bishop by Sir Ralph Assheton, 2nd Bt (c.1606–1680) of Whalley and Downham, and Bishop John soon engaged in the rebuilding of the manor house and its chapel. The date of 1631 and his initials were inscribed onto the main elevation of the house and on a stone gate archway, whilst a domestic chapel, dedicated to the Holy Trinity, was added

FIGURE 63 Great Lever Hall, Lancashire in circa 1690. Photograph of a drawing. The bishop's domestic chapel can be seen on the left-hand side of the range of buildings. Accession number 117.0094. (Copyright Trustees of the Weston Park Foundation.)

FIGURE 64 *Orlando Bridgeman as a boy*, painted by Robert Peake (c.1551–1619) (by permission of the Master and Fellows of Magdalene College, Cambridge).

from 1634 and consecrated in 1636. The bishop's arms were displayed on the plaster ceiling of the room that had been his study, whilst the house's windows also had the family heraldry. In 1662, Samuel Pepys noted a conversation with John Swinfen – who was, coincidentally, a friend of Lady Wilbraham of Weston – in which Swinfen recalled the bishop's activities some thirty years previously:

> Bishopp Bridgeman ... lately hath bought a seat, anciently of the Levers, and then the Ashtons, and he hath in his great hall window (having repaired and beautified the house) caused four great places to be left for coats of armes. In one he hath put the Levers, with this motto, *Olim* [once]. In another the Ashtons, with this, Heri [yesterday]. In the next his own, with this, Hodie [today]. In the fourth nothing but this motto, *Cras nescio cujus* [tomorrow, I do not know which].[10]

Great Lever was a sizeable house, with a total of twenty-one hearths at the time of the Hearth Tax return in 1666. Further additions were made to the lands associated with the property by the bishop, including the acquisition of Highfield Hall Farm, which was purchased soon after 1634.

The house soon became the focal point of life for the Bridgeman family and in 1631 when plague was affecting the surrounding area, Bishop Bridgeman noted on 16 August that:

> my son Orlando's second child (his first son) was born in the chamber next to the Lord's Chamber under the study gallery ... and baptized by name John.[11]

Orlando himself, who had been the second son of John Bridgeman and Elizabeth Helyar, had shown great academic promise as a boy and began his legal career at the Inner Temple, before going on to greater office. He married in 1627/8, his first wife Judith Kynaston, the daughter and heiress of John Kynaston of Morton, an estate located between Shrewsbury and Oswestry. Their first child – later the second Bridgeman baronet – was named after both of his grandfathers.

Bishop Bridgeman was quick to arrest the theft of coal from his Bolton estate – a commodity that future generations of Bridgemans, over the two hundred and fifty years that followed his acquisition, had the bishop to be grateful to – and he was equally quick to begin exploiting its value.[12] The same was true in Wigan where in 1635 he stopped the residents from taking the coal from lands associated with the rectory.[13]

In the following year, his wife Elizabeth died after a long illness and was laid to rest at the southern side of the east end of Chester Cathedral. She had borne the bishop fifteen children, of whom just five survived into adulthood.[14]

The Bishop in 1633 interviewed those who had been accused of witchcraft by Master Robinson in the famous case of the Lancashire Witches, although three had already died in prison. Four of the accused were also taken to London and subjected to a bodily examination by Dr William Harvey.[15]

Throughout his career, Bishop Bridgeman had been able to call upon some of the most important and powerful of contacts, including Lord Strafford, who stayed with his retinue at Chester, shortly after his appointment as Lord Deputy of Ireland, and caused the bishop £100 in expenses,[16] and also Archbishop Laud.

In 1638, as he disclosed in a letter to Laud, he had hoped to purchase the Wigan advowson from Sir Richard Fleetwood but was outbid by Sir Richard Murray DD, Warden of Manchester. At the time, this must have been a bitter disappointment although his son was to have greater success in making an acquisition of the rectory.

The bishop's son Orlando had, by this time, become vice chamberlain of Chester in 1638 before progressing to be solicitor general to Charles, Prince of Wales, and then attorney general to the Court of Wards and Liveries in 1640. During the same year, he was elected as MP for Wigan in both the Short and the Long Parliaments, proving himself to be a committed Royalist. Orlando aided Lord Strange (the eventual 7th Earl of Derby) in resisting the Parliamentary forces at Chester in 1642, and, as a consequence, was excluded from Parliament on 29 August 1642. His father, meanwhile, from 23 until 28 September of that year entertained King Charles I and Charles Prince of Wales at his bishop's palace.

Within the year, whilst Orlando was knighted by Charles I, his father was less fortunate since Parliament passed ordinance to sequester the estates of bishops who had been loyal to the king. Since Wigan, too, was defiantly Royalist, an ordinance was passed by the House of Lords on 28 September 1643 which enabled the rectory of Wigan to also be seized.[17] The Bishop's Palace at Chester and its contents were eventually sold in 1650 for £1,059, the bishop having, meanwhile, sought sanctuary at his son and daughter-in-law's home, Morton Hall in Shropshire. It was here in 1652 that he died and was then buried in the parish church of St Mary at Kinnerley.

During the Commonwealth, the bishop's son and successor in his estates Sir Orlando Bridgeman maintained a private legal practice, specialising in the highly profitable conveyancing of forfeited lands. He was able to maintain an understanding of property transactions and was evidently observing the goings on at Wigan Rectory. His father had been succeeded as rector from 1643 by a nonconformist, James Bradshaw, who had inflamed the Parliamentarian cause in south Lancashire from his pulpit. Bradshaw was, in turn, succeeded by Charles Hotham in 1653 but after his ejection, upon the Restoration of the monarchy in 1660, Sir Orlando was able to purchase the Wigan Advowson from the Hotham family in 1662.[18] He established a trust to own the rectory, within which the Bridgeman family had a prominent place, and gave new rights to the Corporation of Wigan to ensure a satisfactory working relationship between rector and town at that time.[19] Two of the subsequent rectors appointed were, as John Bridgeman had been, also bishops of Chester, John Pearson and Thomas Cartwright. In many other cases, there was a family link, with the rector being either a relation by marriage or blood, or a trusted friend or neighbour of the Bridgemans. Samuel Aldersey (1673–1742), for instance, who was instituted in 1714 was married to Henrietta Bridgeman, daughter of Henry Bridgeman (1615–1682), Bishop of Sodor and Man, himself a younger son of Bishop John Bridgeman. The successor, on Aldersey's death in 1741, was Roger Bridgeman (1700–1750), the second surviving son of Sir John Bridgeman, 3rd Bt, who held it until his death.

The Restoration served to confirm the loyalty of the Bridgeman family to their monarch and Charles II rewarded Sir Orlando with the first baronetage to be created under his rule on 7 June 1660, he being styled as 'of Great Lever, Lancashire'. The new baronet was entrusted in the October of the same year to preside over the trial of the regicides, where his judgement was seen as fair by contemporary observers. Following the trial, he became Chief Baron of the Exchequer and Chief Justice of the Common Pleas. After seven further years, in 1667 he was appointed Lord Keeper of the Great Seal, his tenure commemorated by Pieter Borselaer's portrait, showing him with his burse – or bag – of the Great Seal. The diarist Samuel Pepys recorded him as 'the man of the whole nation that is the best spoken of'[20] and 'a mighty able man'[21] and not only his roles of office but also his personal deportment of them proved this. A strong-minded Protestant, he had reservations about his monarch's

FIGURE 65 Morton Hall, Knockin, Shropshire, seen from the south. The one-time seat of the Kynaston family which passed to the Bridgeman family on the marriage of Judith Kynaston to Orlando Bridgeman (1608/9–1674), first baronet from 1660. Although rebuilt as an estate farm for the 3rd Earl of Bradford in the later nineteenth century, the present house still retains parts of the earlier house, including the brick wing seen on the right of the façade. (Photo: courtesy of the author.)

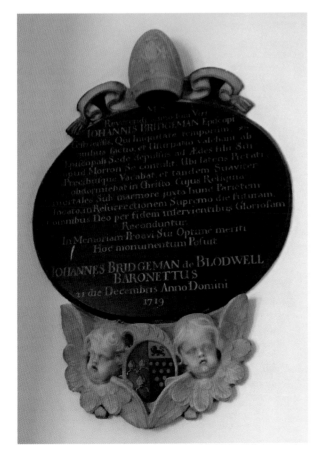

FIGURE 66 Early eighteenth-century monument to Bishop John Bridgeman in the chancel at the parish church of St Mary at Kinnerley, Shropshire. (Photo: courtesy of the author.)

FIGURE 67 *Sir Orlando Bridgeman 1st Bt (1608/9– 1674) as Keeper of the Great Seal*, depicted by Pieter Borselaer (fl.1644–87), oil on canvas, 72.5 x 61 cm. He is seen holding his burse – the purse or bag of office. Accession number 101.0044. (Copyright Trustees of the Weston Park Foundation.)

FIGURE 68 The burse of the Great Seal that was gifted to Sir Orlando Bridgeman following his resignation from office. Framed into a fire-screen by the 4th Earl's wife, the burse was conserved by the textile conservator May Berkouwer for the Trustees of the Weston Park Foundation and it is now displayed in environmentally safe conditions for its long-term conservation. (Copyright Trustees of the Weston Park Foundation.)

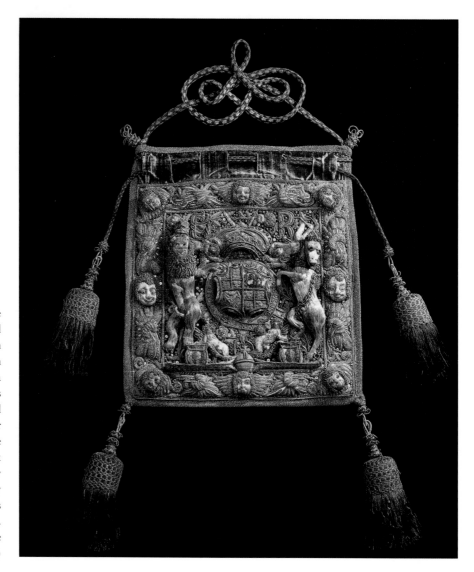

FIGURE 69 Silver stem-cup of late seventeenth-century date, fashioned from the silver of the Great Seal of England at its replacement. The cup's body is engraved with a representation of the burse of the Great Seal. (Copyright Trustees of the Weston Park Foundation.)

associations with France, the Roman Catholicism of his queen and, especially, in the notion of the Declaration of Indulgence, which extended religious liberty to Catholics. In 1672, he refused to apply the Seal to the Declaration and eventually resigned office, to be replaced as keeper by Anthony Ashley Cooper, 1st Earl of Shaftesbury (1621–1683). He was, however, permitted to keep his burse[22] and the seal – a new one being created – with the latter being melted down and refashioned as a weighty stem-cup engraved with the image of the burse. This he specifically referenced in his will, leaving the piece to his eldest son John and calling it: 'that great piece of plate which was made of the great seal which I had inn my custody'.[23]

From 1667, Sir Orlando Bridgeman's private chaplain had been Thomas Traherne, the theologian and metaphysical poet. His *Roman Forgeries* (1673), a criticism of the Catholic Church, was published during his service with Bridgeman. Traherne lived at Bridgeman's Teddington house, a building which remained as 'Bridgeman House' on the main High Street, but which was demolished for tramway widening in the early twentieth century. Both Sir Orlando and Traherne died in 1674, it is thought from smallpox, and were buried at the Church of St Mary with St Alban at Teddington. Sir Orlando, who was sixty-six at the time of his death, is commemorated with a handsome classical monument in the south chancel, whilst both master and chaplain are now also commemorated in twentieth-century figurative stained glass panels in the church's windows.[24] When in 1833 alterations were being made to the church, his sepulchre was opened and the body was found to be well preserved by its embalming, with even his beard surviving the intervening passage of time.

Sir Orlando was succeeded at his death by his eldest son John, who became the second baronet. In 1657 John Bridgeman (1631–1710) had bought Castle Bromwich Hall to the east of Birmingham, in what was then rural Warwickshire, from Leicester Devereux, 6th Viscount Hereford. The house and its estate had been a property of the Devereux family from the fifteenth century, with the core of the present mansion owing to Sir Edward Devereux (d.1622), who 'built a fair house of brick … wherein he resided'.[25] The reason for the purchase, at a remove from the possessions of the Bridgemans in the north-west of England, probably owes to Sir Orlando Bridgeman's second wife Dorothy Cradock, widow of George Cradock (d.1643) of Caverswall Castle, Staffordshire. The Cradocks' daughter Mary – who had been a coheir of her father's Staffordshire estates, which were sold in 1655 – married John Bridgeman and it was probably her fortune that enabled the purchase of Castle Bromwich and

FIGURES 70 & 71 *Sir John Bridgeman (1631–1710), 2nd Bt and his wife Mary Cradock, Lady Bridgeman*, by Wallecomt Vaillant (1623–1677), pastel, each 39.4 x 33.5 cm. Accession numbers 116.0054.1 and 116.0054.2. (Copyright Trustees of the Weston Park Foundation.)

the house's subsequent embellishment.[26] Mary was certainly actively engaged in the process of embellishment, as a notable series of letters between her and the Royalist gentleman architect Captain William Winde (c.1645–1722), written between 7 December 1685 and 17 July 1704, indicate.[27] Winde was married to Magdalen Bridgeman – a daughter of Sir James Bridgeman, younger son of Bishop John Bridgeman – and so in his correspondence Winde refers to Mary, Lady Bridgeman as 'cousin'. The correspondence makes for engaging reading, showing the deliberations of what was and what was not fashionable in terms of painted schemes and types of marbles. In terms of those artists and craftsmen referenced, it also emphasises the quality of the works proposed and the works that were actually enacted. Lady Bridgeman, as patron, was notably grateful to Winde for the value of his advice: 'for we being altogether ignorant in building rely on your judgement …'.[28]

Works had been started on Castle Bromwich Hall from 1672 and a fireback that is now in the hall bears the date 1674 and the Bridgemans' initials. Under William Winde's direction the hall's Jacobean form was reinvented in masterly fashion for the Bridgemans. The plain gabled frontage was given the drama of a stage set by raising the recessed centre's three bays and crowning them with urn-punctuated balustrading with a central pediment carved with the Bridgeman crest. The centre bay of the façade was rebuilt in ashlar with rusticated quoins, and a projecting rusticated porch – crowned by a dainty wrought iron balustrade – was added to the two lower stories. This is a jewel of classical invention, with figures emblematic of Peace and Plenty that were supplied by Sir William Wilson (1641–1710) set in niches on the first floor.[29] Below, the portal into the house is crowned by an open segmental pediment, centred by the family's coat of arms, which is raised upon pairs of Corinthian columns, the inner pair being Solomonic. It is a memorable distraction to the earlier frontage and yet blends well, especially now that it has the patina of age, with the older house.

Within, as the Winde–Bridgeman correspondence evidenced, the house received a series of new interiors, with carving undertaken by Edward Pierce (c.1635–1695), and plasterwork by Edward Gouge (fl.1690). Painted decoration also formed a part of the works: Jan Siberechts (1627–c.1703) proposed for landscape panels and Johann Kerseboom (d.1798), at one point, suggested for decoration in the Closet. Louis Laguerre (1663–1721) was, in fact, commissioned from July 1698 to paint a scene of Cephalus and Eos in Lady Bridgeman's Closet, whilst a ceiling painting of Cephalus and Aurora, derived from Ovid's *Metamorphoses*, was set above the Great Stairs. The furnishings were also discussed, including a looking glass that was supplied by Gerrit Jenson (1667–1715), sculptures that might be supplied to the gardens by Jan van Nost (d.1729), William Larson (fl.1673–89), Richard Osgood (d.c.1724) or Caius Cibber (1630–1700), whilst Winde also liaised with Thomas Tompion (1639–1713) over a watch for Lady Bridgeman. In the gardens George London (1640–1714) – 'ye beste gardiner in Endgland [*sic*]' – was consulted over the Wilderness, and Captain Charles Hatton (d.c.1708) gave advice on plants that might be used to best effect.

Sir John died in 1710 and, at some remove from his death, he and his wife were commemorated by a monument designed by James Gibbs (1682–1754) and sculpted by John Michael Rysbrack (1694–1770) in 1726. This was placed in the parish church of St Peter and St Paul at Aston by their daughter Charlotte (1675–1750).[30] The couple's eldest son, meanwhile, succeeded to the family's estates. He was another John (1667–1747), who had married

FIGURE 72 *Castle Bromwich Hall from the gates*, painted by G.C. Carter in 1853, oil on canvas, 39.4 x 59.8 cm. The porch was added for the second baronet and his lady. Visible to the left is an early eighteenth-century lion sculpture which, with its pair, was removed to Weston Park in the twentieth century and is now to be seen at the Temple of Diana at Weston. Accession number 101.0216. (Copyright Trustees of the Weston Park Foundation.)

FIGURE 73 Castle
Bromwich Hall.
The staircase that
had been created
for the second
baronet and his
wife depicted in a
watercolour of 1867,
32.5 x 44.2 cm.
Accession number
116.0003.1.
(Copyright Trustees
of the Weston Park
Foundation.)

FIGURE 74 Castle Bromwich Hall. The long gallery at the house, shown in a watercolour of 1867, 32.5 x 44.2 cm.
Accession number 116.0003.2. (Copyright Trustees of the Weston Park Foundation.)

FIGURE 75 *Sir John Bridgeman 3rd Bt* (1667–1747), painted by an artist in the circle of Charles Beale (1660–1714), oil on canvas, 69 x 61 cm. Accession number 101.0306. (Copyright Trustees of the Weston Park Foundation.)

FIGURE 76 *Ursula Matthews, Lady Bridgeman* (1673–1719), attributed to Mary Beale (1633–1699), oil on canvas, 74 x 61 cm. Accession number 101.0308. (Copyright Trustees of the Weston Park Foundation.)

Ursula, the daughter of Roger Matthews of Blodwell on the Welsh borders of north Shropshire in 1694. The marriage brought a distinguished Welsh lineage into the Bridgeman bloodline and it also brought the properties of the Blodwell estate. Blodwell added significantly to the acreage of the family's landholdings in north Shropshire, extending them westwards to straddle the border with Wales and the estate included part of the rich limestone escarpment of Llanymynech.

In spite of its territorial advantages, the marriage was a love-match. The couple indulged an enjoyment in gardens, creating the bones of the present gardens at Castle Bromwich, which were being laid out in 1712–17[31] and, in tandem, works were taking place at Blodwell, with the garden house which still survives there being completed in 1718. In the gardens at Castle Bromwich two similar structures – a greenhouse to the north and summer house to the south of the Holly Walk – have the same pedimented form as the Blodwell garden house.[32]

Ursula Bridgeman's death on 31 January 1719/20 at the age of just forty-eight, but after significant illness, seems to have meant that Sir John spent a greater amount of time at Castle Bromwich than at Blodwell and, indeed, his mother-in-law Sinah Matthews died there rather than at Blodwell in 1736.

At Castle Bromwich the church was rebuilt from 1726 to 1731, with what had been a timber-framed structure reinvented as a baroque brick edifice to the design of Thomas White of Worcester (c.1674–1748). The work was based upon a contract dated 18 January 1724/5 and the presence of monuments signed by White to Ursula and Roger Matthews at St Michael the Archangel's church, Llanyblodwel, suggests that the work at Castle Bromwich was probably instigated by the third baronet. The Llanyblodwel monuments themselves are, however, signed 'T. White, Salop', although drawings signed 'Worcester' exist

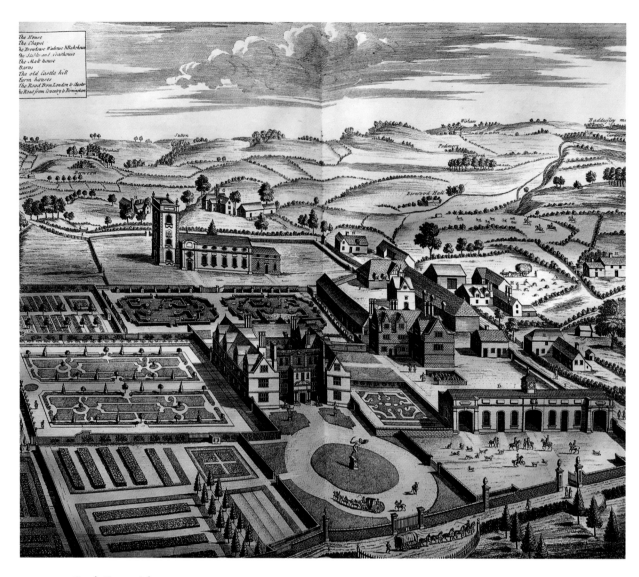

FIGURE 77 Castle Bromwich
Hall and its environs in
circa 1730, from a drawing
by Henry Beighton,
published in William
Dugdale's *Antiquities
of Warwickshire* (1730).
The church, rebuilt in
1726–31, is shown in its
completed state. (Photo:
courtesy of the author.)

FIGURE 78 The garden
house at Blodwell Hall,
Shropshire, which was built
for Sir John Bridgeman,
3rd Bt and Lady Bridgeman.
It is of similar form to two
further garden buildings
at Castle Bromwich Hall
which were also built during
Sir John's tenure. (Photo:
courtesy of the author.)

for them, suggesting that the Salopian and Worcester maker is one and the same.

Sir John had ambitious ideas for the family succession and for the Bridgeman family's advancement. In 1717 he wrote to Richard Newport, 2nd Earl of Bradford to tell him that:

> The great honour and esteem I have for your Lordsps family, makes me propose to ask leave of your Ldsp: to Acquaint you that I have an Ambition to match my eldest son into it.

His intention was to marry his son Orlando to the Bradfords' eldest daughter Lady Elizabeth Newport (1688–1732), although, unbeknown to Sir John, her hand was already betrothed to James Cocks, MP for Worcester, and a marriage followed in the course of the next year. Undaunted though, Sir John wrote again on 1 January 1718, this time: 'to propose my Son to your Lordsps: second Daughter Lady Anne'.

His persistence was rewarded and by the twentieth of that month the marriage was agreed and after settlements were arranged it took place at St Anne's Soho on 9 April 1719.[33] It was to be through this marriage that the Bridgeman family came to be destined to be associated not only with the Newport Earls of Bradford, but with the future of Weston Park and, eventually, with a new creation of the earldom of Bradford.

CHAPTER FIVE

Georgian Weston

Lunacy and Sociability, Arcadia and Industry

At Weston Park, the first half of the eighteenth century witnessed a series of tumultuous family changes, set against the backdrop of a house which was steadily fading. Richard, 2nd Earl of Bradford (1644–1723) and Mary (1661–1737), his Countess – the heiress of Weston – had eventually made the house their home in preference to the Bradford seat of Eyton-on-Severn. When Richard died, his widow continued to preside over her family's estate although she also purchased a newly built house at 17 St James's Square in 1726 for £5,000.[1] By this date, relations with her eldest son Henry (1683–1734), who became 3rd Earl of Bradford at his father's death, had soured. His mother had reputedly disapproved of an unsuitable marriage that he had proposed and, in response, he is said to have 'vowed vengeance on her and her family, which he accomplished by leaving away his immense possessions from his rightful heirs'.[2]

Henry Newport had, however, enjoyed every advantage of a privileged youth, undertaking a Grand Tour to Padua and Rome in 1704–5, in the company of William Pulteney,[3] and he was the favoured grandson of the 1st Earl of Bradford, who settled a considerable amount of property on him. The Newport estates of High Ercall and Eyton became his, together with a Northamptonshire estate at Sudborough and also properties in Wolverhampton. He is known to have slighted the house at Eyton and is said to have lived either at Shrewsbury or at Shifnal when he was in the country.[4] He never did marry, although he produced a son out of wedlock with a Mrs Anne Smyth. The boy, John Newport as he became known, fled to France in 1739, apparently as a Jacobite to support the Pretender's cause, which led to his mother requesting that he should be brought back to England.[5] The Shropshire historian Samuel Garbet, seemingly writing in the following year, suggested that he had fallen 'into the company of rakes, [and] by his wild excesses and repeated salivations … lost the use of his reason'.[6]

It was to him, though, that the Newport estates were left in trust, when his father, the 3rd Earl died of gout aged just fifty-one. William Pulteney, his father's erstwhile Grand Tour companion, was one of the trustees of his estate but he managed the properties as if they were his own, and was able to purchase a reversion of the estate from Anne Smyth. This meant that when 'the lunatick' – as John Newport was referred to – eventually died, the ownership of the properties passed fully to Pulteney and his heirs. To secure his inheritance, Pulteney used his political influence in 1742 to pass the Marriage of Lunatics

Act – which was sometimes known as the Bradford Act – making it legally impossible for any progeny that John Newport might have produced to claim the estates.

Mary, Countess of Bradford lived just three years after her eldest son's death but retained the Weston estate's ownership. She had received the meticulously listed Newport pictures which made their way, in packing cases brought by horse and waggon, to Weston in 1735 after the death of her sister-in-law Lady Torrington. In spite of the prestige of the collection and of her wealth, she chose to make a quiet exit from this world, stipulating that she wanted no pomp at her funeral and that it was only to be attended by her servants, prior to her burial at Weston.[7]

The Weston succession was effectively held in suspense for twenty-five years from Lady Bradford's death. The 3rd Earl's younger brother, and now 4th Earl of Bradford (c.1696–1762), was mentally as incapacitated as his illegitimate nephew. One account, written in 1851, suggested that this was due to him having been thrown from his horse near Cowhay Wood in Weston Park,[8] whilst his contemporary Samuel Garbet, writing in 1740, claimed that, like his brother, he had 'an amour … with a maid of low condition' and that being forced to abandon his relationship had caused the onset of mental instability.[9]

His mother had cared for him at Weston and, with her death, the remainder of his long life – since he lived to seventy-five – witnessed both him and the estate of Weston Park being placed in guardianship. Unlike Pulteney's trusteeship of the Newport estate, the management seems to have been undertaken with great probity, with neighbouring landowner Sir Hugh Briggs, 5th Bt (c.1684–1767) of Haughton Hall – a distant Wilbraham cousin – amongst those maintaining the well-being of both Earl and the estate. Although maintained, the property was apparently little altered as was suggested by the formality of the surrounding landscape on John Rocque's map of 1759, whilst the 1762 inventory suggests an old-fashioned interior within the mansion.[10] Such was the financial liquidity of the property during this period that the guardians could afford to offer a

FIGURE 79 *Henry Newport, 3rd Earl of Bradford* (1683–1734), painted by Michael Dahl (c.1659–1743), oil on canvas, 71.1 x 57.2 cm. Accession number 101.0097. (Copyright Trustees of the Weston Park Foundation.)

loan of £10,000 to the 3rd Duke of Devonshire (1698–1755) to enable him to pay a dowry for his daughter Lady Rachel Cavendish (1727–1805), when she married Horatio Walpole (1723–1809), 1st Earl of Orford of the third creation in 1748.[11]

One of the co-trustees of Weston Park was Orlando Bridgeman (1695–1764), MP for Shrewsbury from 1723 and, following his father Sir John Bridgeman's death in 1747, the fourth Bridgeman baronet and master of the family's Castle Bromwich Hall seat and other estates in north Shropshire and Lancashire. Orlando – as a result of his father's direct approach to the 2nd Earl of Bradford – had married Lady Anne Newport, the sister of the 4th Earl in 1719. The couple, from 1719 to 1725, maintained a house at 5, Soho Square,[12] although at her mother's death in 1737, Lady Anne had received her mother's London house in St James' Square. The maternal will also left her the income on a £20,000 investment, which was left to Lady Anne in trust and with the explicit instruction that Orlando 'shall not in any sort intermeddle'.[13] The old Countess evidently wanted her daughter to have her own liberty as best she could within the strictures of the law. She also made specific reference to the picture collection, which she wanted to be divided into three parts: one third was the collection of her mother Lady Wilbraham, which was to remain at Weston as heirlooms; the further thirds – which would have comprised halves of the remaining Newport pictures – were to be inherited by her daughters Lady Anne Bridgeman and Lady Diana, Countess of Mountrath.[14] Ultimately, like the paintings, the Wilbraham estates that had passed to Mary Countess of Bradford followed a similar course of partition, with Walsall, its manor and the advowson of the parish church there passing to Lady Mountrath, whilst Weston was inherited by Lady Anne Newport's eldest surviving son Henry Bridgeman (1725–1800), the eventual fifth Bridgeman baronet. The decision as to who got Walsall and who received Weston was determined by drawing lots and so Sir Henry's inheritance of Weston Park was down to a degree of chance.[15]

Sir Henry's father died in 1764, just two years after the 4th Earl of Bradford's death, giving him not only the family honours but also the Bridgeman family estates and their income. He also purchased a villa at Ham Common in Surrey, which gave the family an opportunity for the amenities of the country close to London.[16] Henry had married in 1755 to Elizabeth Simpson and the couple went on to have five sons and three daughters. Elizabeth was an heiress in her own right. Her father the Rev. John Simpson (1698–1784) had married a

FIGURE 81 *Sir Orlando Bridgeman 4th Bt* (1695–1764), depicted in a pastel by Francis Cotes (1726–1770), 54.6 x 45 cm. Accession number 116.0014. (Copyright Trustees of the Weston Park Foundation.)

FIGURE 82 *Lady Anne Newport, Lady Bridgeman,* in a portrait by John Vanderbank (1694–1739), oil on canvas, 68.5 x 61 cm. Accession number 101.0309. (Copyright Trustees of the Weston Park Foundation.)

FIGURE 83 *Sir Henry Bridgeman 5th Bt, wearing the livery of the Shrewsbury Hunt Club,* depicted by Daniel Gardner (1750–1805), pastel, 50.8 x 40.8 cm. Accession number 116.0016. (Copyright Trustees of the Weston Park Foundation.)

FIGURE 84 *Elizabeth Simpson, Lady Bridgeman with a favourite spaniel,* drawn by Daniel Gardner (1750–1805), pastel, 50.8 x 40.8 cm. Accession number 116.0015. (Copyright Trustees of the Weston Park Foundation.)

grand-daughter of Admiral John Benbow (1653–1702) and owned the Stoke Hall estate in the Hope Valley of Derbyshire, which passed to the Bridgemans on his death. In addition, Elizabeth's uncle Lindley Simpson's estate at Babworth in Nottinghamshire also passed to the family on his death in 1785 and was inherited by the Bridgemans' younger son John (1763–1850) who adopted the Simpson name.[17]

Although the family's main seat became Weston Park, Castle Bromwich was also maintained. It was visited by John Loveday (1711–1789) on 1 July 1765,

FIGURE 85 Tapestry 'designed after the Indian manner' by John Vanderbank the elder (d.1739). This is presumably one of the tapestries noted by John Loveday of Caversham at Castle Bromwich Hall. It is currently displayed in the Marble Hall at Weston Park and is shown with two of a set of twelve hall chairs, attributed to Thomas Chippendale, which were supplied to Sir Henry Bridgeman, 5th Bt. The pair of gilded torcheres of circa 1770 are part of a set of four and were possibly supplied for the drawing room at Weston Park. (Photo: Paul Highnam/ Copyright Trustees of the Weston Park Foundation.)

not long after the inheritance of Weston, when he noted portraits including Keeper Bridgeman, Bishop John Bridgeman – both sitting and standing – and his friend Archbishop Laud, together with paintings of General Monck, Sir Henry Spelman, Henry VIII, Edward VI, the Earl of Derby, the Earl of Strafford, Charles I in armour and also 'Good tapestry in this house, some by Vandrebanc [sic].'[18]

At the same time that Loveday was visiting Castle Bromwich, the Bridgemans were making plans for the transformation of Weston. One of

FIGURE 86 Lancelot 'Capability' Brown's map of intended improvements at Weston Park, probably at least partly by Brown's draughtsman John Spyers. The plan dates to circa 1765 and shows not only the detail of proposed changes, including pleasure grounds and a new kitchen garden with trees – deciduous, coniferous and weeping clearly indicated – but also, by means of dots, the existing plantings of avenues and also field boundaries that were to be removed if the plan were to be adopted. Accession number SA D1287/M/999. (Staffordshire Archives/Trustees of the Weston Park Foundation.)

the most seismic changes there was the reinvention of the landscape from a formal park, dominated by avenues, to a naturalistic parkland. The works were led by Lancelot 'Capability' Brown (1716–1783), who was brought to Weston Park, probably in the early part of 1765. Under his direction, a proposal map was produced, perhaps by his surveyor and draughtsman John Spyers (c.1720–1798). This enormous plan, measuring nearly a metre by two metres, shows the northern part of the parkland landscape with two pleasure grounds that were intended to be developed to west and east of the house and a vast two-part walled garden to the north. The two pleasure grounds were important transformatory elements – providing, respectively, elevated afternoon and morning spaces of enjoyment from which the family might appreciate the wider landscape at Weston and vistas beyond its boundaries whilst, at the same time, giving a substantial northern belt to protect the park from the intrusion of Watling Street.

The Brown's plan was clearly a discussion document; with dots – little bigger than pinpricks – showing the boundaries, the radiating avenues and the tree plantings that existed, overlaid by the slick hand of one adept at transforming the stiff formality of garden planting and the mundane landscape of a village into an Arcadian vision of beauty and of purpose. Some of the earlier trees were evidently to be left, giving instant maturity, whilst others might be felled. Distinctions are made on the map between deciduous and coniferous trees; the odd weeping willow appears by water, whilst a deft arc of shading is used to denote the form of a sunken fence or ha-ha. An improved approach drive from the north-west, with a pair of flanking roadside lodges was planned but seemingly not enacted, whilst within the intended eastern pleasure ground, an oval clearing is marked 'Menagerie & Dairy' besides a building which did indeed come to fruition.

The map served to sell the notion of improvement to the Bridgemans and a first contract with Brown was dated September 1765, including the building of a dry-walled deer-proof sunken fence for a cost of £765 which included Brown's journeys. This was followed by a second agreement and towards the end of 1767 work ended, when Brown was paid a further £966.[19] Although not specifically mentioned in the contract, the ongoing work evidently included the vast brick-walled enclosures of the four-acre kitchen garden, which stand north of Church Pool as Brown's map indicated they should. The structure still retains stove-houses on the north-eastern side of the inner wall, which would have enabled the wall's southern elevation to be used for tender fruiting plants such as peaches and nectarines. On the western flank of this same wall, a pinery – for pineapples – was built, comprising a central lean-to glass house, embraced by pedimented pavilions with *oeil-de-boeuf* windows above what were originally Venetian windows. This was maintained in production to raise fruit that the family consumed and which they also shipped to relations.[20]

Hand in hand with Brown's landscape enhancements to the immediate surroundings of Weston, went architectural endeavours. In the Shrewsbury Walk, west of the house, is to be found Penderel's Cave, which formed a mineral and shell grotto and was later eulogised about by the house steward John Hall. He, in 1812, wrote a poem suggesting that the cave was home to a hermit called Penderel who was supposedly related to the servants at Boscobel who had aided Charles II when fleeing from the Battle of Worcester.[21]

A further grotto was created as a tunnel from the front of the stables, running below a service drive, and leading into the eastern pleasure ground of Temple Wood. This is known as Pausilip's Tunnel, a name derived from the Grotto of Posillipo, or Crypta Neapolitana, near Naples which was said to have been magically created by the classical poet Virgil. The Weston tunnel is, of course, of much smaller scale, although it was intended to offer an equally transformatory experience in leading into the sensory magic of the eastern pleasure ground of Temple Wood. Here, the path continued, through flowering and scented shrubs to various features. A Coade stone sundial was a later addition to the right-hand side of the path, one costing £28 in 1779, whilst another of the same value was paid for in 1799.[22]

FIGURE 87 Coade stone sundial plinth in Temple Wood. Two Coade sundials were supplied to Weston Park, one in 1779 and the other in 1799. This one stands on contoured ground in the east pleasure ground and is of the same model as plinths at Audley End, Syon Park and Wardour Castle. (Photo: courtesy of the author.)

FIGURE 88 The north front
of the Temple of Diana
at Weston Park, designed
by James Paine. This
engraved elevation, together
with further elevations,
sections and plans, was
published by Paine in his
two-volume work *Plans,
elevations and sections of
Nobleman and Gentlemen's
Houses* (1767–1783).
(Copyright Trustees of the
Weston Park Foundation.)

FIGURE 89 *The south front of the Temple of Diana*, a pen, ink and watercolour drawing by James Paine (1717–1789),
46.5 x 61 cm. Wholly different in character to the north front of the same building, Paine's presentation drawing, illustrated
here, indicates urn, statue and plaque decoration which conform to known Coade designs. None of these embellishments
survive, assuming that they were ever added to the building. This drawing was exhibited by James Paine at the Society of Artists
in 1770. Accession number 116.0067. (Copyright Trustees of the Weston Park Foundation.)

FIGURE 90 The circular tea room of the Temple of Diana, its walls embellished with inset paintings depicting the story of Diana, the Roman goddess of hunting, by Giovanni Battista Innocenzo Colombo (1717–1801). Decorated for the Trustees of the Weston Park Foundation by Janie Money of Sibyl Colefax & John Fowler, the building is now a holiday cottage at the heart of Brown's park. (Photographer: Dylan Thomas; Credit: Sibyl Colefax & John Fowler/Janie Money, associate design director.)

Further into Temple Wood remain two structures that were entrusted to the architect James Paine (1717–1789). Paine's choice as an architect probably owed to Lady Bridgeman's family connections since, until Weston, Paine's country house career had been largely based in the north. Lady Bridgeman's father the Rev. John Simpson had witnessed Paine's new stables and bridge being erected at Chatsworth and he went on to employ the architect to rebuild his own neighbouring Derbyshire family home Stoke Hall in 1751.[23] The success of the works was evidently the reason behind the use of Paine at the family's other properties, with works at the Bridgemans' St James' Square house in the 1770s and at the villa at Ham, in addition to Weston Park.[24] Alterations were made by Paine to the house at Weston, where he supplied chimneypieces and helped to make the house more convenient by adding corridors to the inner walls of the east and south ranges, so that the rooms could be individually entered rather than through a continuous enfilade. It was, though, in Brown's Temple Wood that Paine's most distinguished creations, the Temple of Diana and Roman Bridge, were sited and these were celebrated with engraved depictions in his *Plans, elevations and sections of Noblemen and Gentlemen's Houses* (1767 and 1783).

The Temple occupies the site shown on Brown's plan as intended for 'Menagerie & Dairy'. It is a miniature neo-classical masterpiece of highly advanced design; its ground plan is a play of geometrical form and its elevations to north and south – Janus-like – are of distinctly different elements, intended to be seen as two wholly different incidents on the carriage drives through the landscape. The north front is reinvention of William Kent's 1746 Palladian Temple design at Euston, Suffolk, for the 2nd Duke of Grafton,[25] with an ashlar-faced domed canted-bay breaking forward from a giant pediment. It contains, at its ground floor, a circular tea room, painted with panel decoration depicting the life of Diana, the Roman goddess of hunting, by Giovanni Battista Innocenzo Colombo (1717–1801). Colombo had been a painter at the King's Theatre, Haymarket and was also employed in a similar theatrical setting elsewhere at Weston. Colombo, during his time at Weston, also painted the portrait of Mary Yates, a local woman who had 'lived at the bounty' of Sir Henry and Lady Bridgeman and died at the age of 127.[26]

At the Temple, from the tea room, the family and their guests could watch the exotic birds of a menagerie, disporting their plumage within a netted enclosure on the lawn outside. Birds were an enduring passion of Lady Bridgeman's – as for many society ladies who would acquire them from bird-sellers at the Strand in London – and the 1777 inventory of the house indicates a large birdcage in the entrance hall and also in Lady Bridgeman's dressing room.[27] The menagerie birds were also the subject of a series of paintings which still survive in family hands. These comprised a total of fifteen works, dated 1762 and 1763 and are the work of William Hayes (1729–1799), an artist who also painted the birds in the menagerie at Osterley Park.

Within the Temple, the rooms to east and west of the circular room are, respectively, an octagonal music room and a square room intended for the habitation of a dairy maid. Above is a circular bed chamber – regarded by Paine as 'an exceeding good' one – with a series of vaulted spaces below that were intended to serve as dairies and service rooms for Lady Bridgeman.

On the south elevation, the Temple has a very different and altogether lighter character. Here, the frontage is dominated by the three great arched-headed windows of an orangery that soars the height of the building and is crowned, internally, by a handsome neo-classical decorated plaster ceiling. The front to the park owes its genesis to an unexecuted design that Paine had produced for the Knavesmire Grandstand at York which, at Weston Park, was intended to be ornamented by Coade stone plaques, parapet-urns and statues

FIGURE 91 Giovanni Battista Innocenzo Colombo (1717–1793), *Portrait of Mary Yates (d.1776) aged 127*, oil on canvas, 42 x 36.8 cm, which currently hangs in the Marble Hall at Weston Park. Mary Yates was a local woman who lived to the remarkable age of 128, partly supported by the charity of Sir Henry and Lady Bridgeman. She is also commemorated by a stone tablet in St Andrew's parish church, Shifnal, Shropshire. Accession number 101.0234. (Copyright Trustees of the Weston Park Foundation.)

FIGURE 92 James Paine's Roman Bridge in autumn. (Copyright Trustees of the Weston Park Foundation.)

set in the niches which flank the central projecting bay. These ornaments were shown on Paine's finished elevation of the structure, which he exhibited at the Society of Artists in 1770 and which remains in the collection at Weston Park.[28] The building attracted interest from other artists in the Society, including William Hodges who appears to have viewed the Temple and painted it with timber scaffolding during its construction in a work that he called 'View of a Green House at Weston in Staffordshire'.[29]

James Paine's Roman Bridge, a single arched balustrade bridge set with aedicules, like small sentry boxes, now spans the Temple Pool – created in the 1790s – but was originally bridging but a 'limpid stream'. The drive that it carries originally formed an approach to the house from a former lodge gate on Watling Street, but it now leads solely from the Temple to the Pink Cottage, a secluded place of retreat for the lady of the house. Originally described as simply 'the Cottage' this is thought to occupy the site of a brick-maker's cottage and was adapted firstly by Lady Bridgeman and, again, by her daughter-in-law in the first decade of the nineteenth century.

Paine's architectural works also included the core of the present Shrewsbury Lodge, at the end of the west approach. His classical dog kennel – which was proposed for an undisclosed park location – appears to have only existed on

FIGURE 93 The Cottage in the eastern pleasure grounds at Weston Park. Reputedly built for Elizabeth, Lady Bridgeman, the building was certainly her place of resort as her diaries show. The building originally had a thatched roof, and was extended in the early nineteenth century for the first Bridgeman Countess of Bradford when Morel & Hughes created a tented room inside. The tiled roof is a later nineteenth-century alteration. Later known as the Swiss Cottage, the building is now called the Pink Cottage and has been converted to a holiday cottage by the Trustees of the Weston Park Foundation. (Copyright Trustees of the Weston Park Foundation.)

FIGURE 94 James Paine's
unexecuted design for
a dog kennel at Weston
Park. The arched openings
in the screen walls recall
his gateway and lodges at
Brocket Hall, Hertfordshire,
whilst the elliptical portico
set below a segmental-
arched opening is similar
to that designed on the
dairy at Wardour Castle,
Wiltshire. (Staffordshire
Archives/Trustees of the
Weston Park Foundation.)

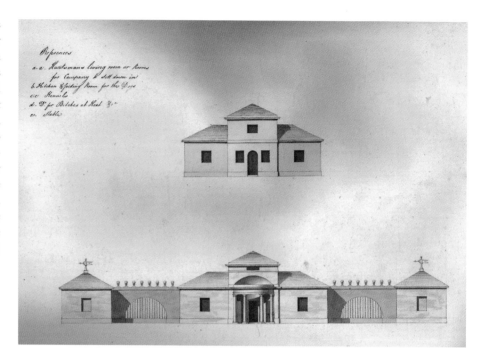

FIGURE 95 The Granary building, Weston Park, seen from the north-east. Originally conceived in 1767 as the model Home
Farm, the northern range – which comprised the great barn with its twin threshing portals – was internally floored to create
a granary in the early nineteenth century. The left-hand tower's upper level was built as a dovecote and still retains its internal
nesting holes. (Photo: courtesy of the author.)

paper. Its design is an essay in accomplished drawing, with central huntsman's house and an elliptical yard for the dogs. It seems likely that Paine was though responsible for the Palladian-style great barn and home farm complex, of brick with stone dressings, which was built in 1767, and is now known as the Granary building. Its main front faces north, with twin pedimented threshing portals and corners marked by pyramid-roofed towers, presenting an elevation with features and massing similar to the Middlesex Hospital that Paine had designed in 1755.[30] The northern façade of the building was a show-front, subtly angled to be seen from the now-lost eastern drive which ran from Watling Street and across the park, over the Roman Bridge and through Temple Wood. The building's southern elevation is much less grand, yet embraced by two three-storey wings which formerly contained ground-floor housing for cattle to the west and for the heavy horses on the east, with granaries above. When writing of Weston Park in 1949 Christopher Hussey described the commodious building as 'one of the noblest architectural products of the agricultural "revolution"'.[31]

Two further farms outside of the park were also evidently rebuilt at this time for Sir Henry and Lady Bridgeman, comprising Weston Park Farm to the east, and also Woodlands to the west.[32] The latter still retains a classic model layout, with a three-bay farmhouse to the south of a U-plan yard which has a classical pedimented threshing barn to its northern centre. The barn was probably originally intended to be an eye-catcher from Brown's belt walk on the west side of the park. Enclosure of land outside of the park was also a part of the agricultural improvements since it was noted in 1782 that all of the parish of Weston-under-Lizard had been enclosed.[33]

Ornamented and improved, Weston Park became the backdrop of a notable musical, theatrical and literary scene. The Bridgemans' friends included the Ladies of Llangollen who would welcome family members to their own home at Plas Newydd, Llangollen, where a portrait of Lady Bridgeman hung in their library.[34] Such was the friendship that, unusually, they spent time away from their home during a two-day visit to Weston Park in October 1784, with Sarah Ponsonby noting that:

> the order and decorum with which so large a family are conducted really surprized us. We attribute it in great degree to the whole family being assembled every night in the Great Hall to Prayers, which were read by Mr G. Bridgeman who is intended for the Church, after which Mrs J. Bridgeman played on the organ.[35]

Besides their clerically minded son, the Bridgemans also had faith-guidance from Rev. Leonard Chappelow (1744–1820), a talented naturalist who served as incumbent of St Mary's, Teddington, and also of Roydon and Burdon.[36] Chappelow was also known to the Ladies of Llangollen and he brought Hester Thrale (1741–1821), Mrs Piozzi, into the Bridgemans' orbit, having encountered her in April 1786 on the Apennines near Spoleto when the Piozzi's coach had broken down.[37] Snippets of life at 'dear charming Weston',[38] as Mrs Piozzi called it, emerge regularly from their correspondence. Anna Seward (1742–1809) – the so-called Swan of Lichfield – was also a part of the family's social circle,[39] as also were Lunar Society member Richard Lovell Edgeworth (1744–1817) and his family. The Edgeworths were distant kinsmen of the Bridgemans but lived as their tenants at Beighterton to the north of Weston and when Richard's second wife Honora Sneyd died, it was at St Andrew's church, Weston that she was buried.[40]

Edgeworth was not the only Lunar Society member known to the Bridgemans, since they also, inevitably, found themselves consumers of the wares of Josiah Wedgwood (1730–1795) and Matthew Boulton (1728–1809).

FIGURE 96 *Rev. Leonard Chappelow (1744–1821)*, drawn
in pastel by James Sharples (1751–1811), 23.6 x 21.2 cm.
The reverend was a loyal friend and spiritual adviser to
the Bridgemans. His correspondence with Hester Thrale,
Mrs Piozzi (1741–1820) gives much detail about the
Bridgeman family's life and social circle in the late eighteenth
and early nineteenth century. Accession number 116.0048.
(Copyright Trustees of the Weston Park Foundation.)

FIGURE 97 One of a pair of white marble and ormolu
candelabra which were supplied to Sir Henry and
Lady Bridgeman by Matthew Boulton (1728–1809).
(Photo: courtesy of the author.)

Lady Bridgeman greatly enjoyed shopping, as is evidenced by her diaries, in
which she frequently mentions her perambulations of the shops in Bath and
London and so, to Georgian entrepreneurs, she was the living embodiment
of eighteenth-century consumer society. From Wedgwood, the Bridgemans
acquired a set of Etruscan-style encaustic ware vases which in 1771 were to
be found in the library and in the anteroom, described as 'Etruscan vases
with historical paintings'.[41] Boulton, who had established his Soho Works at
Handsworth with a refreshment room for fashionable ladies, had flattered
Lady Bridgeman by naming a candlestick pattern of wreathed column form
after her.[42] The Soho Register Books show that Lady Bridgeman visited the
factory on at least two occasions in 1770 and then again in 1780.[43] Of her
purchases, the 1771 inventory lists two ornamental gilt vases 'with Branches,
of Bolton's [*sic*] Manufacture' as being in the Drawing Room and these are
perhaps the white marble and ormolu pair that are still to be found in the
present drawing room. In 1955 a pair of hardstone and ormolu neo-classical
urn perfume-burners of a design produced by Boulton was to be seen in the
library,[44] whilst the house still contains a handsome set of stamped Sheffield
plate candelabra.[45] The Bridgemans were also known to William Withering
(1741–1799), who tended to their daughter Charlotte in 1786.[46] The library

contained a third edition (1796) set of his *An Arrangement of British Plants* ... whilst Birmingham entrepreneur John Baskerville's edition of William Congreve's *Works* (1761) was also on the shelves.[47]

In addition to acquiring family portraits, George Stubbs was commissioned. His *Two Horses Communing in a Landscape* was apparently originally an overmantle picture in the dining room[48] and this remains the pre-eminent work in the house's sporting art collection. High-quality fashionable furniture was also supplied to Sir Henry and Lady Bridgeman as they set about refurnishing the house. Although documentary evidence is lacking, the twelve mahogany hall chairs with out-swept arms and finely carved scrolled legs and backs, have such strong stylistic similarities with documented pieces – especially their Greek key

FIGURE 98 George Stubbs (1724–1806), *Two Horses Communing in a Landscape*, oil on canvas, 124.5 x 123.2 cm. Commissioned by the Bridgemans in 1774, the painting was hanging in the dining room at Weston Park by 1777. Accession number 101.0001. (Copyright Trustees of the Weston Park Foundation.)

carved waists – that they must be from the workshop of Thomas Chippendale (1718–1779).[49] Gillows were certainly involved in providing furniture, with over £70 paid to the company in September 1786, perhaps representing payment for the set of eight shield-backed open armchairs which are now to be found in the Morning Room.[50]

The family's love of fashionable decoration firmly embraced Francophile tastes, as it would continue to do in the next generation. Family rooms at Weston carried French names and it appears that, for a time, the family maintained a French house in addition to frequent visits to Paris.[51] On one of these sojourns, Sir Henry ordered a set of Gobelins tapestries depicting *Les Amours des Dieux*,

FIGURE 99 The Tapestry Room at Weston Park, showing one of the *Les Amours des Dieux* tapestries purchased by Sir Henry Bridgeman from the Gobelins manufactory in the late 1760s. Their current setting was created specifically for them in the nineteenth century, although in Sir Henry's time they were installed in the drawing room, then at the south-west corner of the house. (Photo: Mike Allen.)

the Loves of the Gods. With ground colour of *rose du Barri*, they bear central woven roundels of the Roman deities, derived from cartoons by the French painter Francois Boucher (1703–1770), the tapestries were made under the aegis of Jacques Neilson (1714–1788) and one is woven with: 'Boucher, 1766 Neilson ex'. They are one of six sets commissioned by British patrons, all of which are associated with architectural works by Robert Adam.

In the case of Weston Park, Adam's involvement was confined to the design of a ceiling in 1775, its axial rectangular reserve having a central octagon that was set with a roundel painted with the Three Graces. Of dead-white ground, with green, pink and gilded enrichments, it provided a perfect foil to the colours

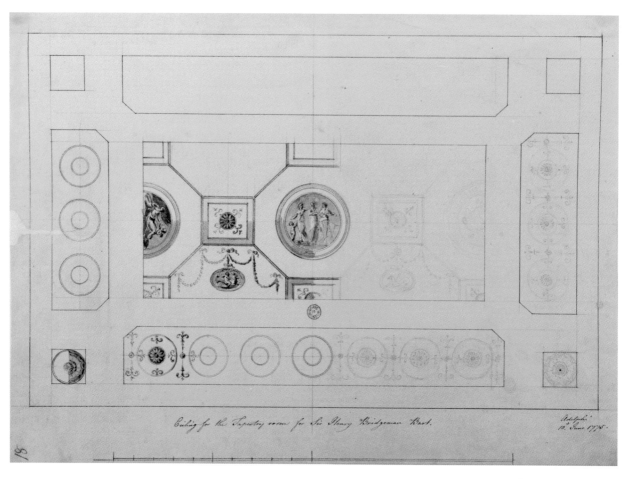

FIGURE 100 Robert Adam (1728–1792), *Design for the Ceiling of the Tapestry Room for Sir Henry Bridgeman*, 1775, pen, pencil and coloured washes, 58.3 x 42.3 cm. The colours of the design were evidently intended to tone with the Gobelins tapestries which remain at Weston Park. Although accounts survive to show that the design was paid for and that plasterers and painters were engaged in its creation in 1775, the ceiling was short-lived and it was removed when drawing room and breakfast room were united to create the Regency dining room (now library). Ref. SM Adam volume 14/18. (By courtesy of the Trustees of Sir John Soane's Museum.)

of the *rose-du-Barri* tapestries. Adam was paid £10 10s, whilst George Halley's bill survives from 1775, detailing the meticulous work involved in the painting and gilding of the ceiling.[52] The room in which the tapestries were located was the drawing room – then the western-most three bays of the south front – where a cellar was created beneath the room to provide good ventilation above.[53] It seems that works on the room's creation were slow to be completed, since the 1777 inventory for Weston Park, whilst noting the tapestries and their protective paper cover, also listed 'Fifty one Painted Paper Panels for Doors & Windows: In the Cupboard', suggesting perhaps *grottesche* decoration which had yet to be affixed.[54]

Although the house and park were in the vanguard of fashion, the Hon. John Byng (1743–1813) appears to have been unaware of the good taste of Weston and its owner when he found himself in the village in 1793, writing that 'As for the Weston House I never heard – or supposed it, to be worth the seeing'.[55] This was perhaps surprising since his niece, the Hon. Lucy Byng had married the Bridgemans' son and heir Orlando five years previously and so the lack of curiosity is notable.

Some sense of the nature of the family and their interests at this time is to be gained from Robert Edge Pine's conversation piece of the Bridgeman family making music, a work that is sometimes described as 'Homage To Handel'. Pine, who is today perhaps best known for the three portraits of George Washington that he painted following his removal to Philadelphia after the Revolutionary War, was then working in Bath and depicted the Bridgemans in an imaginary music pavilion in a parkland setting, gathered to play below a bust of Handel. Their musical efforts have recently been identified, from a reading of the legible score, to have been 'Let The Bright Seraphim' from Handel's *Samson*.[56] Music was a great passion for the family in the late eighteenth century; Sir Henry was a violinist, his daughters Charlotte and Elizabeth played the harpsichord and harp and his eldest son Henry (d.1782) was an able cellist. Sir Henry's musical interests included his election as a member of the Noblemen and Gentlemen's Catch Club in 1761 and also subscriptions to musicians including Johann Erhardt Weippert (1766–1823), whose scores, remarkably, survive in the collection at Weston.[57] Weippert recorded his gratitude to the family by dedicating a score for four sonatas to Lady Bridgeman in 1790.[58]

In Pine's painting, the Bridgeman's daughter Elizabeth is shown as the harpist, and surviving subscriptions indicate her interest in the instrument. Her sister Charlotte, who is seen at the harpsichord, perhaps showed greatest promise as a musician. She was first tutored at the harpsichord by Mattia Vento,

FIGURE 101 Robert Edge Pine (1730–1788), *Homage to Handel* – the Bridgeman family making music below a bust of Handel, oil on canvas, 205.7 x 257 cm. In Sir Henry Bridgeman's time this hung in the breakfast room or anteroom, adjoining the tapestry drawing room at the west end of the south front. Sir Henry wears van Dyck fancy dress, including a plumed hat, whilst his daughter Charlotte plays at the keyboard. Accession number 101.0114. (Copyright Trustees of the Weston Park Foundation.)

FIGURE 102 John Constable (1776–1837), *Portrait of the Hon. and Rev. George Bridgeman (1765–1832), Rector of Wigan*, dated 1813, oil on canvas, 76 x 61 cm. Accession number 101.0030. (Copyright Trustees of the Weston Park Foundation.)

one of the most noted Italian opera composers in London,[59] and also developed an ability as a singer. Charlotte married in 1784 to Henry Greswold Lewis of Malvern Hall, Solihull. Lewis's correspondence suggests a man of irascible character and the couple separated just a year later. Lewis viewed his mother-in-law as the main stumbling block to the union, describing Lady Bridgeman's interference as 'intolerable and insufferable'.[60] There was an eventual reconciliation before Charlotte's untimely death in 1802 at the age of forty-one and the marriage brought two important portraits to the collection. Lewis was a notable patron of John Constable and the portraits of him, and also that of his brother-in-law, the Rev. George Bridgeman, were both works of the artist. In 1813 Constable wrote, with evident pride, to his wife Maria: 'a portrait of the Rev. George Bridgeman, far excels any of my former attempts in that way and is doing me a great deal of service ... It is to go into Staffordshire to Ld. Bradford's seat where in his library he has portraits of his relations and friends. I have one there already [that of Lewis] which Mr Bridgman [*sic*] tells me is preferred to any other in the room ....'[61]

Theatrical entertainments also formed an important interest for the Bridgeman family, something that they shared with other friends, such as the Williams-Wynns of Wynnstay, Denbighshire, in whose plays they were also to be found performing.[62] Like Wynnstay, Weston had its own theatre which when

FIGURE 103 Thomas Weaver (1775–1844), *Portrait of Henry Bowman*, oil on canvas, 75.6 x 62.3 cm. Bowman served the Bridgeman family as their agent until his death in 1820, having also continued to undertake work for his former clients the Dukes of Devonshire. Accession number 101.0244. (Copyright Trustees of the Weston Park Foundation.)

the family and their friends performed the *Tragedy of Tancred and Sigismunda* and the *Comic Opera of the Padlock* in 1775 was 'universally admired'. It had, the report concluded, been 'fitted up under the Direction of Sig. Columba, Painter to the Opera House-London'[63] and as the inventory of 1777 shows it also had its own Green Room. The location of the theatre is not known, although its place in the inventory suggests that it might have been the location of the present servants' hall in what during the late eighteenth century was a part of a detached building to the east of the house.

Underwriting the improvements at Weston Park were developments elsewhere on the family's estates. For the Bridgeman family, the minerals that lay beneath their estates were growing in value as a result of the rise of industry. The iron industry was especially apparent in Shropshire at Coalbrookdale, whilst its allied trades were swiftly developing around the environs of Birmingham, close to the Bridgeman estate at Castle Bromwich. Sir Henry's interest in the potential of iron was illustrated when he invested £50 as a subscriber of Abraham Darby III's Iron Bridge across the River Severn in 1776.[64] As MP for Wenlock in 1768–94, he had shared the seat in alliance with George Forester (1735–1811) whose own Shropshire estate at Willey was mineral-rich and was being developed for the exploitation of industrial minerals and activities.[65] In north Shropshire, the Bridgemans' Llanymynech property's rich limestone quarries had been recognised as providing a source of agricultural fertiliser and for the mineral to be an effective flux in iron-making. The potential of the quarry led the family, with the support of their agent Henry Bowman to improve turnpike roads on the estate and in the 1790s to support the extension of the Ellesmere Canal (subsequently known as the Montgomery Canal). On the canal, a new wharf at Llanymynech enabled cargos of limestone to be transported to ironworks at Plas Kynaston and further afield.

Although, in spite of the Bridgeman interest in development, the Shropshire properties remained largely rural, the situation in Bolton was very different, as the population drawn to the textile industry was growing rapidly. Great Lever Hall, the family's former seat at Bolton, had been partly truncated in circa

1760 and its Chapel of the Holy Trinity fell out of use at this time,[66] indicating the family's preference for living elsewhere. In their absence, the Bolton estate was managed from c.1774 to 1803 by the agent William Hobson who, like Bowman, also worked for the Dukes of Devonshire on their estates. The 3rd Duke of Bridgewater's underground canals provided easier access to collieries and Sir Henry's father Sir Orlando had leased coal-rich lands at Farnworth to the Bridgewaters for the extraction of coal in 1762, whilst Great Lever, too, was also being mined and was producing royalties for the Bridgemans.

John Aitkin, writing in 1793, described how just twenty years previously, Bolton had contained 4,568 inhabitants but that by the time of the 1789 census this had leapt to 11,739 people, drawn by the woollen and muslin trade and its associated activities such as bleaching. 'The extensive crofts are superseded by the art of chemistry', he noted, in what he regarded as a 'wild district'.[67] Taming Aitkin's 'wild district' was attempted by promotion of a Bolton Enclosure and Improvement Act, in 1792, in which Sir Henry Bridgeman was joined by other landowners including the Earl of Derby, John Blackburne, James Lever and Samuel Crooke. They sought to enclose and divide land to the south-west of the town into 126 building lots and, by establishing trustees, to use the rents of the new properties to pay for improvements to the streets, sanitation, and also the regulation of markets and fairs. A two-acre lot was to be used to create a new reservoir, ensuring a clean supply of water for the town.

In addition to the presence of their agents, the family's influence on Wigan at this time was maintained by one of constituency's Parliamentary seats being held by Sir Henry and Lady Bridgeman's eldest son Henry Simpson Bridgeman who was elected in August 1780.[68] With his untimely death in 1782, John Cotes

FIGURE 104 Great Lever Hall, Bolton, Lancashire in circa 1900. The house was truncated for the Bridgeman family in the 1760s and the right-hand wing probably gained its Georgian sashes at that time. On the left of the photograph can still be seen Bishop John Bridgeman's domestic chapel. (Photo: courtesy of the author.)

– a Shropshire neighbour from Woodcote, whose father, Rev Shirley Cotes had been Rector of Wigan 1750–76 – was elected in his stead. In turn, Cotes was joined from 1784 to 1800 by the Bridgeman's younger son and heir presumptive to their estates, Orlando Bridgeman. With Orlando's succession to his father's peerage in 1800, his seat was taken by his brother-in-law George Gunning, husband of Elizabeth Bridgeman.

When Wigan Rectory became vacant in 1790, the Bridgemans' younger son George (1765–1832) was installed. George went on to spend twelve years in improving the rectory house itself, creating a drawing room and apparently sashing the house. In addition to his clerical duties, he also took an interest in the mineral potential of the glebe and in 1806, he drilled two test shafts and discovered coal at a depth of sixty-seven yards and eleven inches.[69] The reverend had married, as his first wife, Lady Lucy Isabella Boyle (d.1801), daughter of the 7th Earl and Countess of Cork, and after her death to (Charlotte) Louisa Poyntz in 1809. The writer Mary Boyle was related to both wives and, describing her visits, she recalled Wigan as 'a frightful, black manufacturing town'. Her aunt Louisa had created gardens around the rectory, but the niece considered that she had 'wounded her horticultural nature on one occasion, when I complained that the rose I had just picked smelt of soot, and blacked my nose when raised thereto!'[70]

By contrast, Lady Bridgeman's diaries give a more rural sense of life at Weston in the late eighteenth century. They do, however, inform of the arrival of furniture from the family's London house in St James's Square which was sold in March 1790.[71] This appears to have been on account of her gambling tendencies which were even a matter of concern to Lady Bridgeman herself. In addition to frequent references to participation in card games, including loo, goose cribbage, whist and pharaoh, she became self-critical in 1766, writing how she 'was horrid stupid lost at Loo one Guinea' and again, later in the same year, she described how, gambling before and after supper, she lost all of her money.[72] References to her gambling continued, and on a memorandum, apparently of 1787, she seems to have written a warning to herself:

> Estates[?] are Landships, gaz'd upon awhile
> Then advertised and auctioneer'd away.
> The wings that waft our riches out of sight
> Grow on the gamester's elbows and the alert
> And nimble motion of those restless joints
> That never tire soon fans them all away.[73]

Matters evidently came to a head two years later when on 21 April 1789 she noted that at Weston Sir Henry Bridgeman 'showd me some letters which affected my spirits'.[74] Having received a letter on 24 May from Sir Henry about a decision on the house, she journeyed to London.[75] On Friday 27 June, after enjoying some of the London season, she noted sadly at St James's Square: 'Ticketed all the things that were to go down to Weston & all other things previous to quitting this dear old Mansion forever.'[76] The St James' Square house was duly sold for £5,250 82s to Sir Philip Francis (1740–1818) with its furniture sent north to Weston, and a house in New Burlington Street was being rented by the family for town visits by 1795.[77] This meant major changes to the way in which the house at Weston was presented, with redecorations including the removal of Chinese wallpaper in Lady Bridgeman's bedroom,[78] when that room became her dressing room. The Temple of Diana also had to take some of the London contents, becoming a repository for the china from that house, whilst Lady Bridgeman amused herself with her Cottage in the eastern pleasure ground at Weston.

After serving as MP for the 'rotten borough' of Wenlock, Sir Henry was ennobled with a peerage in August 1794 and invited to the Upper House as 1st Baron Bradford. His pride in his barony is witnessed by the fine achievement of arms that he commissioned and also in the alteration of the heraldry on twelve of his hall chairs, with the baronet's escutcheon giving way to leopard supporters flanking the Bridgeman shield of arms below a baron's coronet. Lady Bradford, though, was suffering from ill health from about 1790 and correspondence between Leonard Chappelow and Hester Thrale suggests that her affliction was intermittent senility, Reverend Chappelow describing how:

> The intellectual Cement has been crumbling. – All has been deranged – but tis not a ruin that remains …[79]

When Henry, Lord Bradford died in June 1800, the end of an era of both arcadia and industry came for Weston. A different generation came to inherit, with the traits of both parents inherited by their eldest surviving son and successor Orlando Bridgeman (1762–1825). Lady Bridgeman was supported by her family, although her health continued to fail, and she went to live in Bath where she died on 6 March 1806.[80]

CHAPTER SIX

The Early Nineteenth Century
Royalty and an Earl's Inheritance

Orlando Bridgeman, the successor to Sir Henry Bridgeman, 5th Bt and 1st Baron Bradford, was a part of the circle that surrounded the Prince Regent. Although many members of the upper classes claimed an association with the wide and, at times, sycophantic group, Orlando's link was undoubtedly a close one. Besides his friendship with the prince, he also had a connection to one who became close to the prince's heart.

'Mrs Fitz' as Lady Bridgeman called Maria Fitzherbert, appeared in her diary on 29 April 1784 and then the following year she noted in September that 'whilst at Tunbridge the Prince of Wales past 2 days at our House on a visit to Orlando'.[1] In 1786, the prince was calling at the family's house in St James's Square at midnight in what, to Lady Bridgeman's surprise, he considered an 'evening' visit, and in the days following he acted as a messenger to Lady Bridgeman from Mrs Fitzherbert.[2] When June of the same year arrived, he was a guest at Lady Bridgeman's ball, along with Mrs Fitzherbert. She noted that the prince 'came between 11 & 12 & stay'd till 4 o clock but neither danced or sat down to supper'.[3]

There is a suggestion of a visit from the Prince of Wales to Weston Park in 1787, possibly to have been accompanied by Mrs Fitzherbert. Lady Bridgeman noted a number of jobs to be undertaken in her memorandum book of that year, including repairs and redecorating at the Cottage and Temple, honeysuckle to be planted around the trees, pots to be sunk in the subterranean passage, and the essential sleeping arrangements for the royal party, including 'Mrs F' and 'ye P'.[4] No evidence seems to survive to indicate that the hotly anticipated visit actually took place, although the family's associations with the prince and Mrs Fitzherbert continued. On Thursday 4 June 1789, Lady Bridgeman visited her in the day, prior to the family attending the Duke of Clarence's ball at Cumberland House in the evening. Orlando was said to have stood guard outside the drawing room when the prince eventually married Maria in a morganatic ceremony[5] and this loyalty – or perhaps facilitation – was to serve him well.

Aside from royal associations and friendships, Orlando held political office, in representing Wigan as Tory MP from 1784 until 1800 when, on his father's death, he entered the House of Lords as 2nd Baron Bradford. Prior to that time, in 1788 he had married the Hon. Lucy Byng, one of the daughters of the 4th Viscount Torrington (1740–1812) and his wife Lady Lucy Boyle, daughter of the Earl of Cork and Orrery. She proved a capable influence on Orlando's life and two years after the young couple's succession to Weston, Hester Thrale, Mrs Piozzi, wrote that: 'charming Weston … will daily become more beautiful, and its Environs more cheerful under the Auspices of its lovely Mistress'.[6] Lucy's father Lord Torrington had experienced financial embarrassment in having to sell in 1795 the family's main seat at Southill Park, Bedfordshire, where he had spent heavily in the improvement of the park under Lancelot Brown. Much of his life was spent overseas as ambassador in Brussels, but his daughter's marriage was to bring a number of family portraits to Weston Park, including Gainsborough's mesmerising portrait of her mother.

Two years after Orlando's inheritance of Weston Park and his father's peerage, the family's possessions were significantly widened by the inheritance of both the Weeting estate in Norfolk and the old Wilbraham estate of Walsall in Staffordshire. These came to them from the 7th and last Earl of Mountrath (1725–1802), who died at Weston and whose mother had been Orlando's great-aunt. The house at Weeting had been rebuilt in the late eighteenth century by the Earl, when a park was also laid out containing the Belvidere, an octagonal

FIGURE 105 Sir George Hayter (1792–1871), *Portrait of Orlando Bridgeman, 2nd Baron Bradford and later 1st Earl of Bradford of the second creation (1762–1825),* oil on canvas, 91.5 x 68.5 cm. Accession number 101.0027. (Copyright Trustees of the Weston Park Foundation.)

FIGURE 106 Thomas Gainsborough (1727–1788), *Lady Lucy Boyle, Viscountess Torrington* (1744–1792), oil on canvas, 76.2 x 63.5 cm. Painted during Gainsborough's Bath period, the black lace shawl and scarf suggests mourning since Lady Lucy's father, the 5th Earl of Cork and Orrery died in 1762, the supposed date of the painting. Married to the 4th Viscount Torrington, the couple's daughter Lady Lucy married Orlando Bridgeman and ultimately became Countess of Bradford. Accession number 101.0153. (Copyright Trustees of the Weston Park Foundation.)

structure surrounded by a colonnade. This folly – like the mansion – has now long since disappeared. The inheritance was a handsome one in every sense, though, and although architects employed by Lord Mountrath do not appear to have been recorded, reference in a letter of 1784 to 'Mr Linnell' suggests that the cabinetmaker John Linnell might have acted as an upholder for the furnishing of the mansion.[7] With pride flowing from her pen, Lady Bradford wrote to her son George – the eventual 2nd Earl of Bradford – in March 1802 to tell him:

> Your Father tells me the House at Weeting is a very fine one, and most handsomely furnished – large rooms, and hung with Damask, with everything else to correspond with it. The quantity of game is astonishing, I hear, but the Country is not pretty, and the plantations chiefly Fir and Larch, which I am not fond of.[8]

The estate was sold in 1807[9] although some of its contents found their way back to Weston Park where they still remain. Pre-eminent amongst these is a pair of seascapes by Claude-Joseph Vernet which had been commissioned by the late Earl of Mountrath's cicerone and tutor, Dr John Clephane (1705–1758), from the artist in 1745–6. They demonstrate the 'Calm' and the 'Storm', and were tokens of a lengthy Grand Tour in which Mountrath – then styled Lord Castlecoote – had proved hard to stimulate in spite of the remnants of the ancient Roman civilisation. His father, the 6th Earl of Mountrath, had written warning to Clephane in advance of the tour that: 'I am sorry to say Ld Coote requires more looking after than lyes in my power.'[10]

The inheritance of the smart house at Weeting, and the prospect of the capital from its sale, might have provided the Bradfords with the stimulus for major works to Weston Park. For one, such as Lord Bradford, who considered himself to be within the Carlton House circle of the Prince Regent, the Staffordshire house must have felt somewhat out of date. Plans were, therefore, drawn up for a radical remodelling to the designs of John White (1748–1813) and his

FIGURES 107 & 108 Claude-
Joseph Vernet (1714–1789),
The Calm and *The Storm*,
oil on canvas, 96.5 x 132 and
99 x 132.1 cm, respectively.
Commissioned directly from
the artist in 1745–6, the two
paintings were brought to
Weston Park following their
inheritance by the Bridgeman
family from the 7th and
last Earl of Mountrath
(1725–1802). Access numbers
101.0060 and 101.0062.
(Copyright Trustees of the
Weston Park Foundation.)

son and namesake. White was the son of a Shrewsbury carpenter William
White and Anne Pritchard, the daughter of the Iron Bridge's architect Thomas
Farnolls Pritchard (1723–1777). Having moved from Shropshire, White had
been a surveyor responsible for laying out the Duke of Portland's Marylebone
estate, and, as an architect, designed wings for Chiswick House in 1788 to
enable Lord Burlington's villa to function as a proper house for the 5th Duke
of Devonshire (1748–1811). He had also designed a new house at Glevering
Hall in Suffolk in 1792–4, and then went on to design alterations proposed for
the buildings at Fengate House, Weeting in 1801.[11] This Weeting connection
and his Salopian roots may have provided the credibility that led to his work
at Weston, although another possibility is that the Bradford's agent Henry
Bowman recommended him from his work for the Devonshires and, indeed,

White continued to work for them at Buxton, where he designed The Square (1803–6) and St John's Church (1811).

At Weston, White's works spanned the period 1802–8. They included a refashioning of the house's interiors, plus the encasement of the red-brick facades in Parker's Patent Roman Cement to make the building appear as if it was built of ashlar stone, whilst ground-floor window sills on the east front were dropped so that family and guests could walk from the rooms into the pleasure grounds.[12] Within the mansion's walls, the most radical alteration was the creation of a new dining room at the south-west corner, the house's present library. This was achieved by removing a wall between what had formerly been

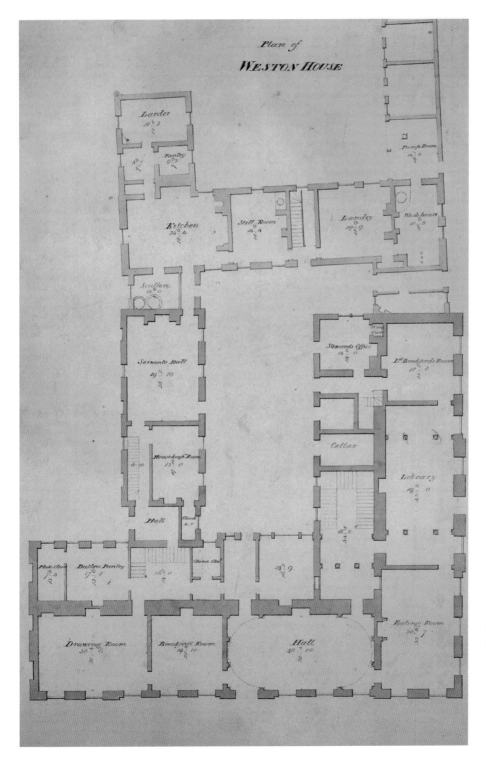

FIGURE 109 John White's 1802 plan of the ground floor of Weston Park as it appeared at the accession of Orlando Bridgeman. As a result of White's changes to the house, the drawing room and breakfast room – lower left of plan – were to be united to form a Regency dining room. After 1866 this became the house's library, which it remains. Accession number SA D1287/M/658. (Staffordshire Archives/ Trustees of the Weston Park Foundation.)

the tapestry drawing room and the anteroom to create a five-bay room. Screens
of columns were inserted at each of the end bays, to give the room a tripartite
plan, whilst a single white marble chimneypiece was centred on the room's
north wall. In creating the new eating room, the tapestries were, of course,
displaced and were relocated to a first-floor room for almost half a century
before being allowed back downstairs. The Robert Adam ceiling, that had
graced the tapestry drawing room, though, was lost forever.

Some of the alterations may have been inspired by alterations that had been
undertaken by Henry Holland (1745–1806) at Woburn Abbey from 1787 to
1802, for the 5th Duke of Bedford (1765–1802). Lady Bradford's sister the Hon.
Georgiana Byng (d.1801) had married the Duke's brother and heir-apparent
Lord John Russell (later 6th Duke of Bedford, 1766–1839) in 1786 and there
were strong ties between the sisters, in addition to shared agricultural interests

FIGURE 111 *Sleeping Ariadne*, based on the ancient sculpture now in the Vatican Museum Collection. This was also supplied by Lignereux and, like the Apollo clock, another version of this model can be found in the British Royal Collection, having been supplied to the Prince Regent. (Photo: courtesy of the author.)

between the Bradford and Bedford families. Certainly, Weston Park's library – which was then in the centre of the east front, in the room that is now the entrance hall – exhibited a strong Woburn influence. Its bookcases, with their Greek key friezes, guilloche pilasters and lion-mask ring handles to the plinths, which still remain at Weston, have stylistic similarities with the cases of the library and ante-library at Woburn. Holland had also been acting as architect to Samuel Whitbread, the purchaser of Southill, also in Bedfordshire, which had formerly been Lady Bradford's family home.

From Weston, as early as February 1802, Lady Bradford had written to her son George to tell him:

> The painter has come, who I told you we expected to clean the Pictures, and he is very much pleased with them. A great deal of the new furniture for the Drawing Room is also arrived, and the room begins to look very comfortable.[13]

Clearly acquisitions were already being made for the new spaces, although far more was yet to come, whilst the progress on the building works was notable and the house was being sashed and externally painted in the summer of 1802.[14]

Although the Wars with France were continuing throughout the period of White's works, there was a brief window of opportunity for travel during the Treaty of Amiens from 27 March 1802 until 18 May 1803, and this the Bradfords seized as a moment in which to visit Paris. Lady Bradford's account book details how they arrived at Paris in November 1802 and that they soon made a number of purchases of gilt and bronze candlesticks and also a print of Bonaparte. She separately recorded a 350 Louis bill to 'Mr Lignereux' and a further 8 Louis 10 Livres bill to him for packaging. This was the marchand-mercier Martin-Eloi Lignereux (1750/1–1809) of 44 rue Vivienne, and the items probably included the Apollo clock garniture – the clock's movement by Charles-Guillaume Manière – and reclining Ariadne sculpture which remain in the collection.[15] Near identical pieces, supplied by Lignereux, remain in the British Royal Collection, having been purchased by George IV, and so royal fashions probably dictated the acquisitions.

Possibly also acquired at this time were the pair of Louis XVI ormolu, patinated bronze and bleu turquin marble three-light candelabra of circa 1785, with bronze figures of Cupid and Psyche after Étienne Maurice Falconet (1716–1791) and with ormolu attributed to François Rémond (c.1747–1812).[16] Likewise, the circular table with patinated bronze gryphon supports, and the commode in the tapestry room – both attributed to Adam Weisweiler (1744– 1820) – were likely also acquired at this time.[17]

By July 1803, the family were also making purchases in England, with £100 spent with 'N. Morel' on 25 July.[18] Nicholas Morel (fl.1790–1830) was a cabinetmaker with French links who worked under the architect Henry Holland on the remodelling of the Prince of Wales' Carlton House and also the prince's hunting lodge at The Grange in Hampshire. He had also worked on Holland's Southill and at Woburn Abbey and so his involvement at Weston was possibly inspired by a desire to emulate the works seen at those houses. In 1805 Morel went into partnership with Robert Hughes (fl.1805–30), trading from 13 Great Marlborough Street, and, until the partnership ended in 1827, the company continued to supply the royal household and other aristocratic houses. The Bradford's were amongst these clients, commissioning a full-scale refurnishing of Weston Park from Morel & Hughes in 1805–7, when Egyptian and *goût grec* styles were employed to create a fashionable sequence of interiors. Their works, which cost a total of £4,126 8s 9¾, included Nicholas Morel's attendance at Weston Park and related to not only the furniture and furnishings, with details as small as the door and shutter furniture in each room. The works comprised all of the main ground-floor family rooms, plus Lady Bradford's first-floor drawing room, and main bedrooms on first and second floors of the house. In the park, provision was also made for the interior of the Cottage, including 176 yards of pink calico for a tented room.[19] A significant number of items of furniture that were supplied by Morel & Hughes still survive in the house and these, along with lost details of the exciting and important Regency scheme, are fully enumerated in the Morel & Hughes Bradford accounts.[20]

In addition to Morel and Hughes, a number of other eminent companies supplied for the refurbishments, including Richard Ovey (fl.1790–1831) the fabric printer, who billed in October 1805, and the wallpaper makers and decorators Robson & Hale, who invoiced in May 1805 for a total of £662–5–5.[21] This mammoth reinvention of the house included works to all of the main rooms, including the drawing room, with works entailing details such as the installation of bronze pilasters and 'a Double Door Ornament consisting of a Circular bronze bas relief with Sphynx and small Pillasters [*sic*] & c. painted in bronze'. For the house bathroom, Robson & Hale charged for putting up a 'Sienna Paper' which appears to have been bordered with a dove marble paper and shaded and varnished by hand. Distinctive leopard-spot patterning was to be found on the blue chintz in the dressing room, main bedroom and drawing room, and also in the Wilton carpet of the billiard room, being, perhaps, a reference to the leopard supporters of the family coat of arms. A section of what is thought to have been the carpet was rediscovered during the restoration of the family's travelling coach, used upon one of the vehicle's folding steps.

Works continued throughout the decade with full regard for fashion but less concern for the previous generation's contribution to Weston. In addition to the destruction of the tapestry room, another casualty was the theatre or 'playhouse' which was taken down at this time.[22] The modernisation works continued for several years, with consideration also given to the services, including heating, with a number of patent register stove grates being supplied in 1809 by Joshua Jowett. These were highly unusual in having inbuilt spark guards that – when not in use – can be revolved out of sight behind the grate

FIGURE 112 The Luncheon Pavilion at The Sytch. This rustic pavilion presides over the lake in the detached pleasure ground to the north of Weston Park, which was laid out for the Bradfords by the landscape gardener and architect John Webb from circa 1813 in tandem with works in the main park. From a photograph of circa 1860. (Copyright Trustees of the Weston Park Foundation.)

itself. Examples of these are still to be seen in the Library, First Salon, Morning Room and Dressing Room.[23]

In the park work was also undertaken. In his later years, Orlando's father had begun to receive assistance from the Staffordshire landscape gardener John Webb, who was first recorded working at Weston Park post-1794.[24] By 20 January 1813, John Webb was involved in the creation of a new detached pleasure ground located to the north of the main park at Weston, on the other side of Watling Street. Comprising woodlands and shrubberies around a lake of the same name, the grounds came to be known as The Sytch.[25] Here, a rustic luncheon pavilion and boathouse were built, overlooking the lake, and two new drives, with lodges, were built to provide a landscape of solitude. Webb continued to work at Weston Park throughout the tenure of both Orlando and his son and successor, with later work for Orlando including the planting up of the eastern end of the park with oak specimens.[26]

Some of the work to the pleasure grounds might have been inspired by brotherly rivalry since Orlando's younger brother John Bridgeman Simpson (1763–1850) – who had taken his mother's Simpson name when he inherited the Babworth Hall estate in Nottinghamshire – had employed Humphry Repton (1752–1818) in the landscaping of his Nottinghamshire estate. In tandem with agricultural improvements that Bridgeman Simpson was making, Repton produced a Red Book of proposals in 1790 which, in its watercolour slides, showed the formerly red-brick house at Babworth being given a lime render and the improvement of the grounds there also included the provision of a Swiss cottage.[27]

For Orlando, a love of fashionable possessions was matched – like his father before him – with a strong and active interest in agricultural improvement. In 1819 Lady Williams-Wynn related how he had examined an ox at the Duke of Portland's estate of Welbeck Abbey,

> in the proper agricultural stile feeling all over … and [took] out a highly perfumed handkerchief … to wipe his hands. The moment he pulled it out the Animal turned upon him and struck at him … Fortunately his cries brought him assistance, and by the united exertion of *six men* the Animal was removed. He was of course dreadfully bruised but not materially, and soon got well, & the Cowman readily explained the cause of the misfortune by saying, 'the poor Cratur never could boide a Stink.[28]

When William Pitt described the state of Staffordshire agriculture in 1817, Lord Bradford's improvements on the Weston Park estate were seen as carrying highly significant influence. He noted the Devon cattle, the Suffolk type pigs, and the Southdown sheep that had been bred from the flocks of the Duke of Bedford and of Thomas Coke, the arable land managed by the Norfolk-system of crop rotation and extensive drainage that had been undertaken to improve the land.[29] Orlando served the Shifnal Agricultural Society as its president from 1805 and he actively made acquisitions to consolidate the estate, purchasing Lizard Grange and Lizard Mill Farms after 1803,[30] with their handsome sets of model farm buildings. These were purchased from the 2nd Marquess of Stafford (1758–1833, created the 1st Duke of Sutherland in 1833) of neighbouring Lilleshall Hall, following the marquess' father's death in that year. The Staffords continued to manage their Lilleshall estate along model farming lines, supported by the land agent James Loch (1780–1855), and together with the Cotes family's Woodcote estate to the north of Weston and the Durant family's Tong estate to the south, the landed estates around and including Weston created a remarkable landscape of agrarian improvement. The evidence of this, with enclosed common land and spruce farmsteads and cottages, still survives and makes a notable landscape contribution all the way from the M54 motorway to the town of Newport, nine miles to the north.

The Bradfords were active in agricultural competitions at that time and the Weston Park collection includes a silver cup, hallmarked in 1812, commemorating a successful showing of livestock by the Earl at the Shropshire General Agricultural Society. A number of portraits of stock and staff by the Shrewsbury artist Thomas Weaver also recall the human and bestial characters of the farming enterprise, including some of the Devon cattle and the pigs with their keeper, Harry Green. The most notable of these paintings, however, depicts the victor of a ploughing contest in 1813 between the ploughmen of Lord Bradford, Richard Lyster of Rowton, Sir Watkin Williams-Wynn of Wynnstay, and Owen of Condover. The winner was Lord Bradford's ploughman John Gee who had settled in Weston, having moved from the old Mountrath estate of Weeting. In December 1803 one of the Weston staff had written that: 'My Lord is sending us from Weeting a new ploughman, three horses a waggon and two ploughs' – the ploughman being Gee. His presence was also noted by William Pitt, who

FIGURE 113 Thomas Weaver (1775–1844), *The Ploughing Match 1813*, 71 x 91 cm, oil on canvas. The Bradford family's ploughman John Gee is portrayed in a match with the spires of Shrewsbury in the distance. The site of the match from the topography shown was probably on either the Attingham or Sundorne estate. Accession number 101. 0303. (Copyright Trustees of the Weston Park Foundation.)

referenced ploughing being done by two horses abreast with 'an able Norfolk ploughman'.[31] Gee lived on the estate until he was tragically killed in 1843, when a waggon accidentally ran over him, although his progeny have lived and worked at Weston ever since, Martin Gee, the current head gardener being his direct descendant.

Although rural life at Weston may have been reassuring, the French Wars of 1793–1815 were something in which the family had a very real involvement in view of the threat of war. Orlando, 1st Earl was appointed Colonel of the First Regiment of the Shropshire Militia in 1804 by the Lord Lieutenant, the 1st Earl of Powis (1754–1839), and he followed the regiment about England as they proceeded on manoeuvres until, in 1813, they departed to Ireland for two years.[32] The Bradfords' youngest son, Captain the Hon. Orlando Henry Bridgeman (1794–1827), had been commissioned into the First Guards at the age of seventeen in 1811 and he saw active service overseas as a part of the wars. He was wounded at the storming of San Sebastián in 1813[33] and went on to serve as ADC to General Lord Hill at the Battle of Waterloo where he was wounded. Whilst he proved a remarkable and able chronicler of the conflict,[34] the brutality of war had its lasting effect on Orlando who in 1815 had been described by Rev. Leonard Chappelow as 'so young – that he carries his Eggshell on his head'.[35] War tragically broke him mentally in what would now probably be recognised as post-traumatic stress disorder. Orlando died just twelve years after Waterloo, his part in the European war recognised by his burial with his ancestor the first Bridgeman baronet, and by his commemoration on Sir Orlando's monument at St Mary with St Alban at Teddington.

Following Waterloo, the family commemorated the British victory by the building of an Obelisk in the Park at Weston. The monument might even serve to celebrate a victory of the Bridgeman family's own since the Earldom of Bradford was revived in their favour in that same year. The Bridgeman family's chaplain, Rev. Leonard Chappelow (1744–1820) wrote, breathlessly, to Hester Thrale, Mrs Piozzi, on 23 November 1815:

> You have heard that Lord Bradford is to be made an Earl, the family title being revived at Last in the Person of the now Earl. – The Regent to whom as a Peer he had a right to demand an Audience received him with the most amiable and friendly manner as the companion of their youthful and early days of merriment when the bottles of Claret and Champaign all ran round the table at Carlton House as if impelled by Magic. What Lord B was going to detail his pretensions to an Earldom &c – say no more said the Prince, it shall be done immediately. Leave the matter to me, it cannot be in better hands.[36]

The family had retained its association with the monarch who, as Prince of Wales, had stood as godfather to the Bradfords' eldest son, the eventual 2nd Earl, George Bridgeman (1789–1865). George was very different to his father in many respects, not least in his father's attitude to sources of money and how it was spent. The wider estate's development, during the 1st Earl's tenure, was largely managed by the family's agents who brought in the income, although this was almost as fast as the earl was spending it and sometimes, apparently, not quick enough. Although in Bolton Edward Charlton negotiated on coalmining agreements in Tonge-with-Haulgh in 1804,[37] the wealth for the family's lifestyle was not so swiftly produced.

During this period, the Bradfords went overseas, on a four-year tour that began in 1814 and which included travel in Belgium, Switzerland, France, Italy and Germany.[38] The tour, aside from giving a change of scene, may also have been borne of financial necessity and to aid Lord Bradford who was suffering from depression. Rev. Leonard Chappelow wrote in April 1814 to Hester Thrale, telling her that Lord Bradford:

> whose finances entre nous – are by no means in a flourishing state, has been at the centre of the Earth – Lower he could not go – he is now in the Moon, in the highest spirits … at Paris, emptying the Champaigne [*sic*] bottles – and I hear this morning, but I hope Lady B – will not hear of it – giving Dinners to forty people at a time.[39]

Lady Bradford maintained a record of the expenses during their travels,[40] but during their absence the acute financial problems came fully to the attention of their son George. His fury permeates his correspondence with his mother in 1817, when he initially accused the family's agent John Heaton of either mismanagement or embezzlement. As the figures under discussion grew, George put his father under pressure and wrote incredulously to his mother in Brussels in March of that year:

> my Father is looking into his affairs in earnest I believe, and seems better inclined than ever to get prudently – this is a grand point, but it remains a perfect enigma to me how £39,000 can possibly have been squandered on personal expenses, and the keeping up of Weston during the last three years.[41]

Lord and Lady Bradford finally returned to Weston Park after four years abroad in 1818.[42] In the following year, there was further spending on the collection, when a quantity of Sèvres porcelain and other French decorative art was acquired from the dealer Robert Fogg. This was invoiced in April 1819,[43] suggesting an improvement in financial prospects – or an impulse purchase.

In 1820, Lord Bradford's health declined and in June 1820 Leonard Chappelow wrote to tell Mrs Piozzi that he was 'now under the roof of Dr Darwin' – this being Robert Waring Darwin (1766–1848), the father of evolutionary theorist Charles.[44] The nature of this illness – whether mental or physical – is not known for certain, although he went travelling to Italy, Switzerland and France in 1821–3. Whilst abroad he made a significant number of purchases including decorative alabaster sculpture in Florence from Joseph Moisé and Pierre Bazzanti, a quantity of prints at Geneva, plus a number of bronzes and also paintings from Genoa.[45] These pictures were mostly religious and historical, including works by Badaracco, Bernardo Strozzi,[46] Cornelis de Wael and Andrea Ferrari, many of which remain at Weston Park, including the study of Bathsheba in a highly colourful formal garden setting that is attributed to Hendrik van Balen. The list of works also includes 'No. 1 Portrait d'un Enfant par Paulo Cagliari Verognese' and 'No 2 Do', which probably refer to the pair of Italian portraits of children that now hang in the Morning Room and which have been attributed to Sofonisba Anguisciola. Perhaps most notable, however, is the *modello* for Anton Raphael Meng's *Annunciation* altarpiece that was painted in 1767 for the Colegiata of Castrogeriz, near Burgos, Spain, and a further version of which is now in the Kunsthistorisches Museum, Vienna.[47] A number of sculpted items were acquired from Lorenzo Bartolini (1777–1850) at Florence during Lord Bradford's travels and these appear to have included the bust of Lady Lucy Whitmore (née Bridgeman), which was produced in several versions, and also perhaps the marble serpent-handled giant tazza.[48]

Following Lord Bradford's return to England in 1823, a bow meeting was held at Nesscliffe on the north Shropshire estate which was flatteringly described as 'one of the most splendid fêtes recorded in this country'.[49] Archery had long been a popular activity for the Bridgeman family, with archery grounds at Castle Bromwich Hall and at Weston, and Lord Bradford was an honorary

FIGURE 114 Anton Raphael Mengs (1728–1779), *Annunciation*, oil on canvas, 75 x 39.5 cm. A study for the altar piece at Colegiata of Castrogeriz, near Burgos, Spain, it was one of a number of works of art acquired by the 1st Earl of Bradford during his European tour of 1821–3. Accession number 101.0251. (Copyright Trustees of the Weston Park Foundation.)

member of the Society of British Bowmen. In spite of such distractions, his health finally failed completely and he died on 7 September 1825, at the age of sixty-four after 'a painful and lingering illness of nearly two years'.[50] His tenure of Weston, which had been marked by many high points, but a dilettante approach to the management of the family's estates, was at a close and a new and more seriously focused era was about to dawn.

CHAPTER SEVEN

A Changing World
The Bradfords, Bolton, Wigan and Walsall

George, 2nd Earl of Bradford's accession to the earldom, Weston Park and the family estates marked a sea-change in their management and one which reflected the socio-economic changes in the world around the Bridgeman family. His character was very different from that of his father, who had emulated the at-times extravagant and whimsical manner of George IV, whose youthful associate he had been. In George, though, there was a seriousness and an earnest nature which is apparent in his correspondence. It is made quite plain in a number of exchanges from son to father, where the older man's outgoing nature, interest in politics and love of worldly show are done down by his eventual successor. The placing of both men's portraits – each the work of Sir George Hayter (1800–1895) – on the piers of the Library at Weston, also exhibits the contrast in their natures, with the 1st Earl's benign countenance seeking to engage with the onlooker, whilst George looks impassively, if not in fact accusatively, in the direction of his father.

As a young man George had gained an understanding of the wider world from travels in 1812–14. He toured Italy and the Mediterranean in the company of his cousin Lord John Russell (the eventual prime minister and later 1st Earl Russell) and with the Hon. Robert Henry Clive, the second son of the 2nd Lord Clive (later 1st Earl of Powis of the third creation). His letters home to his parents from this period were privately printed by his son, the 3rd Earl, in 1875 as *Letters from Portugal, Spain, and Malta*, and they give insights not only into his cultured observations of the countries but also of the progress of the Peninsula Wars. His correspondence with his mother indicates, at times, an incredulity with his father's behaviour – including criticism of his acquisition of a portrait of Napoleon Bonaparte in 1816 – in addition to the worries that he felt over his father's spending and what this might have meant for the estates' future.[1] During his father's period of illness in 1820, the family's trusted land agent Henry Bowman died. This led to the appointment of a new agent, Peter Potter (1773–1843), who had previously worked with John Heaton for the Duke of Devonshire, and also had experience, as a civil engineer, of the laying out of new developments in London including the residential area of Regent's Park and also the Highgate sewers. He was, in many ways, ideally qualified to lead the development of the estates at a critical moment in their history. Although Potter and his family initially went to live at Knockin Hall in rural

north Shropshire, it is telling that he soon moved to a newly built villa, Gorway House at Walsall, from which to oversee the Bradford estates as senior agent. Regional agents were appointed under him, including members of the Twamley family at Castle Bromwich, the Griffiths family in north Shropshire, George Pigott at Bolton, and Alexander Davidson at Weston. Potter was succeeded at his death by his son and namesake, who retired in 1860 and died in 1881, yet with a further three generations of the same family following and who took the Walsall agency into the 1940s.[2]

In 1826, the year after George, 2nd Earl of Bradford's father's death, a sale took place over two days at Weston's farmyard, with the entire flock of Southdown sheep and the Durham cattle together with the farm's implements.[3] The sale raised £2,335.19.6 and it marked a notable change in the policies and management of the estates, with an increased focus on the urban properties and the value that they represented as the century progressed. Although the family had been active in politics, with his father standing for a time as MP for Wigan, George's view of politics was that it was a necessary chore. He had told his father in 1816 that he had: 'no desire to be a Member from any immediate personal pleasure I should derive from it'. Instead, to him, it would be 'a duty … and a point of propriety'.[4] He offered to stand as MP for the rotten borough of Wenlock, local to Weston, which his uncle John Bridgeman Simpson had held, and, indeed, his grandfather Sir Henry Bridgeman before him, although it did not in the end come to pass.

With the growth of urban areas, the nature of politics was changing and there was, inevitably, pressure for reform, especially in the years following the Battle of Waterloo. George, though, was opposed to the notion of measures to reform Parliament and constituencies to give greater voice to urban voters. In 1816 he wrote to his mother, telling her that he feared that social problems lay ahead:

> The Vengeance of Heaven seems to hang over the head of poor England, and a miracle almost seems necessary to ward off the impending ruin.[5]

Three years later, all too close to the family's Bolton estate, on 16 August 1819, crowds had gathered in St Peter's Square, Manchester, demanding reform to Parliamentary representation, and were subjected to a cavalry charge that caused the death of eighteen and severe wounding to seven hundred of the protestors in what came to be known as the Peterloo Massacre. The Bradford's agent at Bolton, George Pigott regarded the main speaker, the Radical Henry 'Orator' Hunt (1773–1835) as 'that great pest to society'. Following Peterloo, Hunt went to court in Lancaster, passing through Bolton and, having been bailed, returned and stayed in the town, attracting a large crowd. The local militia, in which Pigott was involved, was strengthened in the following months, but there was a disturbing incident when two men tried to steal arms from a soldier resulting in one of the soldiers being shot in the hand. Civil unrest, in the growing urban areas, became an especial concern, and the opinion of the 2nd Earl and his agents was that political reform should be resisted since the absence of suffrage might be substituted by social benefits.

Bolton's population grew swiftly, from 17,000 in 1801 to 50,000 in 1841 but, like the Bradfords' Walsall estate where there was a population of 15,000 in 1830, it had no parliamentary representation as an urban borough. This imbalance was something that could not be ignored especially when the neighbouring landowner at Walsall, Lord Hatherton, was in support of reform.[6]

FIGURE 116 Bridgeman Place, Walsall in circa 1890. Built in 1838, the Greek Revival style was reflected in other buildings on the Bradford estate at Walsall at this time. The row of buildings contained an estate office and also residences for members of the Potter family. (Courtesy of Walsall Archives.)

When the vote for reform was approved by the House of Commons in 1831, it was offered to the House of Lords where George, 2nd Earl predictably voted against reform and formed part of a majority that defeated the bill. It was, though, merely putting off the inevitable, so that in the following year Parliamentary reform was achieved and both Bolton and Walsall became part of new constituencies. Regardless of his views on voting, the 2nd Earl took a serious interest in the well-being of those who lived upon the estates, and was supported in this by the eyes and ears of main agent Peter Potter who recognised the need to improve the lot of those living on the urban estates.

In Walsall, what had been an ancient parish gathered around St Matthew's church, had been incorporated as a borough in 1627, and was incorporated as a new borough in 1835 as its urbanisation gathered pace, growing almost six-fold to 86,430 by 1901.[7] This growth was aided by Potter's work in developing the town by laying out new roads – many named after the Bradford family and their other estate properties – in selling building leases, developing the mining and quarrying operations for coal, limestone and ironstone across the estate, and also improving the transport networks from the town to the neighbouring districts of Wednesbury and Darlaston.[8] The development of the road out of the town towards the latter two places led, from 1830, to the building of good villa houses in Bradford Street and Bradford Place.[9] Amongst the developments of Peter Potter the elder, in the heart of the town was Bridgeman Place, a new row of stuccoed Greek Revival houses which arose from 1838. The terrace included the Bradford estate offices, whilst several of the houses were occupied by members of the Potter family. From 1875 to 1878 one of the houses – then owned by the South Staffordshire Railway (later London & North Western Railway) – served as a temporary hospital for the town. The growing scale of Walsall meant that health provision had outgrown the old cottage hospital and so a new general hospital was required. Sister Dora (Dorothy Wyndlow Pattison, 1832–1878), the Anglican nun who devoted her career to nursing, worked at the temporary site.

Tenants living on the estates who worked for manufacturing businesses – many of which were Bradford estate tenants themselves – were not faring well in Bolton. When Potter had visited Bolton and met with local agent George Pigott, he wrote to the Earl in December 1830 to describe the trade disputes that were taking place and how the workmen 'obtain such miserable pittances as scarcely … support life'. The Bradford estate's response to this was to offer small parcels of land, of between a quarter and a half of an acre, to the workers that could be cultivated for growing food.[10]

Potter combined a social conscious with significant business acumen and was able to negotiate in the Bradford estate's favour for the building of canal and rail routes across the estate, as his correspondence indicates. In Bolton town centre, building development initially had grand intentions as an undated and unexecuted plan of development, centred around a proposed Wellington Place and Bradford Square, suggests.[11] The church of the Holy Trinity was already in existence, its site having been given during the life of the 1st Earl, prior to the foundation being laid in 1823. Its dedication was perhaps inspired by that of the chapel that then still existed at the Bridgeman family's Lancashire seat of Great Lever, close to the town, which had been consecrated as such by Bishop John Bridgeman in 1636.

The intended formality of the Bradford estate's Bolton town planning, however, was shelved when the railway with the town's station was built, opening in 1838. The station, at the estate's request, was erected on Bridgeman Street.[12] The well-built early nineteenth-century buildings that survive in Bolton show a concern for good design and the well-being of the tenants. Many of these were built from 1821 on ninety-nine-year building leases. These gave leaseholders some security of tenure to enable quality buildings to be developed whilst, at the same time, empowering the freehold estate to keep overarching control.

In addition to developing land to rent out, the Bradfords also made significant contributions to the well-being of their urban estates throughout the course of the nineteenth century and Bolton was an early recipient of benevolent management, with a site being given for an early hospital in the town's Nelson Square in 1827.[13] In addition to the Church of the Holy Trinity, the family also were active benefactors to a number of other churches, giving sites or funding (and sometimes both) at St Mark's Fletcher Street, St. James' New Bury, St Peter's Farnworth, St Simon & St Jude's Rishton Lane and at St Stephen's & All Martyrs, Lever Bridge,[14] in addition to St Michael's at Great Lever.[15] The latter church also received benefactions from the agent George Pigott, since he was church warden there. This, his position as a Poor Law guardian, involvement in the local militia, and links to the Bolton borough council, meant that Pigott was very much at the heart of the community and a useful guardian of the Bradford family's interests.

During this period, the old family seat of Great Lever Hall was largely tenanted, although in 1848 the old chapel was used, with the family's permission, as a Sunday school.[16] Works to sustain the needs of the people on the estate in Lancashire continued and in 1861 Lever Street Holy Trinity National School in Bolton[17] opened, the estate having given the land and £200 towards the cost of building. The school was later renamed St Mark's. The family were also swift to recognise the value of the public park, something which may have owed to the Shropshire influence of neighbouring landowner and MP for Shrewsbury Robert Aglionby Slaney (1791–1862), who served as an unpaid commissioner for the health of the towns for Prime Minister Robert Peel (1788–1850) in 1843–8. At Bolton the estate established an early park in 1854 with a twin gabled lodge on Radcliffe Road, which has since become known as 'Two cats' from the leopard supporters on the Bradford coat of arms that adorns its façade, and which in the twentieth century was home to renowned steeplejack Fred Dibnah (1938–2004). A further park was opened at Tonge-in-Haulgh, where fifteen acres provided space for cricket and football pitches and for other sporting activities. Bolton's Queen's Park had been suggested in the Bolton Improvement Plan of 1864, and its creation, which included Bradford estate land, was paid for by the council. It was opened by the 3rd Earl of Bradford in 1866 – he having succeeded his father in the previous year – with the earl expressing a wish that it should be 'a great advantage to the operative population'.[18] Facilities for sports at the parks were an important consideration, and the popularity of cricket led to the formation of the Bolton-Bradford Cricket Club at Tonge-with-Haulgh in 1852, whilst the Bolton Cricket Club was established on the estate at Great Lever in the 1870s.

The urban estates were not left solely in the hands of the agents and Lord Bradford did make a number of visits including one in 1844, when he inspected not only the coalmines but also the new churches that were being built with his funding.[19] Mining had hitherto been exploited by third parties taking leases, thus minimising the financial risk to the Bradford Estates, and these leases had included mines at Farnworth that were leased to the Bridgewater Trustees.[20]

By 1833 Lord Bradford was also entering into agreement for the leasing of coalmines in Darcy Lever, Bolton, as well as considering the use of waterpower at Great Lever as a means to pump excess water out of the mines there.[21] However, from about 1839, the Bradford estate decided to work its own coal and a pit, which later became Great Lever Colliery, was sunk on

Raikes Lane at a cost of £10,000.[22] A tramway was established to link into the Manchester and Bolton Railway in 1849, ensuring easy access to markets.[23]

In the Midlands, Walsall similarly grew as an urban centre as a result of the exploitation of the minerals, which here included limestone, coal and iron ore. The Crimean War provided a stimulus for the use of the metals worked by the industries in the West Midlands and as a result of this the pace of growth increased.[24] At Walsall, education, health care and spiritual care were also invested in by the estate. In 1856 new schools were being built at Birchills and Pleck on sites that had been given by Lord Bradford.[25]

The efficient management and presentation of the estates was also reflected in the family's own residences at this time. George had, prior to his succession, been resident at Castle Bromwich Hall and had made a number of improvements to the property, including commissioning the Birmingham hothouse manufacturers Jones and Clark to build a canted-ended conservatory in the garden there in 1824.[26] Upon his succession to the earldom, George commissioned works to modernise Castle Bromwich Hall. Thomas Rickman (1776–1841) with his then partner in practice, Henry Hutchinson (1800–1831), produced designs to improve the old house with the addition of a new kitchen block in 1825. Their work was well received and, from 1830, their attentions were shifted to the main seat at Weston Park.[27]

There, a new west wing was conceived, rising at right angles to and at the full height of the 1671 south front. At ground floor level, the most southerly room was a small sitting room or anteroom. To its north, with a generous

FIGURE 117 *Weston Park from the south in circa 1840*, pen and ink with watercolour, 28 x 33 cm. The house as it appeared after the alterations made for the 2nd Earl of Bradford, showing the new canted bay at the centre of the rebuilt west front. The tower of St Andrew's church can be seen through the trees to the left, whilst one of the Coade stone sundials – later incorporated into garden terraces on the site – can be seen presiding over the drive at a time when the central door of the south front served as the main entrance into the house. Accession number 116.0083. (Copyright Trustees of the Weston Park Foundation.)

FIGURE 118 The domed
iron conservatory at
Weston Park which was
supplied to the 2nd Earl of
Bradford by Jones & Clark
of Birmingham in 1840.
It is shown in a photograph
of circa 1856 by Lady
Lucy and Lady Charlotte
Bridgeman, the daughters
of the 2nd Earl. (Photo:
courtesy of the author.)

projecting canted bay window, which gazed towards the Shrewsbury Walk, was
Lord Bradford's room. Then, north of this, was a new housekeeper's room and
steward's room, whilst on first and second floors were a series of new bedrooms
for the family. The family's agent Peter Potter assisted in sourcing timber
and Westmorland slates for the work, thriftily emphasising to the architects
in 1830 that 'it is desirable that all practicable economy be adopted in the
projected additions to Weston Hall'.[28] Advantage was taken of the presence
of builders to repoint the house's brickwork, and the works continued until
1833. Upon completion, the wing gave the family additional comfort, with a
fitted carpet supplied to Lord Bradford's room, along with a desk with canted
sides, following the form of the bay window in which it was positioned.[29] By
this date, the view from the house and from the new wing took in Park Pool, a
lake that was created partly for aesthetic reasons and also to improve drainage
in the park. It was formed under the direction of John Webb, the landscape
gardener who had worked for the 2nd Earl's grandfather and father before
him and it is a feature which, in its maturity, has frequently been thought to
be part of Capability Brown's landscaping. Unmistakably a product of the
nineteenth century, however, was a structure that was built overlooking Church
Pool in 1840. This was the elegant conservatory that Jones and Clark built, with
metallic framed windows and two wings stretching to either side of the canted
domed centre bay. It proved not only to be a shelter to the tender exotic plants
that it contained, but was also a popular venue for house party guests as early
photographs taken by the family show.

Castle Bromwich Hall was also a focus of further works by the 2nd Earl.
These took place in 1837 and were also entrusted to Thomas Rickman who, by
that date, was in partnership with Richard Charles Hussey (1806–1887). On this
occasion, the ground-floor hall and first-floor drawing room were remodelled
in a careful antiquarian spirit. The drawing room's plaster ceiling was embellished in the manner of Edward Gouge's late seventeenth-century plasterwork

FIGURE 119 The entrance hall at Castle Bromwich Hall depicted in a watercolour of 1867, 32.5 x 44.2 cm. The artist has shown the Jacobean-style chimneypiece and historicist decoration by Thomas Rickman and R.C. Hussey, which was completed for the 2nd Earl of Bradford from 1837. Accession number 116.0003.3. (Copyright Trustees of the Weston Park Foundation.)

FIGURE 120 The drawing room at Castle Bromwich Hall in a watercolour heightened with white chalk of circa 1850, 35.5 x 53 cm. The decorated ceiling, with elements replicating Edward Gouge's late seventeenth-century plasterwork, is shown along with the set of Teniers tapestries that Lord Bradford reputedly acquired from a Spanish palace. Accession number 116.0068. (Copyright Trustees of the Weston Park Foundation.)

FIGURE 121 *St Catherine's,
Windermere*. The Lake
District residence of the
family which was purchased
by the 2nd Earl of Bradford
in 1831, depicted in a
drawing, heightened
with chalk, by his
daughter Lady Charlotte
Bridgeman (1827–1858),
27.8 x 21.5 cm. Accession
number 116.0021.1.
(Copyright Trustees of the
Weston Park Foundation.)

FIGURE 122 The view from St Catherine's, depicted by John Glover (1767–1849) as *Head of Lake Windermere*, oil on canvas,
49.8 x 70.3 cm. Accession number 101.0220. (Copyright Trustees of the Weston Park Foundation.)

elsewhere in the house, whilst for the room's walls, the Earl acquired a set of Teniers tapestries which were said to have come from a palace in Spain.[30] In the hall, a new decorated plaster ceiling and screen was installed. When later chimneypieces were removed, Jacobean ones were discovered underneath which were drawn by the architects and replicated in style.[31]

After Rickman's death in 1841, R.C. Hussey continued to play an architectural role as a trusted adviser to the Weston Park estate during the 2nd Earl's lifetime. He designed the ground-floor north extension of the Weston stables with its central arched door, which provided additional looseboxes, in 1846–7.[32] Later he was asked to consider alterations at Blymhill rectory and was to be found inspecting Tong Castle, following its purchase in 1856.[33]

In addition to his inheritance, George made a number of significant purchases of property during his lifetime.[34] One of these was a small Lake District estate called St Catherine's which he bought in 1831. It centred on a small mansion that had been built of stone, brick and slate in circa 1810, perhaps by the architect George Webster,[35] which had big round chimneys and a veranda that enjoyed fine views across the head of Lake Windermere. After an initial period of tenancy, the house was rebuilt in 1838–9 for the family's use.[36] The advent of railways made it relatively easy for the family to head north, with their carriage[37] taken upon the train, and then for them to be able to enjoy the beauty of the landscape and the society that it afforded. Amongst the visitors that they welcomed to the house was William Wordsworth, and his portrait by Thomas Heathfield Carrick found its way into the family collection. By 1856 however, a valuation of timber had been conducted and part of the estate offered for sale as building plots; this was not successful and a further attempted sale in the following year for the whole property also proved abortive. The family, in fact, continued to actively use the house and retained ownership into the twentieth century, with the 3rd Earl's daughter Lady Mabel Kenyon-Slaney eventually inheriting the property.

The 2nd Earl's other acquisition, much closer to Weston Park, was the neighbouring three-thousand acre estate of Tong Castle for which he paid £171,500 in 1855. Relations with Tong's owners, the Durant family, had become

FIGURE 123 *William Wordsworth*, painted by Thomas Heathfield Carrick (1802–1874), oil on canvas, 16.5 x 14 cm. Wordsworth was a friend of the family and visitor to St Catherine's. Accession number 101.0363.2. (Copyright Trustees of the Weston Park Foundation.)

increasingly tense, especially in 1840 when the Bradfords were purchasing property at Neachley, which adjoined the Tong estate. At that time, the agent Peter Potter had received a letter from George Durant junior containing veiled threats that purported to emanate from his son Ernest Durant who, the father claimed, 'would delight in exhibiting the effigies of His Lordship's maternal ancestor the unfortunate Admiral Byng on a gallows under his windows [at Weston Park]'.[38] At Tong, the medieval castle, which had been rebuilt in the Tudor period by Sir Henry Vernon – who also held Haddon Hall, Derbyshire – had been rebuilt in gothick style in the 1750s for George Durant senior to Capability Brown's design. As early as 1796, John Byng had been critical of the house's size versus its acreage, although the property contiguous to the Weston estate made for a logical purchase by the Bradfords. Their bid for the property was successful and on 11 September 1855, the Earl's daughter Lady Charlotte Bridgeman was able to write that:

> Not only has Papa got it, but got it for £10.500 less than he would have gone to. It has gone for £171.500. Hurrah for the Tong Knoll! We may walk straight to the top as often as we like. Mr. Jones, of Shackerley & Ruckley was the other bidder we were afraid of. They say the tenants at Tong were very anxious Papa should get it, which is a good beginning. Davidson or Cattell, or somebody or everybody are in such a state of glee that the bells have been ringing ever since & a feu de joie has been fired.[39]

George's art collecting interests were largely restricted to portraits, with Hayter a favoured artist. The mountainous landscape around St Catherine's perhaps inspired the acquisition of the painting *Head of Lake Windermere* by John Glover, and also two great canvases by Theophilus Lindsey Aspland (1807–1890) of *Honister Crag* and *Langdale* of 1853. He was a keen purchaser of decorative art pieces throughout his life, enabling houses that were altered to be furnished to his and his family's tastes.[40] These purchases included china and furniture from Edward Holmes Baldock (1777–1845) of Hanway Street, a dealer who had also been patronised by George IV and William Beckford of Fonthill Abbey. Lord Bradford acquired a number of items that were invoiced from 16 April 1838 until 1841, much of it intended for his London house at 43 Belgrave Square. These included 'a Beautiful Buhl Cabinet 2 Glass doors & a Centre one of Buhl £60', and also '2 Encoignures and Slabs inlaid and turquoise china inserted £80', all three of which can now be found in the Marble Hall at Weston Park. A number of bureau plats also remain in the collection – one of classic Baldock form, stamped 'EHB' – whilst one of a pair of Continental porcelain arbours can also be found in the house, which also came from Baldock.[41]

George also bought a pair of ebony cabinets with mosaics from the Emanuel Brothers, and from R.M. Butt came a bronze of Hercules and the Erymanthean Boar and an elaborate Cellini-esque pair of bronze vases – the latter three now in the Entrance Hall – which were invoiced on 25 May 1838 and were paid for that same day.[42] Also in that year, J.G. Fearn sold him a bronze clock with the figure of Hector,[43] and he purchased from Garrard the equestrian figure of the Duke of Wellington.[44] Of the contemporary makers, Perrys provided chandeliers for the house and Gillow & Co. supplied furniture. Whilst most acquisitions were made in London, he also added to the collections through the patronage of the Birmingham sculptor Peter Hollins, one of the founders of the Royal Birmingham Society of Artists. Hollins had, in August 1846, been commissioned to create the remarkably fine stele monument to the Earl's first wife and mother of his children, Georgina Moncreiffe (1790–1842). The family visited his studio on 21 August that year to inspect the piece prior to its installation in October within St Andrew's church at Weston.[45] Hollins also sculpted

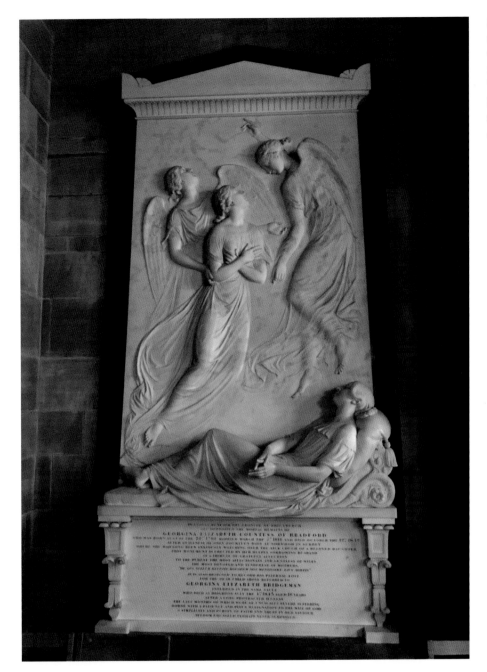

FIGURE 124 Memorial to Georgina Moncreiffe, Countess of Bradford (1790–1842) in St Andrew's church, Weston-under-Lizard by Peter Hollins of Birmingham, sculpted from 1846. (Photo: courtesy of the author.)

the Earl's portrait, with sittings commencing 25 September 1849, but its likeness was not thought to be especially good by his daughter Lady Charlotte. When Hollins came to Weston to set it up on 5 November 1850, she observed that 'I don't think it so like as the first clay was.'[46]

The 2nd Earl was not always easily persuaded to make a purchase and his astute sense of awareness must have warned him that the ancient carved oak bed carved with the Bridgeman arms, which he was offered by the dealer George Shaw of Upper Mill in 1848,[47] was too good to be true. It prevented the family from owning a historicist fake although others, including the Duke of Northumberland, were content to make an acquisition when similarly propositioned by Shaw, who assured his would-be customers that the bed had their heraldic achievements carved upon it.

In 1849, Lord Bradford married for a second time. His wife was Helen Mackay, daughter of Captain Æneas Mackay, who, at first, was not well received by the children. Matters eventually eased, so that Lady Lucy and Lady Charlotte

Bridgeman were able to photograph the couple in their landau outside the original front door on the south side of the house in the 1850s. His tenure at the helm of Weston Park proved to be a stabilising era that lasted for forty years. It was marked by sensible acquisitions and embellishments which almost all had a purpose beyond the mere aesthetic. At the time of his death in 1865, it was noted that his funeral was attended by his agents, 'Potter, Pigott, Twamley, Griffiths and Davidson'[48] indicating the scale of the bureaucracy that was now required to manage the estates, especially in view of the urban growth. A toast to 'Lord Bradford, the Just' was drunk by the mourners afterwards, and the generations that followed had equal reason to be grateful for the sense of balanced judgement that he shared with his agents.

In the meantime, throughout the nineteenth century, at Wigan a similar pattern of urban expansion and leisured patronage was also being maintained on the family's behalf and continued triumphantly beyond the date of the 2nd Earl's death. In that Lancashire town, the family's interests had been overseen by the Bradfords' cousin,[49] Rev. Sir Henry John Gunning, 4th Bt (1797–1885), who was inducted in 1833 and retired in 1864. Gunning's Wigan Rectory Act of 1837, which enabled the rector to grant leases for the mining of coal under the Mesnes – or demesne land – had proved unpopular. These were, in part, motivated by a need to raise £2,000 of capital with which to repair Wigan Hall,[50] although the mining was to prove the building's undoing. The growing population in Wigan meant that the parish church was unable to adequately

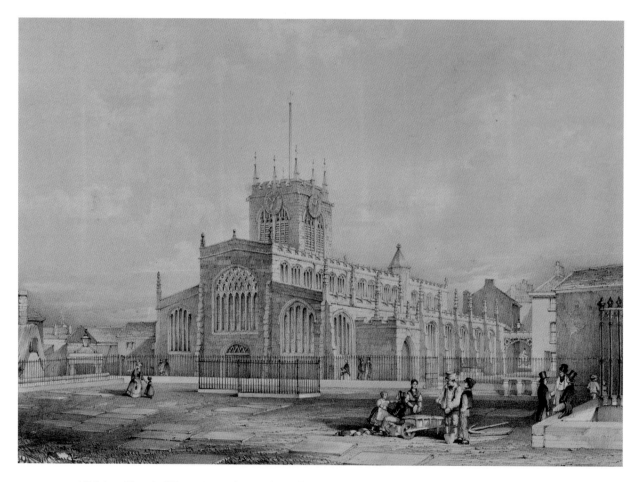

FIGURE 125 All Saints Church, Wigan, Lancashire in the mid-nineteenth century, shown in a lithographic print, 31 x 42 cm. The contribution of the younger sons of the family to Wigan – especially the 2nd Earl's younger son the Hon. and Rev. G.T.O. Bridgeman – was notable for the development of the town and for attempts to resolve social problems at that time. Accession number 102.0103. (Copyright Trustees of the Weston Park Foundation.)

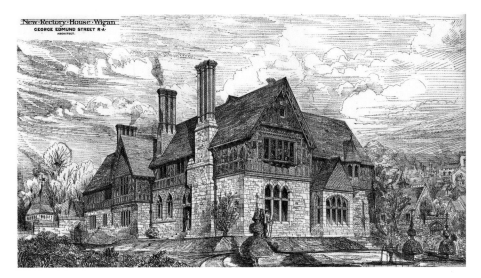

FIGURE 126 G.E. Street's design for the new Wigan Rectory or Hall, as engraved for *Building News* of 3 October 1873. (Photo: courtesy of the author.)

serve the town, and so new chapels of ease were built. Sir Henry Bridgeman, 1st Baron Bradford's younger son, the Hon. and Rev. George Bridgeman, had already overseen the building of St John's Pemberton to designs by Thomas Rickman in 1832, whilst others now followed. These comprised St David's at Haigh, St John's at Abram and St Catherine at Scholes. This growth of the town meant that, towards the end of Gunning's tenure, the manorial rights of the rectory were sold in 1860 to the Corporation of Wigan, but the family's connection with the town was maintained in a benevolent fashion by 2nd Earl's younger son, the Hon. and Rev. George Thomas Orlando Bridgeman (1823–1895).

G.T.O. Bridgeman had begun his clerical career on the Bradford family's Lancashire estate, as curate at Bolton-le-Moors from 1850, becoming, successively, rector at Willey in Shropshire, at Blymhill on the Weston Park estate from 1853, and then rural dean of Brewood in 1863, the year prior to his Wigan appointment. He was a keen antiquarian and when travelling in the Holy Land had acquired cedar seeds from Mount Lebanon which were grown and planted on the west face of the Knoll in Weston Park.[51]

As rector, from 1864 until his death, G.T.O. Bridgeman took up the office in Wigan and played an important role in the town, passing his own Rectory Glebe Act in 1871, which enabled him to sell a part of the glebe,[52] some of which was for the granting of building leases, and also for a new market place and a public park, Mesnes Park. The Act also made provision, though the sale and through the security of mine rents, for financing the building of the grammar school and enabling the rebuilding of the rectory in 1875–6, following significant damage as a result of mining subsidence. The architect of the new rectory was G.E. Street, who had designed a number of churches built in Shropshire and Staffordshire in the 1850s and 1860s, as a part of his wider practice. He had restored the church at Barrow on the Willey estate in 1851–2 and St Mary's, Blymhill in 1856–9, and was later to restore St Andrew's at Weston-under-Lizard in 1869–70.

At Wigan Rectory or Hall, a new gatehouse was built and the house itself retained the service wing of the earlier house.[53] The new house, in Tudor gothic style, had main rooms, gathered around a handsome gothic staircase with a tiled floor ornamented with encaustic tiles emblazoned with the Bridgeman arms. The house's decoration incorporated earlier decorative features, many of which still survive in the house, including Swiss stained glass of mid-sixteenth century date and a Jacobean overmantle in the former dining room which is thought to have come from the earlier house. Some of the stained glass

FIGURE 127 Pair of Lübeck panels, of late fifteenth- or early sixteenth-century date, which were originally the outer wings of a triptych, acquired by the Hon. and Rev. G.T.O. Bridgeman for the chapel at Wigan Rectory. Conserved as part of a project with funding from the National Lottery Heritage Fund, the panels are now on display in All Saints Church, Wigan. (Photo courtesy of the Rector and Churchwardens of Wigan parish church.)

was probably acquired by G.T.O. Bridgeman from Wardour Street dealers in London, and it may have been from this source that the pair of Lübeck late fifteenth- or early sixteenth-century altar panels came. These – the outer wings of a triptych altarpiece, with eight carved figures of saints on the inner side and paintings on the outer sides – were formerly in the Green Room of the Hall. They were conserved with Heritage Lottery Funding in 2014 and are now on display in All Saints parish church itself. The rectory cost £9,249 8s 9d, and the gatehouse £1,275 8s 8d, with a further £1,214 9s expended on the building of a new wall to separate the rectory's grounds from two new streets, New Market Street and Parson's Walk. The costs were more than had been allowed by the Court of Chancery, and the rector himself paid the difference.[54]

G.T.O. Bridgeman demonstrated philanthropic concern throughout his career, with a keen interest in the working population around him. He was one of the founders of the Lancashire and Cheshire Miners' Permanent Relief Society – of which he was president until his death[55] – and understood the needs of the growing urban community, recognising that different sections of that society had varying needs. The 1781 classical chapel of ease of St George's had already become the church for a new parish in 1864, whilst the chapels of ease built during Rev. Sir Henry Gunning's time around Wigan now also became churches for self-administering new parishes. In 1878 Rev. Bridgeman also gave the site for a new church, St Michael and All Angels, and he provided a site out of the glebe for a new National and Blue Coat School for two hundred and fifty children in a building that was designed by G.E. Street. In 1887 his work aided women's advancement by the founding of the Church High School for Girls, and in the same year he also encouraged the Sisters of the Community of St Mary the Virgin to establish a branch house in the parish, to work closer and more empathetically with women, and for this purpose All Saints' Mission House in New Market Street was built for them.[56] The changes that he effected around the glebe also included an Act for Sewerage, New Streets and the Provision of Gas at Wigan in 1874.

The influence of the rector at Wigan, together with the activities of agents and family on the urban estates at Bolton and at Walsall, witnessed transformational change that was to define the futures of each town. The Bridgeman legacy of this period can still be found at each place, continuing to provide a lasting heritage that bears witness to social change and investment. Although at a distance geographically and in its rural location, Weston Park was to benefit enormously from the developments of the urban estates as the nineteenth century progressed and the reign of Victoria dominated the family's country house life.

CHAPTER EIGHT

The Reign of Victoria
Enrichment, Tragedy and Disraeli

For many traditional landowners, who were reliant on agricultural incomes, the second half of the nineteenth century proved to be a financially uneasy time. In the aftermath of the repeal of the Corn Laws, the flood of cheap grain from America and Canada created difficult trading conditions for farmers and this, in turn, adversely affected those who owned the land itself. For the Bradfords, however, their ownership of urban properties and mineral reserves meant that their income levels remained stable throughout the nineteenth century, with only the rise in taxation towards the end of the century as a growing threat. Whilst agricultural incomes began to depress, the income from ground rents and from minerals grew in Bolton and Walsall. In both places, developments continued apace, with a new coal mine sunk at Walsall Wood in 1874, generating both rental income and royalties from shares that the family held in the site's mining company.[1]

As a result of this wealth and the capable control of the urban estates by agents and junior family members alike, life for the family at Weston Park was one of great stability and constant improvement. There was never, it seems, a grand plan to rebuild the house at any stage but rather a contentment with the bones of the seventeenth-century house and an intention that the house should work for the family, their guests and for the servants as a result of organic alterations.

The 2nd Earl's eldest son and heir Orlando (1819–1898) became, in many ways, the model Victorian landowner. The eventual 3rd Earl of Bradford, Orlando was an exact contemporary of his eventual monarch Queen Victoria. In his lifetime, he gave public service as MP for South Shropshire from 1842 until his succession to the earldom in 1865. He also served his queen in a number of positions which culminated in two terms as Master of the Horse, firstly in 1874–80 and then in 1885–6 following the death of the 1st Duke of Westminster. In 1852, during the 14th Earl of Derby's premiership, Lord Newport was made Vice Chamberlain of Her Majesty's Household and also sworn of the Privy Council. He had a second term of office in this role in 1858–9. As Vice Chamberlain, he was deputy to the Lord Chamberlain, supporting his duties of making arrangements of state occasions. He also had a responsibility for acting as a line of communication from Queen Victoria to the House of Commons and vice versa.

In 1866, the year after his father's death, he was elevated as Lord Chamberlain and held the office until 1868. As such, his role entailed supervising the departments which supported and advised Queen Victoria and also acted as a conduit between the monarch and the House of Lords. His office was responsible for organising all ceremonial activity including state visits, award and honour ceremonies, royal weddings, and the State Opening of Parliament.

He had married the Hon. Selina Weld-Forester, daughter of the 1st Lord Forester and his wife Lady Katherine, daughter of the 4th Duke of Rutland in

FIGURE 129 *The Hon. Selina*
Weld-Forester, Viscountess
Newport and later Countess
of Bradford (1819–1894),
painted by Robert Thorburn
(1818–1885), watercolour
on ivory, 47 x 31.5 cm.
Accession number 116.0122.
(Copyright Trustees of the
Weston Park Foundation.)

1844, and the couple went on to have two sons and two daughters. Orlando's life
spanned the ages of painted depiction and of photography and it is intriguing to
look at his painted image in the portraits that survive of him by John Ferneley
and his hunting friend Sir Francis Grant (1803–1878) and also to observe him
as the subject of photographic images too. He and his wife, in fact, were the
subjects of some of the very earliest calotype photographs since his sisters Lady
Lucy and Lady Charlotte Bridgeman were pioneering photographers. William
Fox Talbot had developed the calotype method of photography and the two
Bridgeman ladies took a great interest in the new techniques, coached by their
sister-in-law's brother the Hon. and Rev. Townshend Forester (later 4th Lord
Forester). Lady Charlotte noted in her diary of 2 October 1855:

The photographing mania strong upon us all. Lucy and I received instructions from Mr Forester and watched his proceedings narrowly. Lucy even did one. Did various groups ...

Some of the processes required a dark room and the sisters, looked about at Weston to find a suitable place. Finally, on visiting the Temple of Diana in the park, Lady Charlotte wrote in her diary on 7 November 1855:

shuttered myself up in the Temple to see if the stone parlour would do for photograph messing in – for Colonel Pennant has kindly made us a present of his machine but it has not arrived yet ...

The room proved satisfactory and the equipment – which may have been a solar enlarger – sent by Colonel Pennant (later Lord Penrhyn of Penrhyn Castle, in North Wales)[2] duly arrived although was unfortunately damaged en route.

Their photographs included family, friends and servants, together with scenes at Weston Park and elsewhere. They were given to friends and family, finding their way into various albums that are now in private and public collections, with an important group in the Philadelphia Museum of Art and also another at the Victoria & Albert Museum.[3]

FIGURE 130 Lady Lucy and Lady Charlotte Bridgeman, from a contemporary photograph – possibly a self-portrait of circa 1855. (Copyright Trustees of the Weston Park Foundation.)

FIGURE 131 Lady Lucy and Lady Charlotte Bridgeman's photograph of the upper servants at Weston Park. From left to right, Lucy Thompson, Harriman, unknown, Davies and Mrs Austin. In her diary for 16 February 1856, Lady Charlotte had written: 'We photographed in the dining room the upper servants in a group and then me. Both successful. We also did Miss Hope after luncheon before going out …' The Dining Room in 1856 was located in the room now used as the Library. (Copyright Trustees of the Weston Park Foundation.)

Tragically the photography came to an abrupt end in 1858 when a spark from the drawing room fire caused Lady Charlotte's crinoline dress to catch light. Her sister Lucy tried to save her but was also badly burned. Charlotte died on 26 November and her sister followed her to the grave on 3 December.[4] They were commemorated in the parish church at Weston and also at Blymhill, where their friends erected a stained glass window in the north aisle to their memory. Their tragedy, which had been enacted in the heart of the family home at Weston Park, may have been one of the factors behind the many alterations that the house at Weston was to have throughout the second half of the nineteenth century.

The Ladies' elder brother Orlando was keenly interested in hunting and prior to 1849 he purchased a house at Melton Mowbray that he rebuilt as Newport Lodge.[5] Here, in the early 1850s, Sir John Leslie (1822–1916) painted the dining room wall with a fresco which depicted twelve of the so-called 'Belvoirites', including many subjects from the Ladies Lucy and Charlotte's photography such as the Orlando's brother-in-law the 2nd Lord Forester, and also the Duke of Rutland and Seymour Egerton (later 4th Earl of Wilton), all of whom were celebrated for their hunting prowess.[6] Perhaps unsurprisingly, although Newport Lodge is known from photographs, it was the interior of the stables, with favourite hunters 'Tom of Lincoln' and the 'Engineer', that was captured in paint by John Ferneley. Newport Lodge remained a property of the family into the second half of the nineteenth century, although was increasingly tenanted from 1869.[7] Lord Newport kept a hunting diary from 1845 to 1865 which was eventually privately published and which enumerates his hunters – several of which are immortalised in paintings at Weston by John and Claude Ferneley[8] – together with the challenges of the field and also the eminently sociable aspects of the sport. Not only was the painter Francis Grant amongst his companions of the chase, but other social luminaries were present. On the eighth birthday of the Newports' son George – the eventual 4th Earl of Bradford – when he went hunting for the first time, the party was joined by the Duchess of Cambridge (1797–1889) and her daughter, fourteen-year-old Princess Mary Adelaide (1833–1897) in February 1853.[9]

FIGURE 132 Newport Lodge, Melton Mowbray, Leicestershire, seen from the garden in a photograph of circa 1860. The house was a favourite residence of Viscount Newport, prior to his succession to the earldom in 1865, on account of its access to the hunting field and its attendant social scene. (Staffordshire Archives/Photo: courtesy of the author.)

FIGURE 133 John Ferneley Senior (1781–1860), *Interior of the stables at Newport Lodge, Melton Mowbray, in 1852*, oil on canvas, 110.5 x 165.1 cm. The artist shows some of the favourite hunters including Tom of Lincoln and the Engineer. Accession number 101.0003. (Copyright Trustees of the Weston Park Foundation.)

Orlando's interest in the natural world included that of birds and this interest, combined no doubt with a desire to add to the plate books collected by his father, led to an association with the ornithologist and early lithographer John Gould (1804–1881). As a result, the family's library was added to with all of Gould's works as they were published, and the author in gratitude gave the Earl a case containing a pair of stuffed lyre birds which remain in the collection.[10]

When not hunting or in London, Castle Bromwich Hall was the residence occupied by Orlando and Selina as Viscount and Viscountess Newport, although for a time they also rented Davenport House in Shropshire, which gave them a home closer to Lord Newport's father at Weston Park. Towards the end of his life, the 2nd Earl had embarked upon further works to Weston in May 1862.[11] This comprised a new family staircase at the north east corner of the house, and – linking with it – a new easterly wing which stood at right angles to the main block of the house. Designed by his favoured architect R.C. Hussey and built by Richard Yates of Shifnal at a cost of over £10,000, the wing contained a new breakfast room – linking with the staircase – and a grand new saloon with a south facing canted bay window, two fireplaces and a tripartite plan divided by Corinthian columns of scagliola.[12] The chimneypieces were supplied in 1864–5 by the sculptor James Forsyth, working to Hussey's designs – each with monopodia jambs, one with lions and the other with goats. Following the death of the 2nd Earl on 22 March 1865 – when he was laid in state in his new saloon – the bills for the chimneypieces totalling £799 17s had not been settled and they seem to have caused some rancour between architect and the new Earl. Hussey was asked to account for the expense and acknowledged to Lord Bradford that:

> The amount is certainly large, but the work is very costly & Elaborate, & I think quite worth what is charged for it ... The first sketches, which I made for these chimneypieces were of much less costly character but they were not approved [by the 2nd Earl], & I was directed to provide others. I did not know what the expense of them would be until I received Forsyth's bill.[13]

Forsyth, when approached, refused to take back the chimneypieces, offering instead to exhibit them in his gallery and to sell them on commission. Eventually the new Earl retained the chimneypieces, dispensing instead with Hussey's services. He also decided to demolish the new wing just four years after its commencement.

The 3rd Earl turned instead to the Scots architect William Burn (1789–1870) and his nephew and successor in practice John MacVicar Anderson (1835–1915), whilst continuing to use the Shifnal builder Richard Yates. Burn had become the favoured Tory country house architect and in Staffordshire had designed Sandon Hall in 1852 for the 2nd Earl of Harrowby (1798–1882). Sandon was a Tudor-style house, whilst at Weston the practice remained classical in its intent, but like all of Burn and MacVicar Anderson's work the alterations were planned for convenience and were well executed in first-rate materials.

Their early plan of 1866[14] suggested a short new east wing upon the ghost footprint of the Hussey wing which was indicated in red ink. Further drawings evolved the wing, including elevations suggesting small paned sash windows to match those of the main house. Eventually a final drawing, showing an easterly progress of apsidal-ended waiting room, Lord Bradford's room, housekeeper's room, Mr Cattell's Room and Steward's Room was produced, annotated that it was a revision of July 1866 and endorsed as a contract drawing by the builder Yates.[15] The wing provided first-floor bedrooms for guests and also, by ingeniously linking to the earlier northern service building, gave adjacent accommodation for the guests' servants. Hussey's wing was demolished and the new wing, faced in stone ashlar and with four-pane plate glass sashes, replaced it.

The work did not end there and, at the same time, the orientation of the main house was also changed, with a new entrance porte-cochère added to the east front of the house. Balustrading was also added to the roofline above, flanking the giant pediment and matching that on the new wing. Within, what had been the Library, became the Entrance Hall. In turn, the former Regency Dining Room became the Library, whilst the adjoining old Entrance Hall was given a parquet floor and additional plasterwork and became the Drawing Room.[16] The old Drawing Room was adorned by the Gobelins tapestries that had been consigned to a first-floor bedroom in the first decade of the century, with one of the Hussey-designed Forsyth chimneypieces from the ill-fated saloon installed. A new Dining Room was created in the 1830 west wing, by removing the internal walls that had previously separated Lord Bradford's Sitting Room from the Small Sitting Room or Ante Room and from the Housekeeper's Room and by the insertion of iron girders to take the weight previously borne by the walls. Here, the other of the short-lived saloon's chimneypieces found a home, set against a sienna and Carrera marble foil of inferior quality carving to Forsyth's fire surround, whilst oak panelling adorned the lower walls.

An internal courtyard, at the heart of the house, was partly roofed over to make a billiard room, with mechanical ventilation provided by G.H. Haden of Tunbridge Wells on its leaded roof. To afford the family comfort in the interior decorating, the company of George Trollope was commissioned.[17] Trollopes provided not only painting and decorating, but also French polishing services,

FIGURE 134 Weston Park House seen from the east in circa 1870, following the 3rd Earl of Bradford's initial campaign of building works under the architects William Burn (1789–1870) and John MacVicar Anderson (1835–1915). The house retained the Roman cement render applied during the tenure of the 1st Earl of Bradford, but has been given a balustrade parapet, new porte-cochère and the addition of the east wing, today known as the Victorian Wing. The carriage ring has been created on the site of the Regency flower garden, its southern boundary defined by the balustrading of William Brodrick Thomas's upper terrace, whilst the drive is closed by gates supplied by the Coalbrookdale Company in 1869. (Copyright Trustees of the Weston Park Foundation.)

FIGURE 135 The drawing room at Weston Park in circa 1890. The Ionic columns and deep entablature survive from James Paine's reinvention of the space for Sir Henry and Lady Bridgeman, when it was the entrance hall. MacVicar Anderson replaced the room's marble floor with parquet, installed a new white marble chimneypiece, and gave the room new ceiling, over-door and panel-framing plasterwork as a part of its transformation to a drawing room for the 3rd Earl and Countess of Bradford in the late 1860s. (Copyright Trustees of the Weston Park Foundation.)

FIGURE 136 The Library in the early twentieth century. The appearance of the room is surely much as it would have been in the time of the 3rd Earl and Countess of Bradford. Selina Countess of Bradford's portrait by Edward Clifford (1844–1907) can be seen on the easel to the left of the chimneypiece.

The room had been the Regency dining room – in turn created from the eighteenth-century drawing room and breakfast room. (Copyright Trustees of the Weston Park Foundation.)

upholstery, the supply of furniture and literally hundreds of yards of Brussels carpet for corridors, staircases and rooms. On the first floor, the south-east corner room, where the Gobelins tapestries had been hanging, gained the Forsyth chimneypiece from the lost 'new breakfast room' of Hussey's wing, whilst the walls were clothed in a Chinese wallpaper of similar type to those installed at Sandon Hall and at Bowhill, where William Burn had also worked, suggesting his hand in its supply.

In the following year, MacVicar Anderson produced designs for new service areas to the north of the house, including a game larder and a new courtyard with an octagonal dairy which remained unexecuted.[18] One structure which did make it off the drawing board, however, was the Orangery with an arcaded loggia linking it to the west side of the house, which was designed in May 1867[19] and built in the months thereafter. The iron roof was supplied by Turner & Co of Marylebone at a cost of £1,129.[20] The total cost of this first phase of works with Burn and MacVicar Anderson was £15,636, and the reinvention was not to stop.[21]

Outside, Hope the head gardener was given assistance by William Brodrick Thomas (1811–1898) in 1866 in the design of new formal balustraded terraced gardens, which took the place of the old carriage sweep to the south of the house. These works resulted in the creation of the southern terrace and rose

FIGURE 137 The first-floor boudoir at Weston Park. This room was given the early nineteenth-century Chinese wallpaper during the 3rd Earl and Countess of Bradford's time and the decorated plaster ceiling was possibly also a part of works. The chimneypiece is that supplied by the sculptor James Forsyth for the breakfast room in the 2nd Earl of Bradford's short-lived east wing. (Paul Highnam/Copyright Trustees of the Weston Park Foundation.)

FIGURE 138 The Orangery designed in 1867, which stands to the west of the house at Weston Park. The tower of St Andrew's church can be seen rising above, whilst to the left a path leads off into Capability Brown's west pleasure ground, the Shrewsbury Walk. The Italian Garden, with its central fountain, laid out by head gardener James Hope following direction from William Brodrick Thomas (1811–1898), occupies the terrace in front of the orangery and was restored in 2017 by the Weston Park Foundation following major repairs and restoration of the Orangery's cast iron roof. (Copyright Trustees of the Weston Park Foundation.)

garden with the great sweep of the balustraded Plane Tree Lawn beyond, which enclosed a section of the park with a giant mature oriental plane tree within it.

The south front of the stables, which had long been hidden behind a thicket of shrubs to allow the house dominance in Capability Brown's landscape, was once more exposed to view as a part of the changes effected to create a carriage ring before the new entrance on the east front of the house.[22] Although the Coalbrookdale Company was commissioned to supply a new gate-screen for the carriage ring before the east front in 1869, further changes were planned within the decade.[23] By 1877 plans were sent from MacVicar Anderson for alterations to the entrance carriage approach. Gate pillars, with lion sculptures were proposed and Edward Kempe was also consulted, in 1878, on alterations to the approach to the east front.[24]

Railway development had been a preoccupation of the wider estate and, inevitably, the Bradford's agent, Peter Potter maintained a keen interest in the development of railway companies and their potential impact – both the positives of the financials and the negatives of aesthetics – by attending meetings of their directors. Where the development of the Shropshire and Montgomeryshire Railway was concerned, this was built across estate land to the north-west of Shrewsbury. The proprietor and engineer Richard Samuel France neglected to pay the estate for some of its land, although he used the cache of the family's status to name two of his Manning Wardle steam engine locomotives 'Bradford' and 'Viscount'.

For some of the family, namely Orlando's sister Lady Charlotte, railways were a thing of potential danger as her diary for 16 July 1847, recalling an exchange with the family's Castle Bromwich agent Zachariah Twamley, illustrates:

> After dinner we strolled to the new buildings at the barn & met Mr. Twamley & Mr. Smallwood. The latter gave us a long rambling description of the dreadful railroad accident near Wolverton at which he was present. At breakfast this morning in talking over railway accidents it was proved that the chances were a million to one on our side against being killed on the North Western Railway. As for 18 or 19 years, ever since the first bit of it was opened, 5 million people have travelled by it & 5 persons only have been killed on it.

Yet the advent of the railways, for all country houses, meant an easing of journeys, with swifter and simpler travel between London and the provinces than the coaching roads had ever allowed. This, of course, led to an increase in visits, not only from friends and acquaintances but from their attendant growing retinue of servants. In turn, this meant that more accommodation was required within houses like Weston for the guests and their servants and, as house parties developed, activities like playing billiards and smoking came to require their own specific rooms within the house. For Weston, the opening of Shifnal Station, in 1849, had meant that the house enjoyed better connections to the wider country and, inevitably, increased the numbers of guests and servants staying.

The reinvented Weston welcomed many significant guests, as the visitor books testify. Queen Victoria's grandson Prince Christian of Schleswig-Holstein (1831–1917) was recorded on 19 December 1872 in a party which also included the Marquess of Westminster (later 1st Duke of Westminster). All of the group were also subjected to the scales, with their weights recorded in the house book of weights and measures, a practice then common in great houses but which would horrify a modern generation of visitors.

A regular visitor in the 1880s and 1890s was Alice Wodehouse (née Powys), who stayed with her husband the Rev. Frederick Armine Wodehouse (1842–1921) and the couple's eldest son Arthur Powys Wodehouse (1881–1915).[25] Mrs Wodehouse was a niece of Sophia Norman, wife of 4th Lord Forester, and also of Lady Grant, second wife of the 3rd Earl's old hunting companion the painter Sir Francis Grant, and so appears to have been an intimate of the family. Her husband's nephew was the author P.G. Wodehouse, who is known to have spent time with his aunt and uncle during his parents' time in Hong Kong, lending further credibility to the suggestion that Weston Park was indeed the inspiration of the fictional Blandings Castle.[26]

Another literary association of the Victorian era – and perhaps Weston Park's most important and well-known guest – was with the great Victorian statesman, prime minister and author Benjamin Disraeli (1804–1881) who is recorded staying on five occasions between 1873 and 1878. Disraeli had been elected MP for Shrewsbury in 1841, as his second seat in Parliament. Selina, Countess of Bradford's brother, John George, 2nd Lord Forester, had made the nomination for his candidacy and he actively supported Disraeli through what was a tumultuous and at times openly anti-Semitic election contest. The premier recalled this in 1874, remembering: 'He was my earliest supporter, and never changed or faltered.'[27] The enduring support given meant that Disraeli came to be a friend of the Forester family, including with two of Lord Forester's sisters, Selina and Anne. The former was, of course, Lady Bradford

FIGURE 139 *Benjamin Disraeli, later 1st Earl of Beaconsfield* (1804–1881), painted by Theodore Blake Wirgman (1848–1925), oil on canvas, 35.5 x 28 cm. The elder statesman was a regular visitor to Weston Park and a prolific correspondent to both Selina, Countess of Bradford and her sister Anne, Countess of Chesterfield. Accession number 101.0025. (Copyright Trustees of the Weston Park Foundation.)

FIGURE 140 Disraeli's parrot. The Conure parrot was a live gift from Disraeli and it lived in the Orangery at Weston Park. Long presumed to be male, it began laying eggs towards the end of its life and was preserved at its death by the taxidermist Rowland Ward. (Copyright Trustees of the Weston Park Foundation.)

and the latter was also married to an earl and became Countess of Chesterfield. Following the death of his own wife Mary Anne Lewis in 1872, Disraeli took up a correspondence with both countesses, and commissioned their portraits, that of Selina being by Sir Francis Grant. Lady Bradford was then fifty-five and her sister Lady Chesterfield seventy. In the case of Lady Bradford, the correspondence amounted to some 1,500 letters and his devotion was both chivalrous and sincere; when without her company he wrote that 'Not to see you is a world without a sun.'

In his writing, he aptly summed up Selina's character, describing her in May 1874 as being possessed of:

> a sweet simplicity, blended with high breeding; an intellect not over-dralled, but lively, acute and picturesque; a seraphic temper, and a disposition infinitely sympathetic ...[28]

Within the correspondence, candid details of affairs of state are discussed, whilst the ageing monarch is referred to as the 'Faery', her court revolving around her needs. At Christmas one year, as the letters inform us, Selina gave Disraeli a pair of slippers and she would also knit for him.[29] In turn, Disraeli's fondness for the Bradfords resulted in the generous gifts of an oriental-pattern Aubusson carpet and a paperweight composed of a piece of rock crystal on a gilt bronze sleigh raised upon a piece of lapis, both of which still remain in the house. More unusual was a Conure parrot that he gave and which lived to a long age in the orangery at Weston. Towards the end of its life, the bird – which had long been considered male – began to lay eggs, one a day for twenty-three days. On the final day of laying the bird breathed its last and its last rites were given by the taxidermist Rowland Ward who prepared the bird for immortality, with its eggs.

Aside from Weston, Disraeli was also visitor to the family's various houses in London and in the country. In August 1874 he took the train to Windermere, to stay with the Bradfords at St Catherine's, and was met at the station by Lord Bradford and a great crowd of onlookers. Writing to Lady Chesterfield, he described St Catherine's:

> The House here is not a very small one and there is accommodation enough ... Its grounds are considerable and look more extensive than they are, being well arranged and well timbered, with a mountain birk tumbling through the ferny rocks, gurgling and fretting and foaming.
>
> The view from the drawing-room windows is one of the most beautiful I ever beheld: the mountains of various and captivating outlines and the banks of the lake richly wooded.[30]

Later, in staying with the royal family at Balmoral, he wrote flatteringly to Selina to tell her that, whilst the Tay valley there was very fine, 'nothing now satisfies me now but Windermere'.[31]

At Castle Bromwich Hall, his presence is said to have been the reason for the then-village possessing the first post office outside of London to have a telephone, so that Disraeli might maintain contact with government.[32]

Weston, however, was his true favourite and he – who purported not to like country house visiting – was a regular visitor, memorably writing in 1878:

> You will find Weston beautiful ... It is a place that always pleased me.[33]

By this time, the embellishment of Weston had also included the enlargement of the park, which was undertaken for the 3rd Earl to incorporate the high ground

FIGURE 141 Knoll Tower, Weston Park, which was built, following a suggestion by Disraeli, on an elevated site to the south of the main house in 1883. The 3rd Earl and Countess had already extended the park to include the Tower's site – Tong Knoll – in 1866–7. The southern elevation of the tower, shown here, now includes the single-storey extension added for the trustees of the Weston Park Foundation by clerk of works David Buckle, and which includes a kitchen and bathroom that enable the structure to be inhabited.

Knoll Tower is now a holiday cottage and enjoys exceptional views of the park and surrounding countryside. (Copyright Trustees of the Weston Park Foundation.)

of Tong Knoll to the south of the mansion in 1866–7. Incorporating land that had been formerly a part of the Tong Castle estate acquired by his father, this expansion of the parkland may have been prompted by the unwelcome presence of charcoal burners on the Knoll Side who were present until the enclosure. One observer recalled their 'fires covered with turves, and the smell of burning wood'.[34] George Durant junior of Tong Castle had built a monument on the summit of the Knoll to celebrate a low award of alimony when he divorced his wife and this was blown up by his son Ernest following his death in November 1844.[35] Later, on one of his visits, Disraeli is said to have suggested the building of a tower on the Knoll, as an eye-catcher from the house and this duly happened, but in 1883, two years after the former premier's death. It occupies a site to the west of the Durant monument's site, where a few scattered dressed stones still stand testimony to the monument. The succeeding Tower is of red sandstone, rising through three stories and with a taller angle-turret to afford fine views across Shropshire and Staffordshire.

Deer had roamed the park since medieval times and continued to do so, but they also gained some additional livestock company at this time. In about 1870, a flock of Jacob sheep arrived as a gift from George Fitzwilliam of Milton, Northamptonshire, and these still remain a notable feature of the park.[36] In 1880 Joseph Ridgway Bridson (1831–1901), a Bolton resident and businessman – who also maintained a conspicuous presence in Windermere, close to the Bradford family's St Catherine's – gave Selina Countess of Bradford some of his St Kilda sheep from Windermere. These were the ancestors of the other distinctive flock which remain resident in the park at Weston and from the wool of which, throughout the late nineteenth and twentieth centuries, the gamekeepers had their shooting suits woven.

The parish church of St Andrew's was also restored under the patronage of the 3rd Earl. This was done in 1869–70 by Street and it was then further enlarged in 1876 to Ewan Christian's designs at a cost of £3,500, when the Bradford Chapel and vestry were added to south and north respectively, and a new reredos was gifted by Lord Bradford's brother the Hon. and Rev. John R.O. Bridgeman (1831–1897).[37] In Weston, the family's paternalistic benevolence also extended to rebuilding many of the cottages and to the village school. An early nineteenth-century school had been established by the family and a new school, of red brick with stone dressings, was built and opened in 1873 to the north of the Watling Street. In the following year, on the opposite side of the road, a row of four almshouses was built as the gift of Selina, Countess of Bradford.[38] This sedate single-storied building, originally with rustic-branch decorated loggia – emulating the porches of many of the estate cottages of that time – still survives as a group of tenanted houses with a generous garden set before them.

The family's concern for those around them in less fortunate circumstances extended to artists and craftsmen who had played a part in the supply of works for the family in previous years. One of these was the Birmingham sculptor Peter Hollins, who had initially been patronised by George, 2nd Earl. When Hollins as an old man could no longer work, his fingers racked with rheumatism as a result of a life of working with wet clay, the 3rd Earl sought to assist him by making purchases of items that had been sat in his workshops. Of these items, a sculpture of Sabrina, goddess of the River Severn, was gifted to Shrewsbury in 1873, where it can still be seen in the Dingle of the town's Quarry Park. His other purchase is more intriguing, in being a bust of the Hon. Caroline Norton (1808–1877), writer, poet, and ultimately early champion of women's rights following appallingly abusive treatment from her husband who implicated

FIGURE 142 The bust of Caroline Norton (1808–1877) by Peter Hollins, purchased by the 3rd Earl of Bradford to aid the sculptor in his later life. The bust had gone uncollected in the sculptor's studio although, according to surviving correspondence in the Bradford MS, Mrs Norton had been specific about its sculpting and the eventual siting of the piece. It has recently been restored to the Marble Hall at Weston Park. (Copyright Trustees of the Weston Park Foundation.)

FIGURE 143 *The Investiture of the Sultan of Turkey with the Order of the Garter, 17 July 1867*, by George Housman Thomas
(1824–1868), oil on canvas, 42 x 63.5 cm. One of a number of works by Thomas in the collection at Weston Park, Lord
Bradford had the artist insert his own portrait, standing behind and to the left of HM Queen Victoria. The prime version of the
painting, in the British Royal Collection (RCIN 406336), does not include Lord Bradford's portrait. Accession number 101.0186.
(Copyright Trustees of the Weston Park Foundation.)

her in 'criminal conversation' or adulterous behaviour with Lord Melbourne.
Although the Forester family had been part of the Melbourne circle, there is
currently no known evidence to link the Bradfords to Mrs Norton. Yet her
bust – which came from Hollins with specific instructions as to its carriage by
train and its display as Mrs Norton had wanted it seen – remains an important
if little known sculptural treasure at Weston Park.

The 3rd Earl's devotion to the monarch that he served is exemplified by his
patronage of the artist and engraver George Housman Thomas (1824–1868).
From him he acquired sketches, including the intimate study sketch of Her
Majesty watching from the balcony of the Edward IV Chantry at St George's
Chapel, Windsor, which was a preparatory sketch for *The Marriage of the
Prince of Wales*, 1863, in the Royal Collection, and portraits of his queen, in
addition to commissioning his own version of *The Investiture of the Sultan
with the Order of the Garter, 17 July 1867*.

Similarly, in 1867, following the lead set by his monarch at Frogmore near
Windsor, Lord Bradford began to consider building a Mortuary Chapel or
Mausoleum at Weston with his architect MacVicar Anderson.[39] The churchyard
of St Andrew's church had been closed in 1866 and so the site selected was
within a new burial ground accessed from the Watling Street, north-west of
the House. Initial designs were gothic, showing a gabled building in the lancet
style, although in the event a classical temple with tetrastyle Tuscan portico
was built.[40] The correspondence relating to the project is highly detailed and
the building, when eventually begun, was finally completed in July 1872.[41]

Three years after the mausoleum's completion, as a result of the intervention of Disraeli,[42] Lord Bradford was invited to be Lord Lieutenant of Shropshire in 1875, representing his monarch within that county. It was a role that he fulfilled until 1896. During his lieutenancy, he also served his two terms of office as Her Majesty's Master of Horse and the Court role evidently led to patronage of artists favoured by the royal family. Lord Bradford commissioned Jean-Édouard Lacretelle (1817–1900) to paint Chippendale and Retreat in 1884, winners, respectively, of the 1879 Hardwicke Stakes at Ascot and the 1882 Doncaster Cup. Lacretelle also painted *Creams and Blacks*, a record of the cream stallions and Hanoverian Blacks that were used as carriage horses, in the Royal Mews at Buckingham Palace, whilst Charles Lutyens, father of the architect Sir Edwin, painted *The Putting To*, showing a state landau being put to the horse at the Royal Mews, a suitably modest painting to commemorate Lord Bradford's service to his queen.[43]

The 3rd Earl's interest in horses had, by this time, developed into a passion for racing which was eventually run on formal lines with assistance from the trainer Thomas Wadlow, who operated from Stanton Lawns near Shifnal. His initial efforts, though, were so disheartening that Disraeli write to Lady Bradford on 29 July 1875 to say:

> I cannot understand why a great noble with his brains and knowledge of horses, does not command the turf. I don't want him to have a great stable but I do want him to have a famous one.[44]

The premier, after further Bradford racing disappointments, was more direct in October 1876: 'Bradford really should leave the Turf. His position becomes more ludicrous there.'[45]

FIGURE 144 The Mausoleum in the private burial ground at Weston Park, seen from the north-west. Commissioned by the 3rd Earl of Bradford from the architect John MacVicar Anderson, correspondence relating to the structure began in 1867 and the building was finally completed to a classical design in July 1872. (Photo: courtesy of the author.)

FIGURE 145 *The Putting To*, by Charles Lutyens (1829–1915), oil on canvas, 99.7 x 125.7 cm. Painted to commemorate the 3rd Earl's terms as Master of the Horse to HM Queen Victoria, the work shows one of the coachmen with a state landau in the Royal Mews at Buckingham Palace, as it is put to the Hanoverian black carriage horses. Accession number 101.0047. (Copyright Trustees of the Weston Park Foundation.)

Gradually, though, the situation had improved, with Chippendale's win at Ascot in 1879. Disraeli then wrote that he 'was glad to see Bradford had won a good stake, which will at any rate lighten his trainer's bill'.[46] In October of the same year, Chippendale went on to win the Cesarewitch, with members of the Bradford and Disraeli households having placed bets. Disraeli noted that Bradford was reported to have won £1,000 and wrote to Lady Bradford that 'I expect to see you in a tiara and the young ladies in several new dresses'.[47]

The various horses of the turf were immortalised in paint, with many painted by W.H. Hopkins, some showing the jockeys perched upon the horses in the Bradford colours of white silks with red sleeves. One of Hopkins' works, *Mares and Foals*, shows a group of horses in the park at Weston, some with their names painted onto the canvas. One of the foals, however, showed even great promise and eventually, as a rank outsider, he won the Derby in 1892, beating the favourite La Fleche. Sir Hugo, as he was known, had to have his name scratched onto the painting's mount, although no fewer than five other paintings of him in the collection at Weston made up for the earlier oversight. The Derby winnings paid for a new clock for the church at Hughley near Much Wenlock, whilst Sir Hugo's progeny was grandly continued when he was put to stud with some of Queen Victoria's horses.

The year 1892 was auspicious in other ways for the family, since the Bradford's grandson Laddo (the eventual 5th Earl of Bradford) had left Harrow and gone travelling for eighteen months with a tutor, whilst granddaughter Margaret ('Mollie') became engaged to John, Lord Dalkeith (1864–1935, the eventual 7th Duke of Buccleuch), marrying in the following year. The Buccleuch marriage would later result in the birth of Lady Alice Christabel Montagu Douglas Scott (1901–2004), who in 1935 married HRH Prince Henry, Duke of Gloucester (1900–1974). The family's links to their monarch and to the British royal family continued to be close in the late nineteenth and early twentieth century. In 1875, on the birth of Hon. Helena Mary Bridgeman (1875–1947), daughter of Viscount and Viscountess Newport (the eventual 4th Earl and Countess of Bradford), HRH Princess Christian, the third daughter and fifth child of HM Queen Victoria and Prince Albert, stood as her godmother. Six years later in 1881, the Bradfords' younger daughter, Lady Florence Katherine Bridgeman married Henry Ulick, Viscount Lascelles (and later 5th Earl of Harewood). Their son, Henry, eventual 6th Earl of Lascelles, made a royal marriage to HRH Princess Mary, Princess Royal, the daughter of HM King George V and HM Queen Mary.

During the period of the 3rd Earl's tenure as master of the estates, there was a notable shift in the financial importance of the urban estates at Bolton and at Walsall. In both locations, the rise in industrialisation and urbanisation, which had begun in earnest under the 2nd Earl, continued apace. At Walsall, the suburb of Pleck had been growing through the 1850s and 1860s with increasing

FIGURE 146 *Mares and Foals in the Park at Weston in 1889*, painted by William Henry Hopkins, oil on canvas, 76 x 126 cm. Many of the horses depicted, which formed a part of the 3rd Earl of Bradford's racing stud, had their names painted onto the canvas of the work including Duvernay, White Heather, Manoeuvre and Hemlock. The notable exception was the foal with the white nose-marking, right of centre; this was Sir Hugo who went on to win the 1892 Derby for the family. His name was later inscribed in pencil onto the gilt mount of the painting. Accession number 101.0293. (Copyright Trustees of the Weston Park Foundation.)

rents. From the mid-1880s more houses were being built there on long leases, upon newly laid-out roads such as Ida Road, whilst at Chuckery, there was Lumley Road and Scarborough Road, all three streets named after Lady Ida Lumley, daughter of the Earl of Scarbrough, who in 1869 had married Viscount Newport, the eventual 4th Earl of Bradford.[48] The building leases had clauses to ensure standards by requesting that the houses were built to a certain specification and that the occupant ensured that the gardens were well maintained.[49] Walsall, unlike Bolton – where public parks had been created on land leased from the estate from 1854 – was slow to have a public park that had associations with the Bradford estate. However, after protracted negotiations, a derelict mining site at Reedswood was eventually given to the people of Walsall for a nominal fee, in 1882, by the Earl of Bradford as a space for recreation, and by 1888 it had a swimming pool and changing rooms.

Benefits for the urban tenants in Bolton had also included a friendly society for waggoners and colliers established by the Bradford estate, which provided sick pay and funeral expenses during the 1860s and 1870s, in return for a modest subscription.[50] The town's hospital, having outgrown its central site in Nelson Square, was also relocated with help from the Bradford estate, to a new site adjoining Queens Park, where the estate, in tandem with the Church Commissioners, provided the site. For some of this period, from 1885 until

FIGURE 147 The dining room at Weston Park in the early twentieth century, looking to north. The room's height had been increased in 1893 in anticipation of the Golden Wedding celebrations in the following year. The chimneypiece's lower frontal section is one of three supplied to the 2nd Earl of Bradford for his short-lived east wing by the sculptor James Forsyth (1827–1910). (Copyright Trustees of the Weston Park Foundation.)

FIGURE 148 The Golden Wedding Celebration Party in 1894, photographed outside the Orangery loggia at Weston Park. The 3rd Earl and Countess of Bradford, celebrating fifty years of marriage, are seated at the centre of the group; their son and daughter-in-law Viscount and Viscountess Newport, whose Silver Wedding anniversary was the same year – are seated at the extreme right of the group, he in a bowler hat; the Hon. Orlando Bridgeman (the eventual 5th Earl), for whom the year marked his coming of age, is standing looking to left to the right of the 3rd Earl, with hand on the back of his chair. Behind the Hon. Orlando, bearded and in stovepipe hat, is the Hon. and Rev. G.T.O. Bridgeman, Rector of Wigan. (Copyright Trustees of the Weston Park Foundation.)

1895, the MP for Bolton was a younger son of the 3rd Earl and Countess of Bradford, Brigadier-General the Hon. Francis Bridgeman (1846–1917), this ensuring a close understanding of the town.

Funded largely from the urban estates' incomes, further building works were undertaken at Weston Park. In January 1882, MacVicar Anderson produced drawings which resulted in alterations to the arrangement of the Tapestry Room's windows, resulting in the form of the room as it appears today.[51] Nine years later in 1893, probably anticipating celebrations that were to take place in the following year, the Bradfords summoned MacVicar Anderson back to Weston to produce a scheme to raise the height of the Dining Room. This was done by eliminating the first-floor bedrooms, taking the Dining Room's ceiling halfway through the floor above, whilst using the lower sashes of the former first-floor windows to now give light into the lofty space below.[52] It improved the room's proportions enormously, creating a grand and essentially double-cube entertaining room from what must have previously been a long and low space.

In 1894 the family, their tenants and friends celebrated the Golden Wedding of the Earl and Countess. This year was in fact, simultaneously, also the Silver Wedding anniversary of their son and daughter-in-law, Viscount and Viscountess Newport (later 4th Earl and Countess of Bradford), and the coming of age (twenty-first birthday) of their grandson the Hon. Orlando

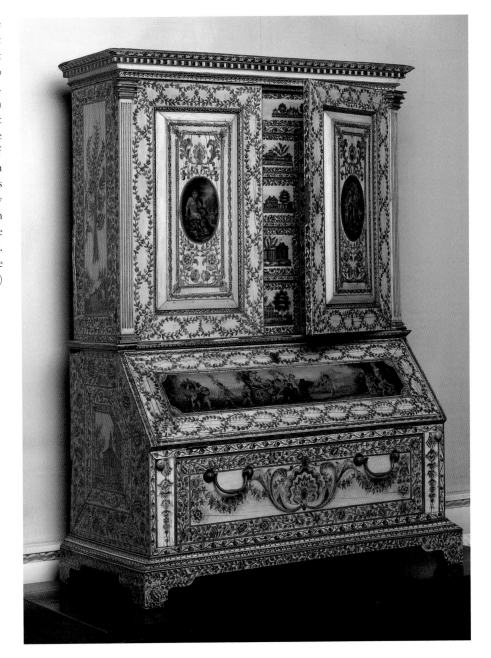

Bridgeman (the eventual 5th Earl of Bradford). Lord Bradford's ill health
had meant that the Golden Wedding was unable to be celebrated in the April
of that year and so, under the secretaryship of the agent George Griffiths, a
joint celebration for the three events was planned for Saturday 6 October. The
village was decorated, triumphal arches were set up at the entrance to the park
and a succession of activities took place from twelve-noon. These involved
presentations, a dinner for eight-hundred tenants and workers, followed by a
tea for women and schoolchildren, a parade of the family racehorses, sports for
the men and boys, an organ recital, a thirty-foot bonfire and fireworks at the
Knoll and then dancing.[53] Harkening back to the theatricals at Weston in the
eighteenth century, a temporary theatre 'capable of accommodating more than
1000 people' provided a stage for John Radford's Company's performance of
Simon Lee.[54] Amidst the merriment were speeches. Colonel Francis Bridgeman,
addressing Orlando Bridgeman, emphasised to him how 'power and wealth
had their responsibilities', whilst Lord Newport, in his speech, cast an ominous
warning that:

those who may some day be called upon to inherit great estates, were passing through a time of great change and great difficulty … problems were almost certain to arise in connection with the ownership and occupation of land.[55]

The presentations were made by tenants and employees. The latter were made by John Clayton, a ninety-five-year-old, who was brought to the house in a bath chair but recalled being present at the 2nd Earl of Bradford's coming of age in 1810.[56] In addition to the handsome, yet predictable, illuminated addresses from staff, tradesmen and tenants, the collection at Weston retains a number of items which were gifts at this momentous occasion, ranging from a longcase clock in the staircase hall that was presented by the tenants of the Walsall estate, a pair of tables in the Tapestry Room that were the gifts of the 330 tenants and employees of the Weston estate, and a desk set which was a gift from the household staff. The item that perhaps trumps all other gifts is an Anglo-Indian miniature bureau bookcase in the drawing room, which was a gift from the 1st Duke of Westminster.[57] This had been made at Vizagapatam a century earlier but now has later polychrome decoration and it had been acquired by the duke from the Chester dealer D. Sherratt & Co. in April 1894.[58]

The celebrations, in one form or another, continued for several days afterwards. Most of those attending were from the agricultural estates in Shropshire and Staffordshire, although a deputation from Walsall was noted as having attended at the Hall.[59]

The happiness of the celebrations was sadly to be short-lived, since on 25 November that year Lady Bradford died. Her widower, on 28 May in the year after her death, handed over the Knockin and Castle Bromwich estates to his son and heir Viscount Newport.

In January 1898, there was one more reason for celebration when the Newports' daughter Helena Mary married Osbert, Viscount Molyneux (the eventual 6th Earl of Sefton) to whom she had become engaged in the previous year. Just two months later, though, Lord Bradford died on 9 March 1898. His remains were placed, with those of his late wife, in the Mausoleum at Weston and commemorative glass was installed in St Andrew's church. Lord Bradford's elder daughter Lady Mabel – who had married William Kenyon-Slaney of Hatton Grange, Shropshire in 1887 and who inherited St Catherine's – commissioned a commemorative window at St Mary's Windermere.

The 3rd Earl was succeeded by his eldest son George, Viscount Newport who, as 4th Earl of Bradford, together with his Countess and family, left Castle Bromwich Hall for Weston Park on 28 March 1898.[60]

CHAPTER NINE

Edwardian Weston
An Indian Summer and Dark Clouds of War

The 4th Earl and Countess of Bradford's reign at Weston started in a manner that must have appeared to be a continuation of the previous regime. After twenty-nine years of marriage, the couple had observed life at Weston and saw little reason to change it, albeit that they adapted the house for their own times.

The couple had become engaged in June 1869 and they were married in September of the same year. Lady Ida Lumley, who came to be known to her grandchildren as 'Guida', was the gentle and vivacious daughter of the 9th Earl and Countess of Scarbrough, who took a great deal of personal interest in the family history and collections of her husband's family. Initially the couple lived at Weston Park with the Bradfords, and when in London resided at 43 Belgrave Square. As a young married couple, they had travelled, visiting Rome and Continental Europe in 1870. Their first child Beatrice Adine (1870–1952) was born in the same year, followed two years later by another daughter Margaret Alice (1872–1954). Just a year later, the son and eventual heir Orlando – known as Laddo – was born, to be followed by two sisters, Helena Mary (1875–1947) and Florence Sibell (1877–1936), and then two more boys, Richard (Dick) Orlando Beaconsfield (1879–1917) and Henry (Harry) George Orlando Bridgeman (1882–1972).[1] The distinctive third name of the second son was a compliment to Benjamin Disraeli, Earl of Beaconsfield, who stood as godfather.

With their first daughter still a baby, they moved to 20 Lowndes Square in January 1871 after furnishing the house.[2] Amongst the visitors in 1874 was Disraeli who described Lady Ida's home as 'with many evidences of art and a love for it'.[3] From September 1876 the couple also had Castle Bromwich Hall which Lady Ida adored, writing a descriptive article about the house for the *Pall Mall Magazine* in 1898 which shows her passion for the old mansion and its gardens.

Leaving his wife with their young family in 1887, Lord Newport travelled to Tangiers and Spain with Montagu Corry, 1st and last Lord Rowton (1838–1903, who had been Disraeli's private secretary) and Lord Claud Hamilton,[4] and their travels were humorously recalled in a privately published journal, *The Travels and Adventures of Messrs Brown, Jones and Robinson*.[5] The journey proved fruitful for carpets and rugs that made their way initially to Castle Bromwich, and it was followed by a further expedition to Vienna in 1898, where some folding screens were acquired for the rooms at home in England.[6]

FIGURE 150 *George Cecil Orlando, 4th Earl of Bradford* (1845–1915), painted in earl's robes in the library at Weston Park in 1902 by Frank Brooks (1854–1937), oil on canvas, 260 x 168 cm. Accession number 101.0195. (Copyright Trustees of the Weston Park Foundation.)

After Lord Newport's succession to the earldom and to Weston in 1898, the 4th Earl and Countess of Bradford, as they became, made further alterations to the house. In 1899 they brought John MacVicar Anderson back to Weston Park to rework the mansion to the needs of their family. This included practical works to the service areas but also some major works to the main rooms. The most important was the replacement of the former staircase with a new marble flight, railed with an elegant French-inspired ironwork balustrade and mahogany handrail. The marble treads may have been inspired by French examples or perhaps of that commissioned by Ferdinand de Rothschild at his London house at a reported cost of £20,000, of which Disraeli had written

favourably to Lady Chesterfield in 1876.[7] At Weston, by placing the ascending
flight against the courtyard wall, the staircase hall was then able to be opened
up into the entrance hall via a new arched opening.

In the ensuing work in the entrance hall, the room's chimneypiece was
moved from the west wall to the south wall, whilst a pair of Aubusson tapestries
were installed, framing the arch to the new staircase. In the remainder of the
central courtyard, north of the 3rd Earl's billiard room, a further roof was
added to create a new ground-floor smoking room, adorned by a handsome
eighteenth-century chimneypiece with central tablet of Diana and her hound.
This has reduced proportions and was probably salvaged from Tong Castle.[8]
The smoking room was accessed from the entrance hall via a new passage way
which had water-closets for ladies and gentlemen accessed from it. His work
also linked the Victorian wing built by his father, at first-floor level, to the rest
of the mansion and he added a new back staircase close to the kitchens, which
connects to an existing staircase at first floor level.[9]

FIGURE 152 The marble staircase at Weston Park in the early twentieth century. The staircase was created for the 4th Earl and Countess in 1899 by the architect John MacVicar Anderson. The sixteenth-century cassone or marriage chest, to the right of the picture, was acquired by the 4th Earl and Countess in Lugano in 1906. (Copyright Trustees of the Weston Park Foundation.)

FIGURE 153 The entrance hall at Weston Park in the early twentieth century, following alterations made by the 4th Earl and Countess of Bradford. The alteration of the main staircase enabled the staircase hall and entrance hall to be linked via the newly created archway. (Copyright Trustees of the Weston Park Foundation.)

During the upheaval that the works entailed, the family went to live at Knockin.[10] There, on the north Shropshire estate, Lady Bradford had already given her name to an alkaline chalybeate well, Lady Ida's well, which had been discovered near the village of Kinnerley, and which was marketed for a short period from 1896 as a mineral water which could benefit anaemics. When first discovered, it was suggested that Lord Newport would provide bathing facilities, and grand comparisons with Baden-Baden and Aix-les-Bains were made.[11]

At Weston, as works progressed on improving the house, services and new technology were also given consideration. Electric light was installed and was finally switched on in July 1908, whilst in 1903 a steam fire-engine had been supplied by Merryweather.[12] Transportation also began to witness changes, with the advent of the motorcar and for the Bradfords, their first motor was a Daimler that was delivered in May 1906.[13]

In the following year, their eldest son Orlando went to fight in the Second Boer War having joined the 3rd (Militia) Battalion of The Royal Scots (Lothian Regiment), in which he was made a captain on 29 April 1899. His battalion was embodied in December 1899, specifically to serve in the Second Boer War, and it left Queenstown, Ireland in March 1900 on the SS *Oriental*, destined for South Africa. Bridgeman fought in the war after his arrival in 1900, and again in 1902, returning from Cape Town to Britain with most of his regiment in May 1902.

His younger brother Richard, known within the family as Dick, meanwhile, had followed a naval career, having passed out second into HMS *Britannia* at the age of thirteen in 1892,[14] and his service was to take him around the world.

During this period, the portrait painter Frank Brooks was commissioned. Initially in 1900, this was to paint the Bradfords' daughter Lady Florence, and also Lady Bradford.[15] His work clearly pleased his clients, leading to a somewhat regal full-length of the Earl and a half-length of Viscount Newport in 1902, followed six years later by his portrait of Richard Bridgeman.

In 1901, HRH Mary, Princess of Wales asked Lady Bradford to serve as her Lady of the Bedchamber. Lady Ida had known the princess for much of her life and, at her wedding, the princess had given her a mother-of-pearl and lace fan.[16] She shared many interests with her royal mistress, not least that of antique china. Her Royal Highness regularly visited Shropshire since her brother, Adolphus, 1st Marquess of Cambridge (1868–1927) and his wife Lady Margaret Evelyn Grosvenor (1873–1929) lived to the north of Shrewsbury at Shotton Hall, Harmer Hill. This brought her regularly to Weston and on one occasion, on proceeding to visit the Temple of Diana, she neglected to decline her head when entering Pausilip's Tunnel with the result that her hat got knocked off – an incident which was still recalled by the family in the 1940s.[17] During Lady Ida's royal service she wrote detailed and eminently charming letters to her husband, telling him of the engagements that she attended, with each missive signed 'Wifie'.[18]

The engine-room of the family's estates and of Weston Park continued to be the urban estates and the exploitation of minerals, which continued to play an important part in the family's finances. However, the development of the coal, iron ore and limestone, which had increased rapidly from the late eighteenth century and through much of the nineteenth century, was on the wane. New developments were stimulated, though, including the Hoffman Kiln which was built on the family's north Shropshire estate at Llanymynech in 1899 and operated until 1914.

Yet, more tellingly, at Bolton, the Hacken, Five Quarters, Gravel Hole and Aqueduct Collieries, which had been managed directly on the family's behalf from the 1860s, had all closed by 1890. Great Lever Colliery at Bolton, which had initially opened from circa 1839 in the time of the 2nd Earl, and had been modernised in the 1880s, was still functioning. By 1896 it employed 173 underground and forty-five at the surface, and in 1913, on a royal visit and exhibition of local industries in Bolton, the 4th Earl of Bradford proudly described the colliery's activities to the royal party. However, even there the quality of coal was lessening and, ultimately exhausted, the colliery was finally closed in 1922.[19] Benefactions to Bolton continued, with estate land donated for a new park at Great Lever in 1910/11 which, upon its completion by the council, was opened by Lady Bradford in 1913.[20] Great Lever Hall itself had found a new use as a Conservative Club, and in about 1900 an oak table, dated 1649, that had been in the house was taken to Weston where it remains.[21]

In 1903 George Carter, the agent who had joined the estate in 1884, after a career as a bank manager, died. He had been agent for the Bolton, Weston-under-Lizard and Knockin estates.[22] In the same year, though, a new purpose-built estate office in red terracotta brick was opened in Bolton, on Silverwell Street, replacing an earlier estate office at Bridgeman Buildings where it had existed since 1865.[23] Its rebuilding marked an intention that the Lancashire urban estate should continue to fulfil an important part in the economy of the Bradford family's estates.

For the family there were celebrations in 1904 when the Bradford's eldest son and heir Orlando, Viscount Newport, became engaged to the Hon. Margaret Bruce, the daughter of Lord Aberdare, in June and the couple married in the following month. Lord Newport had been serving as Assistant Private Secretary to Robert Gascoyne-Cecil, 3rd Marquess of Salisbury (1830–1903) when Secretary of State for Foreign Affairs (1898–1900) and then during his brief tenure as prime minister in 1902. Following Salisbury's resignation from the

FIGURE 154 The Bradford Estate Office, Silverwell Street, Bolton. Built in 1903, the Bradford coat of arms is prominently displayed over the doorway. The building ceased to be the estate office in the late twentieth century. (Photo: courtesy of the author.)

premiership, Lord Newport became private secretary to Salisbury's successor Arthur Balfour for three years from 1902.

In 1905, the year after the heir's wedding, Lady Bradford was to confide in her journal on 5 April that her husband's 'illness began'.[24] This period of ill health was to last for ten years, until his death of a heart attack in 1915 at the age of sixty-nine. A clock had clearly begun counting down and so, in 1906, the Bradfords went to Corsica, Lugano and Athens and took the opportunity to make acquisitions to add to the collections at Weston. These included the sixteenth-century marriage chest of cedarwood, some ivories and two Greek cups.[25] Corsica was clearly a happy time for the couple, referenced in the 4th Earl's will[26] and recalled also by a collection of shells that Lady Ida had picked there and, on her return, displayed and labelled with their origins in one of the cabinets at Weston.

At Weston, Lady Ida took a great interest in the collections and sought to emphasise the key elements in their placement within the house's rooms so that future generations would be able to understand their significance. The burse of the Great Seal, which had been presented to the first baronet, was framed up into a fire-screen for the Smoking Room by her.[27] She created an annotated inventory of the decorative arts at Weston in 1910, and clearly the house's porcelain collections were her greatest passion. Her leather-bound volume 'Oriental Porcelain' of 1912, is, itself, now a part of the collections, bearing her bookplate with its quote from Bryan Waller Procter, 'All Round the Room my Silent Servants Wait: My Friends in every Season Bright and Dim'. Its bound pages of typescript and watercolour celebrate, in a highly personal way, the finest Chinese and Japanese porcelain, whilst also noting the scope of the collection, its possible origins and its continuation with assistance from her son Dick. He added to the family's china collection with items that he had sent from China in 1909. Amongst these were *famille rose* plates, and

FIGURE 155 One of the plates from Lady Ida's leather-bound book 'Oriental Porcelain', which contains her watercolours of the collection. The item shown was one of a pair of matching Qing Dynasty ruby-ground *famille rose* vases and covers, with similar chargers, which were noted by Lady Bradford as having attracted the attentions of the dealer Joseph Duveen. His offer was not accepted and the actual pieces remain in the Tapestry Room at Weston Park. (Photo: courtesy of the author.)

FIGURE 156 Designs for the Coalport armorial dessert service commissioned by Lady Bradford in 1908 to match an existing eighteenth-century Sèvres drinking service in the collection at Weston Park. The armorial bearings were based upon advice received from the Rev. Ernest Bridgeman and his brother Charles G.O. Bridgeman, sons of the Hon. and Rev. G.T.O. Bridgeman. (Staffordshire Archives.)

saucers painted with butterflies,[28] plus jars and bowls that were displayed on the chimneypiece in the smoking room. His own cataloguing work, entailing descriptions of no fewer than 1,561 pieces in a modest notebook, is alluded to within its pages.

Lady Bradford also noted, in relation to the Chinese Qing Dynasty (1644–1911) ruby ground *famille rose* Chinese chargers, vases and covers that remain in the Tapestry Room, that: 'Mr Duveen offered 2,000 Guineas for them, and to make replicas which could not be detected.' Joseph, later 'Sir' and eventually 'Lord', Duveen was of course the highly predatory art dealer who sold much to American clients. It is known from Lady Bradford's son's diaries that he was in communication with Duveen in 1919, probably at a time whilst he was seeking funds with which to pay inheritance tax due following his father's death and so this may have been the date of Duveen's offer. The offer was declined, although Duveen had greater success, further north in Staffordshire, when he persuaded Lord Burton to sell similar pieces which, with others of the type, found their way to the Frick Collection in New York.[29] For the Weston pieces, Lady Ida created a new glazed cabinet from a former doorway in the Tapestry Room. She also painted watercolours of the tapestries in the Tapestry Room itself, maintaining an interest in the fate of the Earl of Coventry's similar set of tapestries when they were sold from Croome Court, Worcestershire, and initially found their way to Paris.

Lady Bradford's interest in the collections led her to commission an armorial dessert service from Coalport in 1908. Its design was based upon her own sketches, with armorial assistance provided by the Rev. Ernest Bridgeman and his brother Charles. Lady Bradford wanted the service to have a 'Sevres pattern gold border'[30] and it was clearly intended to match the eighteenth-century white and gold Sèvres drinking service in the collection. A lengthy correspondence survives between Lady Bradford and Coalport in 1907–8, and she evidently delighted in the service's craftsmanship, later noting that the signatures of the

FIGURE 157 Siblings at the Delhi Durbar of 1911. From left: the Hon. Henry Bridgeman; Lady Helena (Nellie), Countess of Sefton; the Hon. R.O.B. (Dick) Bridgeman. (Copyright Trustees of the Weston Park Foundation.)

painters were to be seen in grey on some of the plates, whilst the gilder, too, had inscribed their initials on the back of one of the plates. It was such a success that six further matching dessert dishes were made by Coalport in 1912.[31]

With the death of the King Edward VII on 6 May 1910, the British throne passed to his son, who succeeded as King George V. The succession meant that Lady Bradford was now in service to the Queen, whilst the title of the new King, as Emperor of India, was to be celebrated by a Delhi Durbar in the following year. The 1911 Durbar was the last of three; the first, in 1877, had been to proclaim Queen Victoria as Empress of India, whilst that in 1903 had celebrated the succession of King Edward VII and his Queen, Alexandra of Denmark, as Emperor and Empress of India. The final Durbar, however, was the only one attended by the monarch as Emperor, and for the Bridgeman family it proved memorable since it was attended by three of the Bradford siblings. Dick Bridgeman was appointed first lieutenant of HMS *Medina*, a new steel screw-steamer that conveyed the King and Queen to India, whilst at the ceremony itself he was in command of the naval guard of honour. His younger brother Henry served as an extra ADC to the Viceroy, 1st Lord Hardinge of Penshurst, and was personally requested for interview by Queen Mary following the Durbar's formal proceedings, whilst Lady Helena (Nellie) was also present with her husband, the Earl of Sefton.[32] Following the Durbar, in 1912 Dick was promoted to commander and took command of HMS *Druid*.

Within three years of the Durbar, the international mood had changed. As the dark clouds of the First World War began to gather in 1914, though, all three of the Bradford sons prepared themselves to defend their country. Lord Newport served with the 3rd Battalion of the Royal Scots (Lothian Regiment). This was a reserve regiment and only saw service in 1917, with much of the prior period of the war spent on training manoeuvres in Scotland, at Weymouth and in Ireland.

Dick had arrived home from Portuguese East Africa on 30 June 1914 for three months leave, but on 15 July he left the safety of Weston Park forever and was never to return. Initially he was based on HMS *Hyacinth* at the Cape Station, and then in 1915 he was involved in reconnaissance on the German SMS *Königsberg* using seaplanes. His sketches of the vessel and its location enabled the allies to severely damage the ship, as a result of which Bridgeman was awarded the DSO.

Henry, meanwhile, was promoted to captain and was given command of a battery in France. In 1915 he was advanced to major and was transferred to the 47th Divisional Artillery. The following year he was decorated with the Military Cross (MC) and then, in January 1918, with the Distinguished Service Order (DSO). During the course of the war he was mentioned in despatches five times and afterwards was awarded the Order of Prince Danilo I of Montenegro, an award that was gifted to prominent champions of the preservation of Montenegrin independence.

As the war progressed, the Earl of Bradford's health declined. He suffered severe ill health from New Year's Eve 1914 and on the 2 January 1915, he died. His properties were left primarily to his eldest son, although Dick inherited his Newmarket residence, Clarendon House, and Henry succeeded to African investments with the Messina, Transvaal Development Company.[33]

Lady Bradford had, until that point, been engaged in organising Red Cross meetings around Weston Park through which the intention was to make and collect supplies that might support the troops. She now resigned herself to the fact that a new generation would need to take on Weston and so left the house, just over a month after her husband's death, for Castle Bromwich Hall, on 6 February. The Earl was commemorated by stained glass windows by

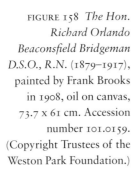

FIGURE 158 *The Hon.*
Richard Orlando
Beaconsfield Bridgeman
D.S.O., R.N. (1879–1917),
painted by Frank Brooks
in 1908, oil on canvas,
73.7 x 61 cm. Accession
number 101.0159.
(Copyright Trustees of the
Weston Park Foundation.)

Powell & Co, at the parish churches at Weston-under-Lizard, Castle Bromwich, Hughley, Tong and in the west wall of Knockin Church which were dedicated in the following year.

The succeeding 5th Earl and Countess already had a young son and eventual heir, Gerald (1911–1981). Although a daughter, Joan, was born to the new Earl and Countess on 29 May 1916, giving a granddaughter to the Dowager Countess, more tragedy was to follow. This initially came just two days later, when Midshipman The Hon. Cecil Richard Molyneux, grandson of Lady Ida and the son of the Earl and Countess of Sefton, was killed in action on board HMS *Lion* at the Battle of Jutland. Worse, though, was yet to come.

On 6 January 1917, Dick Bridgeman together with Flight Lieutenant Edwin Rowland Moon RNAS undertook a reconnaissance mission of the Rufiji Delta in their seaplane, *Short 8254* operating from HMS *Himalaya*. On their return, the engine failed and so a forced landing had to be made on a creek. Since the engine could not be restarted, and due to the close proximity of Germans, the two men decided to burn the seaplane and make an advance both on foot and by swimming to the mouth of the river. They made a raft but this was swept out to sea where Bridgeman tragically died. Moon survived and was captured by German Askaris on the 9 January.

The tragic news came through to Weston Park by a telephone call from the Admiralty on the eve of the 5th Earl's departure for France.[34] Eventually, Commander the Hon. R.O.B. Bridgeman's body was borne by HMS *Mersey* to its final resting place at the British Military Cemetery, Dar es Salaam. A brass memorial commemorates him in Dar Es Salaam cathedral, whilst a touching memorial, which depicts his seaplane, can be seen in the parish church of St Andrew at Weston-under-Lizard. Later that same year, further tragedy came on 26 June, when the Seftons' only daughter Lady Evelyn Molyneux (1902–1917) died of tuberculosis aged just fourteen. Then, in September, Brigadier-General the Hon. Francis Bridgeman (1846–1917), the second son of the 3rd Earl of Bradford and former MP for Bolton, also died, his age

being a more senior seventy-one. The Brigadier-General was commemorated by a stained glass window by Christopher Whall (1849–1924) depicting St George in the parish church of St Andrew's at Weston. Whall learned of the armistice as he completed the window and included the discreet inscription: '1918 Novr.11.11 a.m. Deo Gratis. C.W.W.'. It was a fitting conclusion to a turbulent and tragic period for the house of Weston Park.

Following the 4th Earl of Bradford's death, change had inevitably followed. The family's London house at 44 Lowndes Square was sold as an economy, with many of its contents brought to Weston Park.[35] Lady Ida, the Dowager Countess continued to take an interest in the family's destiny from Castle Bromwich, where the house and its garden became her absorbing passion. There, she commissioned armorial glass from Hardman of Birmingham for the landing windows in 1920, and restored the iron gates in the north garden in 1926, using the services of a craftsman from Lichfield, whilst electric light was also installed in the house that latter year.[36] It was from Castle Bromwich,

FIGURE 160 Christopher Whall's stained glass memorial window to Brigadier-General the Hon. Francis Bridgeman (1846–1917) in the south wall of the nave at St Andrew's church, Weston-under-Lizard. The window bears the discreet inscription '1918 Novr.11.11 a.m. Deo Gratis' since it was completed on the Armistice. (Paul Highnam/Copyright Trustees of the Weston Park Foundation.)

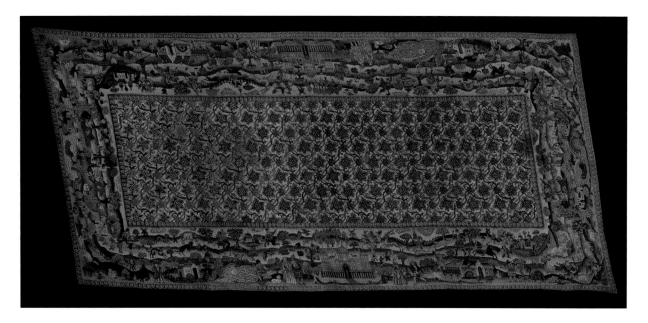

FIGURE 161 The Bradford Table Carpet, an early seventeenth-century decorative table covering. The piece has no heraldry, suggesting that it was made for general consumption by those able to acquire such a high-quality textile work. Formerly at Castle Bromwich Hall, it was sold to the Victoria and Albert Museum in 1928. Dimensions 179.5 × 422 cm. (© Victoria and Albert Museum, London.)

though, that one significant item emerged to meet some of the duty that had become payable on the Earl's death, this being the Bradford Table Carpet. Dating from the early seventeenth century, little seems to be known about the provenance of this remarkable treasure, although in 1928 it was acquired, with support from the then National Art Collections Fund (now Art Fund) by the Victoria & Albert Museum, where it remains a jewel amongst the museum's holdings of textiles.[37]

Lady Ida continued with her royal duties and these included hosting her royal mistress and guests at Castle Bromwich, with the Queen staying in the company of her brother and sister-in-law the Marquess and Marchioness of Cambridge, for a week in August 1927. Lady Bradford, in turn, would stay in the royal households and she fondly recalled a visit to Windsor Castle on 23 April 1928, where she was in the room adjoining Queen Mary: 'Next day, Princess Elizabeth, just two [later HM Queen Elizabeth II], and the Lascelles boys played in my room.[38] When, eight years later, Lady Ida died at the age of eighty-eight, her loss was felt by the royal family. Queen Mary, to whom she had bequeathed a Japanese cupboard, wrote to thank her son, telling him:

> I was so fond of dearest Ida and we had been great friends for many years and her friendship meant much to me. I grieve her loss deeply …[39]

CHAPTER TEN

The Reality of the Twentieth Century
From Private to Public

Orlando, 5th Earl of Bradford faced a series of challenges following the death of his father in 1915. The international events of the First World War, and the new earl's personal involvement in the conflict, kept him away from Weston Park for significant periods of time when matters of inheritance tax and settlements were pressing. With the war in the past and its consequences ongoing, it became a time of modernisation that also involved embracing social and economic change. Following his political work for Lord Salisbury and for Arthur Balfour earlier in the century, Lord Bradford had taken his seat in the House of Lords following his father's death and became a government whip from 1919 until 1924. He had been asked to be chamberlain to HRH Princess of Wales in 1901 but had refused the role,[1] choosing instead throughout later life to balance public duty linked to the management of the family's estates with his young family. He and Margaret, Lady Bradford had four children who survived to adulthood: Lady Helen Diana (1907–1967); Gerald, the eventual 6th Earl (1911–1981); Lady Anne Pamela (1913–2009); and Lady Joan Serena (1916–1935). A further daughter, the Hon. Ursula, had sadly died at Castle Bromwich in 1912 at the age of three.

For Lord Bradford, the introduction of the motor car proved to be a positive and, indeed, a particular passion from an early point in its history, and his leather-bound volume 'My Motor Rides' charts excursions with a 22–28 HP Crossley car in 1905. His notes on one particularly burdensome journey detail how: 'She travelled grandly though very heavily laden.'[2] Unfortunately, other journeys were less happy, including a run from London to Weston in which he and Lady Bradford endured no fewer than four punctures. A veritable cavalcade of cars was owned by the earl, ranging from a Wolseley in 1919, a Fiat Shooting brake in the following year, then a Standard Coupe, whilst in 1925 a Sunbeam, Morris Oxford, Daimler, and a Chrysler were to be found in the motor-house at Weston Park. When his daughter Lady Diana celebrated her twenty-first birthday on 22 June 1928, her father presented her with a Morris Cowley two-seater – that he had surely test-driven himself – whilst later in the same year he acquired a 20 HP Rolls and then a 40/50 Phantom Rolls, with an MG, a Lancia, and an Isis being run alongside the smarter cars in the years that followed.

In spite of this apparent extravagance, the finances of the estate in the aftermath of the 4th Earl's death were being reassessed. Art dealers, acutely

aware of the possible implications of death duties, contacted the family including in 1915 Godfrey Kopp. He was a less than straightforward character, who wrote to Lord Bradford from Zurich, claiming to be acting for a friend in Paris, with offers to buy the Gobelins tapestries.[3] His offer was turned down, although four years later Joseph Duveen was visiting. On 7 March 1919, Lord Bradford noted that Duveen had offered £380 for 'the oak from Tong' – whether this was for a now-forgotten carved or panelled oak interior at Tong Castle or for the choir stalls at St Bartholomew's church is not recorded. Duveen was also noted as visiting Weston on 22 June, with a further meeting scheduled on 27th.[4]

Where the estates were concerned, an attempt had been made to sell Tong Castle with four hundred acres in the 4th Earl's lifetime in 1913.[5] This proved unsuccessful and so in 1918 the lead was stripped from the castle's roofs and its fittings sold. The 5th Earl was, however, able to expand the acreage close to Weston by the purchase of the adjacent property of Boscobel House in 1915. This brought to the family not only additional land marching with the core estate but also the famous seventeenth-century timber-framed hunting lodge. Built by the Giffard family of White Ladies, the house had originally been set deep in a wood – hence its Italian-inspired name – and it was here that

FIGURE 163 *The Hon.*
Margaret Bruce, Countess
of Bradford (1882–1949),
drawn in pastel in 1905
by Edward Francis Wells
(1876–1952), 73.8 x 63 cm.
Accession number 116.0072.
(Copyright Trustees of the
Weston Park Foundation.)

Charles II was concealed by the Giffards' servants, the Pendrell family, after he
had fled the Battle of Worcester. The oak tree that had originally concealed
him, and which subsequently lent its name to legions of British public houses,
was by that date represented by a successor tree. When HRH Princess Mary,
the Princess Royal (1897–1965) married Lord Bradford's first cousin Henry,
Viscount Lascelles (later 6th Earl of Harewood) on 28 February 1922, his eldest
daughter Lady Diana was a bridesmaid and the couple stayed at Weston Park
for the first week of her honeymoon. During the couple's stay, the princess
occupied the room then known as Bedroom D which is today known as the
Boudoir, distinguished for its Chinese wallpaper, and the Bradfords took their
royal guest to see Boscobel.[6]

Receiving royal and non-royal guests had meant that the house at Weston
Park required adaptation to make it suitable for a new generation. The works
were thorough, even though just twenty years had elapsed from the works
commissioned by the 4th Earl and Countess at their succession. Fundamental
works took place in 1919, when the drains were renewed, new kitchen apparatus
for cooking was purchased, and also the heating systems were upgraded by
Jones & Attwood of Stourbridge.[7] By 1 September 1919, the house was at
such a state of satisfaction that Lord Bradford was able to note in his diary
that the family were able to move into the place and that the servants arrived
from London.[8]

On the north side of Temple Pool, two new tennis courts were laid out on a site formerly occupied by an archery ground, whilst at the house, in 1925 a squash court was created from the former brew house[9] – the creation of these sporting amenities signalling the family's intent on maintaining house parties with fashionable ideas of recreation. New wrought iron gates, that had been designed by Lady Bradford and made by Bayliss, Jones & Bayliss of Wolverhampton, were installed at the lodges in 1929,[10] whilst old wooden gates and doors yielded to iron gates, between the carriage ring and stables, and as entry points to the south terrace and also the Rose Walk. Some rationalisation of the formal Victorian garden planting schemes occurred at this time, whilst the great early nineteenth-century cast iron Jones and Clark conservatory overlooking Church Pool was found to be in a parlous state. Its magnificent dome was removed in 1935, the ironwork cleared away, but its footings were retained to form a foundation for a new hardwood conservatory built by Foster & Pearson.

Lady Bradford made a number of discoveries in the collections as she began to take the house from the Edwardian period into a newer incarnation. In the stables, a pair of eighteenth-century chairs were found and reupholstered with needlework that she had undertaken. In 1924, her husband found a box of old glass in the Temple of Diana's china room and this was restored by Delomosne to create three chandeliers – one intended for the Tapestry Room, and a pair for the Drawing Room – together with a pair of candelabra.[11] In 1921 Lord and Lady Bradford consulted the architect Philip Tilden (1887–1956) about the restoration of the Drawing Room which, it seems, led to the removal of some

FIGURE 164 HRH Princess Mary, Princess Royal and Viscountess Lascelles, later Countess of Harewood, with her husband Viscount Lascelles and party at Boscobel House, Shropshire in 1922. The princess is seated third from right. Behind her stands the 5th Earl of Bradford, whilst seated left of her is Lady Ida, Dowager Countess of Bradford, who was then Lady of the Bedchamber to the princess's mother HM Queen Mary. Boscobel House had become a part of the Weston Park estate in 1915 and was gifted to the nation in 1954. Accession number 117.0171. (Copyright Trustees of the Weston Park Foundation.)

of the more excessive plasterwork of the Victorian period, and this work was evidently followed by a redecoration, with Herbert Keeble of Keeble & Co., recorded as meeting with Lord Bradford in January 1925.[12]

The Gobelin tapestries, which had been stitched as fixtures to their backing in the Tapestry Room, were rehung and fitted with press-studs to enable their swift removal in the case of a fire, whilst ten years later the Aubusson panels of the seasons – then displayed to either side of the staircase hall arch in the entrance hall – were restored and re-backed by the Cambridge Tapestry Company. Aside from restorations, the collections also benefitted from conservation, with the portrait of Sir George Carew conserved and cleaned by the artist and conservator Nico Jungman (1872–1935),[13] prior to certification by Professor Paul Ganz that the work was by Holbein the younger in 1931. Henry Alexis Hornfeck (1860–1940) also worked on the collections, conserving the wall paintings at the Temple of Diana and also working on other smaller works in 1933.

During all of the reassessment of the inheritance, the letters that had been written by Disraeli to Selina, Countess of Bradford and to her sister Anne, Countess of Chesterfield were also finally brought to public attention. The letters had been passed to Selina's son, the 4th Earl of Bradford who on his death in 1915 left them to his youngest son Richard (Dick) since he had been Disraeli's godson.[14] Richard dying just a year later meant that the letters passed to his elder brother Orlando. In 1929, edited by the 1st Marquess of Zetland – who was married to Lady Ida Bradford's sister Lady Lilian Lumley – the letters were finally published in two volumes.

FIGURE 165 The Drawing Room at Weston Park in circa 1940. Advice on the restoration of the room was sought from the architect Philip Tilden in 1921 and plans for redecoration were obtained from Keeble and Co. in 1925. It appears that this work resulted in a removal of some of the Victorian plaster ceiling decoration and also the over-door decoration. The chandelier is one of two created for the room by Delomosne from old glass that had been found at the Temple of Diana. (Photo: courtesy of the author.)

FIGURE 166 Hans Holbein the younger's portrait of *Sir George Carew, Captain of the Mary Rose*, oil on panel, 33 cm diameter. The painting was conserved for the 5th Earl and Countess by Nico Jungman prior to certification of its authorship by Professor Paul Ganz in 1931. Accession number 101.0152. (Copyright Trustees of the Weston Park Foundation.)

The house's structure was also the subject of works. In 1936 the estate staff had begun to remove the Roman cement that the 1st Earl had applied to the exterior elevations. In the following year, the architects Trenwith Wills (1891–1972) and Lord Gerald Wellesley (1885–1972, later 7th Duke of Wellington) were appointed and the building company Wilson Lovatt of Wolverhampton completed the removal of the stucco in 1937–8.[15] Internally, electric heating was installed in the Victorian Wing, with even the house's servant bedrooms provided with hot- and cold-water basins. As work progressed, however, it was hindered by unattractive discoveries which also had to be remedied, such as a dry rot infestation under the Tapestry Room and Entrance Hall.

Gerald Wellesley was also responsible for designing the Ionic seat, or Aedicule, overlooking Temple Pool, which bears the date of 1938 and, in the same year, James Paine's Roman Bridge was restored. There was a clear strategy of gradual restoration, with the Pink Cottage commenced in 1939. Here, only the roof was completed by the time of the outbreak of the Second World War,

FIGURE 167 The Aedicule, dated 1938, designed by Lord Gerald Wellesley (1885–1972) – later 7th Duke of Wellington – overlooking Temple Pool at Weston Park. (Copyright Trustees of the Weston Park Foundation.)

FIGURE 168 John Fowler's unexecuted design for recreating a tented interior at the Pink Cottage in the east pleasure ground of Weston Park, pen and ink, 21 x 28 cm. Accompanying correspondence indicates that the outbreak of the Second World War in 1939 meant that the scheme was shelved. Accession number 116.0151.1. (Copyright Trustees of the Weston Park Foundation.)

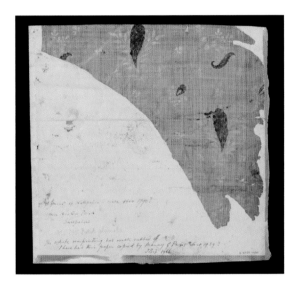

FIGURE 169 A fragment of wallpaper discovered by John Fowler at Weston Park and considered by him to have been of 1790–1800 date (left). His inscription suggests that it might have been found in 1939. The paper, ornamented with stylised sprigs of French lavender, was reproduced by Mauny for Fowler (right) and both samples were gifted by Fowler to the Victoria and Albert Museum in 1966. (© Victoria and Albert Museum, London.)

although Lady Bradford had the intention of reinstating the Morel and Hughes tented room within the building. The young John Fowler visited Weston Park at this time and supplied Lady Bradford with sketches for the work, showing how the tented draperies might be held from a central ceiling rosette. Sadly, the commencement of the Second World War seems to have prevented this project from progressing further than the jaunty drawings.

John Fowler did, however, evidently make improvements at the house, as is evidenced by the wallpaper samples from Weston Park that he gifted to the Victoria & Albert Museum; one is an early nineteenth-century paper decorated with sprigs of French lavender, perhaps from the 1st Earl and Countess's time, and the other is a copy of it by Mauny, one of Fowler's favoured French *papier peint* wallpaper manufacturers. The replication was as much an indication of the Bradfords' historicist tendencies as it was of John Fowler's. At about the same time, the architect and decorator Guy Elwes, was also involved in the house's redecoration, with his contribution including the pine graining of the Library and also the fumed-oak graining of the boudoir anteroom. The Library was especially successful, with a sage green walls and white woodwork scheme yielding to Elwes' wood grain to create a club-like interior of great warmth and charm.

The reinvented house formed a backdrop to parties throughout the twenties and thirties which were attended by fashionable society figures. Within this setting, the family's three daughters Diana, Joana and Anne shone. Admired for their beauty and for their accomplishment, Diana perhaps was pre-eminent amongst the three, her mother having published *The Poems and Paintings of the Lady Diana Bridgeman* in 1920, when Diana was just thirteen years of age. Dedicated to her pet Pekingese dog Yenèe, the works chart her childhood fascination with fairies. In the 1920s she was admired by Henry 'Chips' Channon, who whimsically proposed to her on repeated occasions and was a frequent visitor to Weston Park. In 1926 he visited several times, describing the place as 'a pleasant brown house with an old-fashioned flavour'.[16] On another visit later that same year, he and Diana fantasised about living in the Temple of Diana together: 'We have chosen our rooms and how to do them up and have, in short, planned an exquisite, unreal life together.'[17] Diana maintained her artistic interests as a painter and was photographed by the fashionable lenses of Cecil Beaton and Madame Yevonde. Beaton included her in *The Book of*

FIGURE 170 The library at Weston Park, looking eastwards to the drawing room in 2021. The room's grained decoration, imitating pine, owes to Guy Elwes, working for the 5th Earl and Countess of Bradford. (Paul Highnam/Copyright Trustees of the Weston Park Foundation.)

FIGURE 171 The Countess of Bradford with her children by the south terrace sundial in circa 1920. Her eldest daughter Lady Diana stands beside her, holding her pet Pekingese – perhaps Yenèe – whilst in front are Gerald (later 6th Earl of Bradford), Lady Anne and Lady Joan. The sundial, which vanished in 1939, was rediscovered in the gardeners' compound and was restored by the trustees of the Weston Park Foundation with funding from Arts Society Wrekin, being reinstated in 2021. Accession number 117.0052. (Copyright Trustees of the Weston Park Foundation.)

FIGURE 172 *Lady Diana Bridgeman, Lady Abdy* (1907–1967), photographed by Madame Yevonde (1893–1975) Accession number 117.0120. (Copyright Trustees of the Weston Park Foundation.)

FIGURE 173 *Lady Joan Bridgeman* (1916–1935), painted by her sister Lady Diana, oil on canvas, 59.7 x 49.5 cm. Accession number 101.0341. (Copyright Trustees of the Weston Park Foundation.)

Beauty (1933), describing her as 'leonine large and pale, sullen with flowing ash hair and richly curving lips. Her movements are panther like, and in many other ways she resembles Greta Garbo.'[18] James Lees-Milne encapsulated her personality in his diary after drinks at her London house in 1949, when he noted: 'She is always affectionate and always sparkling like a nymph by a fountain in a landscape by Lancret.'[19]

By that date she was Lady Abdy, having married as his second wife the divorcee art dealer Sir Robert Abdy, 5th Bt (1896–1976) in 1930, and she divided her time between Newton Ferrers in Cornwall and a Paris flat at 44 Avenue Kleber.

Five years after Lady Diana's marriage, the Bradfords faced tragedy in 1935 when their daughter Lady Joan died aged just nineteen. She had suffered illness for some years and had undergone several operations. In her memory, her parents commissioned Bakers of Codsall to create a rock garden at the west end of Temple Pool which is now known as the Garden of Memory. It is a place of solitude and great beauty, with a small waterfall adding continuous life and movement to the garden.[20]

In 1936, Lady Ida, Dowager Countess of Bradford died and her much-loved home of Castle Bromwich Hall became vacant. The house's proximity to the urban expansion of Birmingham meant that, although canvassed, no member of the family was willing to live there. Lord Bradford's brother, Henry was one of those offered the property, but, instead, he initially lived at Harehope and then, in 1946, acquired Fallodon, Northumberland, a house that had been the home of Sir Edward Grey, Viscount Grey of Fallodon (d.1933).

Yet Castle Bromwich's architectural importance and significance to the family was recognised and so it remained a matter to be resolved. In the meantime, in 1939 at the outbreak of the Second World War, a number of items of garden statuary were taken to Weston Park, whilst in the following year the early eighteenth-century lions from Castle Bromwich's turning circle also made their way to the Temple of Diana. The house at Castle Bromwich was requisitioned by the army during the war and it did not fare well. When the National Trust's Historic Buildings Secretary, James Lees-Milne visited, just after the end of the war on 22 September 1945, he noted:

> The house is empty, having been vacated by the troops, and in consequence is in a filthy mess. Every window, and these were casemented and quarried, broken by several bombs dropped in the garden. All the heraldic glass has been destroyed ...[21]

Dry rot was causing problems and the garden was badly neglected. Lady Bradford, who was aware of the futility of generating income from a tenancy only to see the funds consumed by punitive taxation, was keen to see the house gifted to the National Trust. Her husband, though, was more reticent[22] and, eventually, whilst covenants were given to the National Trust, the house remained a little longer in the family's ownership.

In 1944, the year before Lees-Milne's visit, the Bradfords had sold most of the Walsall properties, raising £75,460, in a disposal that was partly to offset capital tax liabilities affecting the family at that time.[23] This followed protracted negotiations with the family's agents and solicitors over Walsall Wood Colliery, which was subject to a settlement in 1934.

During the Second World War, Lord Bradford served as colonel commanding the Weston-under-Lizard Home Guard, for which the stables served as HQ. The park was requisitioned, with land beyond its southern end off Offoxey Road acting as a satellite landing ground, 33 SLG, for RAF Cosford from 1942 to 1945. Here aeroplanes that included Spitfires, manufactured close to the Bradford's other estate at Castle Bromwich, could land on a mown strip outside of the park wall and then be towed by tractors into the park and concealed by the foliage of the trees. An aircraft hangar was created and disguised by being painted up to look like a farmhouse, whilst the quarry within the park was used for rifle practice. A part of the house was requisitioned by the army at this time although its use was not, mercifully, intensive.[24] The Bradfords' son and heir Gerald, Lord Newport had meanwhile been commissioned into the Shropshire Yeomanry in 1938. He had travelled extensively in Europe after university and went on to fight with the Royal Artillery in Italy, being mentioned in despatches and awarded the Territorial Decoration, before being demobilised in 1945 with the rank of major. His eventual bride Mary Montgomery, whom he married in 1946, had been in the Women's Land Army. She was a brilliant linguist, serving as such at Bletchley Park, and ended the war in a high position within the Austrian Section of the BBC.

The advent of war and wartime service posed particular challenges to the way in which country houses like Weston Park were run. This led to the Bradfords wisely adapting the house, with the former servants' quarters converted to flats. In doing so, it enabled older married couples to occupy the accommodation and to assist the family at a time when younger people – who ordinarily might have been in domestic service – would have been performing war service. In 1943 the rooms over the laundry at the north side of the house became home to Mr and Mrs Plevin and their two daughters, with a smaller flat created for the remaining laundry maid Miss Williams. The east end of the former dairy wing became a cottage that was created from the one-time gunroom, and this was occupied initially by the house carpenter and his family and then, later, by the married butler who served Lord Newport. In March 1947, the Newports themselves took to occupying a flat that had been created from the entire top floor of the main house[25] and this remained their family quarters, even after their succession to the earldom.

FIGURE 174 *Gerald Orlando Michael Bridgeman, 6th Earl of Bradford* (1911–1981), painted by Frank Eastman (1878–1964) in 1956, oil on canvas, 91.5 x 76.3 cm. Accession number 101.0202. (Copyright Trustees of the Weston Park Foundation.)

During the war, the Temple of Diana – in spite of repairs earlier in the century – was found to have serious structural issues owing to dry rot and woodworm. The centre of the ceiling of the China Room had collapsed in 1944 smashing much of the china.[26] Repairs were finally put in hand under the aegis of the Birmingham architect S.T. Walker, using the builder Griffiths of Wolverhampton, with works commencing in 1951 and completed in October 1952.[27]

By this date, Lord Bradford was a widower, Lady Bradford having died in 1949 aged just sixty-seven. He continued to maintain Weston and its collections, undertaking the restoration of the Vanderbank tapestry in 1955 when it was restored by Anglo Persian Carpet Company. When he himself died in 1957, his son and daughter-in-law took up the reigns.

The new Earl and Countess had, respectively, outside and inside interests which were to be of great benefit to Weston Park. The abiding – and, indeed, award-winning – interest of Gerald, 6th Earl was in arboriculture and he shared his knowledge widely, being a Crown Estate Commissioner 1956–67, President of the Country Landowners' Association, President of the Timber Growers' Organisation 1962–4, and as Chairman of the Forestry Committee of Great Britain 1964–6, and President of the Soil Association. At Weston he augmented the parkland planting with a wide range of species. These included *Nothofagus Procera* introduced from Chile – plus leylandii and dawn redwoods, with some species being more successful than others. A tree nursery was established on the Knockin estate in addition to that at Weston. There, the north Shropshire estate remained at 4,500 acres and still retained its own land agent, Captain Evelyn Beresford-Peirse, who served until 1955, and was followed by Ralph Higginson until 1987.[28]

Whilst other aristocrats and members of the landed gentry faced the harsh reality of twentieth-century taxation, Lord Bradford found himself in a position to pick up some of the pieces of the break-ups as a result of his management skills and use of land mortgages. His purchases were, in themselves, of notable estates. From his distant cousin the Duke of Bedford, he acquired a significant part of the Tavistock estate in the Tamar Valley of Devonshire.[29] In Staffordshire, the decision of the Morris-Eyton family to settle in Zimbabwe provided the opportunity to buy their Wood Eaton Manor estate, whilst in Shropshire, with the departure of the family of Humphrey Lloyd for Gloucestershire in 1947, Lord Bradford was able to purchase that family's Leaton Knolls estate to the north of Shrewsbury.[30] The big house at Leaton, a Greek Revival pile designed by Edward Haycock with significant input from its owner J.A. Lloyd, which overlooked the River Severn, initially became flats but its maintenance eventually proved too costly and so it was demolished in 1955. The estate was well regarded for its trees in the nineteenth century and this must have further endeared its acres to Lord Bradford. It eventually passed to Lord Bradford's younger son, the Hon. Charles Bridgeman RICS, who, like his late father, has a keen interest in arboriculture and who has driven the estate forward into the twentieth century. In Scotland, close to Inverness, the Dell estate came into the 6th Earl's ownership and this was, in due course, settled on his late daughter Lady Serena Andrew.

The importance of the urban properties to the family had, by this time, significantly diminished. Properties at Bolton remained, managed from the Edwardian purpose-built estate office at the heart of the town and family still took an interest in civic developments there, with Lord Bradford opening Bishop Bridgeman School in Rupert Street in 1972.[31] Closer to Weston, Castle Bromwich Hall was finally sold in 1962, becoming the regional headquarters for Bovis Homes and then, later, it eventually became a hotel. Its gardens, in the meantime, had suffered neglect until rediscovery in 1983 and the establishment of the Castle Bromwich Hall Gardens Trust two years later enabled the restoration and opening of the gardens to the public. With the disposal of Castle Bromwich, the Pieter and Franz van der Borcht 'Fins Teniers' tapestries from that house were offered for sale at Sotheby's in November 1962.[32]

FIGURE 175 Lady Bradford in the entrance hall that she had redecorated, admiring the rehung van Dyck portrait of Thomas Killigrew. (Copyright Trustees of the Weston Park Foundation.)

At Weston Park, Lady Bradford concentrated her efforts on the house and its internal redecoration and re-presentation. To her generation, the Victorian and Edwardian interventions of the 3rd and 4th Earl and Countess were anathema and she attempted to erase these generations' works by redecorating in a neo-Georgian style, working with the Curzon Street decorators Bird Iles. Her endeavours were not merely superficial but involved major works including structural interventions, with architectural oversight provided by S.T. Walker and Partners of Birmingham, and new plasterwork that was created by Jacksons.[33] In the entrance hall, in 1961 she altered the capitals of the columns by adding a collar of anthemion motifs, whilst a new frieze was introduced around the room, the walls of which were painted a light green. The two Aubusson tapestries that had been framed to flank the staircase arch were removed to the former billiard room to flank its chimneypiece.

Both this latter room, and its neighbour the former smoking room were subject to a thorough remodelling that began in 1957. The billiard table was removed and acid-etched glass doors, which had divided the billiard room from the Marble Hall were banished to the stables so that the spaces linked.[34] The oak boards in both rooms were removed, to be replaced by a dazzling new terrazzo floor that emulated the black and white marble chequerboard floor of the Marble Hall. Above, new lay-light fenestration was installed, whilst Jacksons provided wall frame-mouldings in the old billiard room and new

tympanum plasterwork above a new pair of mahogany double doors, that united the spaces, and also in arched panels in the former smoking room. The rooms were renamed, as First and Second Salons, and were treated as galleries of some of the old master paintings, whilst selected pieces of furniture were displayed against the walls of each room.

FIGURE 177 The Morning Room at Weston Park. Known by Lady Bradford as the Breakfast Room, she redecorated the room with additional plasterwork and the present handsome salmon pink silk damask, which forms an excellent foil to the smaller pictures in the collection. The shield-back chairs – recently conserved by the Weston Park Foundation – conform to a late eighteenth-century Gillow design. Above the chimneypiece hangs John Riley's portrait of Sir Orlando Bridgeman, 1st Bt in robes as Lord Chief Justice. (Paul Highnam/ Copyright Trustees of the Weston Park Foundation.)

In the breakfast or morning room, decorative fanned plaster panels were added to the ceiling and the room's walls were covered in a pink silk damask to produce a hugely effective foil for the display of some of the smaller paintings in the collection. On the south front, the drawing room was the least successful of the alterations. Here plaster wall panels, which defined the room's proportions, were removed and the walls uniformly papered in an ivory colour, with matching silk damask curtains that flowed below flat panelled pelmets. The ceiling's plasterwork was partially picked out in pastel colours whilst the seat furniture was reupholstered in a sage green damask.

Of the ground floor rooms, it was the dining room that witnessed the most dramatic transformation. Here Lady Bradford's work was a reworking in the aftermath of a disastrous dry rot infestation on the outer wall, which had been caused as a result of blocked rainwater hoppers. S.T. Walker and Partners liaised over the insertion of a new beam in the room in 1959–61 and eventually the room was redecorated from 1965. Removing the oak panelled dado – which found new purpose at the Church of St John the Baptist at Finchingfield, Essex – Lady Bradford's work involved the addition of a new lower dado. Above it, the room was bound with a new urn and swag frieze, created by Jacksons, below the room's cornice. The old curtains were replaced below new pelmets that had been inspired from the tester of a French bed that Lady Bradford had admired, whilst the room's door cases were given new neo-Palladian pedimented doorcases of an extremely high quality. After deliberations about fabric wallcoverings, Cole and Son produced a version of their Trieste wallpaper to a colour especially devised under Lady Bradford's supervision, whilst a complexed colour palette, with details of the ceiling picked out in pastel and lavish gilded highlights, was implemented. It was a hugely ambitions scheme and served as a foil for some of the best portraits in the collection, including the exceptional group of van Dycks. Whilst initially an ormolu chandelier was considered, Lord Bradford acquired a chandelier from the sale of nearby Longford Hall.[35] Lady Bradford, however, preferred a loaned Regency chandelier that came from Apley Park and which was in the room for many years. The Longford chandelier was hung, for a time, in the Orangery before taking the place of the Apley chandelier when that eventually returned to its owners.

FIGURE 178 The scene that confronted the Bradford family in the dining room in the late 1950s. Dry rot, exacerbated by blocked external downspouts, had led to the removal of the internal plaster. (Copyright Trustees of the Weston Park Foundation.)

FIGURE 179 The redecorated dining room in circa 1980. Lady Bradford's work included the Cole & Son 'Trieste' pattern wallpaper to a special colour run, the Jackson & Son urn and swag plaster frieze, the lower dado and the reframing of the Robert Edge Pine conversation piece of Sir Henry and Lady Bridgeman and their family. (Copyright Trustees of the Weston Park Foundation.)

FIGURE 180 Tent Bedroom, a first-floor bedroom in the Victorian east wing of Weston Park, which was created by Lady Bradford with yellow silk hangings supplied by Charles Hammond Ltd. (Copyright Trustees of the Weston Park Foundation.)

Lady Bradford's decorating work at Weston Park also extended to the bedrooms, to introduce late twentieth-century comfort. Pre-eminent of this work was the creation of Tent Bedroom, a realisation of the Regency Morel and Hughes scheme for Pink Cottage and which John Fowler had attempted to revive prior to the outbreak of the Second World War. Lady Bradford brought about the vision with great aplomb – and expense – with assistance from Charles Hammond Limited.[36] It is said that the cost of this work prevented the refurbishment of the Tapestry Rom in 1970, where Lady Bradford had planned on installing the Louis Laguerre ceiling painting that had come to Weston from the staircase of Castle Bromwich Hall, and also intended changing the room's chimneypiece.[37]

The fabric repairs to the structure of the house had been partly funded by a Historic Buildings Council grant, and conditions attached to this were amongst the reasons that the family decided to open the house to the public from 9 May 1964. Much publicity was generated about the opening and, in doing so, it carried the emphatic sentiment that 'Lord Bradford is adamant that there will be no gimmicks' – a subtle aside at his distant cousins, the Duke of Bedford at Woburn and the Marquess of Bath at Longleat, where safari parks had become a part of the visitor offer. Weston, the Bradfords were determined, would be presented as a home and not as a museum. The estate though, was already showing itself to be a master at public awareness, with even the sanctuary of the walled gardens, which continued to produce fruit and vegetables for the house and for local sale, quietly generating interest. Here, the head gardener Roland Smith, well-known as a judge of produce at county and national shows, became a familiar face to BBC viewers as one of the experts on television shows broadcast from the kitchen garden at Weston Park during the 1950s.

For the house opening, a curator was appointed. Mr D.H. Trumble OBE was a retired colonial civil servant with thirty years' service as state treasurer and then resident at Brunei[38] and he produced a guidebook in addition to masterminding the conversion of the orangery into a tea room for visitors to the house. Other logistics also had to be considered for what was forecast, initially, to be a thousand visitors a day, with a target of 40,000 visitors for the first season. A 'dress rehearsal' for 150 invited guests took place on 28 April, before the public were formally admitted, and Lord Bradford publically praised Mr Trumble and his team in the press.[39] The actual opening was a success too, with the predicted daily numbers met and, after a successful Whit bank holiday weekend, Mr Trumble commented that:

> Monday was a terrific day. Visitors were going through the house bumper to bumper, as you might say. There were people picnicking in the grounds and they didn't leave much litter.[40]

By the end of the year, 32,000 visitors were recorded as having visited Weston Park – significantly lower than Ragley Hall where 47,842 visited, Berkeley Castle's 85,600 visitors and Harewood's 85,375 visitors and, even locally, at Hodnet Hall which received 35,000 visitors.[41]

Where the house and its collections were concerned, there were rationalisations and also favourable reconsiderations of contents. The most exciting of the latter came in 1958, when a Weston Park's portrait was recognised as the prime van Dyck version of Sir Thomas Hanmer's portraits following cleaning by Horace Buttery – having been previously wrongly identified as Colonel West painted by Robert Walker – whilst another portrait of Hanmer, formerly at Barton Hall, Suffolk, in the meantime had been previously considered to be the prime version.[42] Similarly, Weston's van Dyck portrait of Thomas Killigrew was recognised to be that which had provenance from the seventeenth-century painter Sir Peter Lely's sale and, in so doing, it came to be accepted as the more important work than the portrait in the collection of the Dukes of Devonshire at Chatsworth which had, wrongly, previously claimed the Lely provenance.[43]

FIGURE 181 Roland Smith, head gardener at Weston Park, broadcasting from the walled garden for the BBC. (Courtesy of Brian Smith/ Weston Park Foundation.)

Seven years after public opening, the profitability of the estates was a matter of concern, when Lord Bradford commissioned Strutt & Parker to undertake a feasibility study in 1971. At this time, the Weston estate, which then ran to 14,242 acres, was just about breaking even although Lord Bradford had been disappointed by visitor numbers of 49,000 in 1970 and 47,000 in 1971. He wanted to increase the figure as a possible means of improving profitability since the public admission account had shown a deficit in each year since opening began in 1964. Strutt & Parker noted the children's playground near Church Pool as being 'of the garish swings and slides variety' to which a separate admission charge was levied, and they also considered the additional attractions, including the antiques shop, pets' corner, pottery studio, catering in the orangery and the gift shop, all of which were running at losses.

The recommendation was that a new business plan, with higher quality attractions, a better circulation route and higher tariffs should be coupled with new facilities created. This would involve injecting up to £50,000 of capital. Amongst the 'improvements' it was suggested that the car park to the south of the house should be moved to the walled garden, where the loss-leading market garden would be shut down and replaced by spaces for 800 cars and twenty coaches. Here the Granary building could be reinvented as the visitor entry point, gift shops and café, with the stables transformed into a museum of agriculture or carriage museum. These plans were not adopted, although a local history museum was established in the stables, and an aquarium attraction – of which Strutt & Parker were dismissive – was created under the orangery. A miniature railway was also added to Temple Wood which, along with a butterfly farm, was run as a franchise. Of the report's suggestions, a new adventure playground in Temple Wood was in fact created, whilst a need for advertising and better publicity was also heeded.[44]

To finance some of the changes and to sustain other outgoings, sacrifices from the collection had to be made. Books – including a collection of the eighteenth-century plays that must have been performed in Sir Henry Bridgeman's eighteenth-century theatre at Weston – were offered for sale at Sotheby's, and prints, too, had been sold in 1967.[45] By far the most notable item to have left the house at this time however, was the Holbein drawing, then assumed to be of Anne Boleyn, which Lord Bradford sold to the British Museum in 1975.[46] Further sales followed later in the decade at Christie's, with a number of entries of books from the library, the most regrettable of which was on 11 October 1978 when lots 138–22 comprised eighteenth- and nineteenth-century travel books from the house's collection.[47] A rationalisation of paintings was also undertaken, and a number of items from the family's collections was offered for sale at Christie's from November 1980 to January 1981.[48]

Weston Park, by this time, had become a highly regarded visitor attraction that played an important part in the heart of England's tourism economy. It was still a vibrant and much-loved family home set at the heart of a series of estate businesses that covered a wide territorial area and offered support to the house itself. Within months of the Christie's picture sale in 1981, however, Lord Bradford's unexpected death would cast a shadow of doubt over the future of the house and collection.

CHAPTER ELEVEN

The Weston Park Foundation
Forging a Hospitable Future from the Past

With the 6th Earl of Bradford's death, the family faced significant death duties. His eldest son and successor Richard, who became 7th Earl of Bradford, had forged a successful career as a restaurateur, opening Porters English Restaurant in Covent Garden in 1979, and he developed a series of popular gourmet evenings at Weston Park, where he himself would chef for paying guests. He and Lady Bradford had a young family and had taken the decision not to live in the house, where the Dowager Countess remained until her death in 1986. Instead, they established themselves at one of the principal estate farms, which they altered for their family life, away from the public activity at the big house. The extent of the tax liability, however, was such that, even with the greatly increased levels of business activity that the family were now engaged in at Weston Park, the income was proving to be wholly insufficient to clear the debt.

Other measures of raising capital were actively explored and this led to the Bolton estate being largely wound up in 1983, with the closure of its estate office in Silverwell Street and an auction sale of properties at Farnworth, Bolton and Great Lever in some sixty-five lots. At that time, those properties had been generating an income of £31,000 per annum.[1] As the family and their advisers looked to find a way forward for Weston Park, there was one sad casualty from the collection, the severance of which is to be deeply regretted. This was the sale of the Jacopo Bassano *Way to Calvary*, which left the house, seemingly forever, in 1983 when it was sold to the National Gallery in London.

The fragmentation of the important collections, though, was not something that the family wanted and eventually Lord Bradford chose to make the generous sacrifice of gifting the house, thousand-acre park and the majority of the collections to the nation with terms agreed by the Capital Taxes Office. In 1985, the government through Lord Gowrie, Mrs Thatcher's Arts Minister, offered a grant of £25 million to the National Heritage Memorial Fund. This sum provided funding for the national acquisition and maintenance of the collections of a number of heritage assets deemed to be of national importance. They included the Chippendale furniture at Nostell Priory, West Yorkshire, Robert Adam's masterpiece Kedleston Hall, Derbyshire, and also for Weston Park. Nostell's mansion was already owned by the National Trust and so its collection of furniture was transferred to the Trust, as was Kedleston.

FIGURE 182 *Richard Bridgeman, 7th Earl of Bradford* (b.1947), painted by Paul Benney (b.1959) in 1999, oil on canvas, 109.5 x 86.5 cm. Accession number 101.0215. (Copyright Trustees of the Weston Park Foundation.)

At Weston Park, though, the solution was a different one, with the core heritage assets being vested in a newly established independent charity, the Weston Park Foundation, which would be accountable to central government and which was also provided with an endowment fund by the NHMF. The intention was for the charity to have conservation objectives and also to fulfil an educational purpose, giving public access and enjoyment to the property and collections whilst at the same time being able to generate the necessary funds to enable the altruistic activities to viably take place. With the support of Lord Bradford – who not only sacrificed his ancestral home but also contributed £1 million to enable the new Charity's existence – the deal was finally completed on 12 December 1986, when Weston Park became the property of the Weston Park Foundation. The management of the foundation was to be through trustees appointed initially by the NHMF but who would then be self-perpetuating. The charity's first chairman was John (later Sir John) Dugdale, Lord Lieutenant of Shropshire, who was joined by the founder trustees: the Earl of Scarbrough, the Earl of Plymouth and Peter Bridgeman, the son of the Hon. Henry Bridgeman, a younger son of the 4th Earl, and the owner of Fallodon. In addition, further specialist expertise was provided by two other trustees: the solicitor Peter Mimpriss of Allen & Overy – who had undertaken all of the initial legal work to enable the establishment of the Foundation and its acquisition of the property – and also Richard Sawtell, county secretary of Shropshire County Council and who also served as clerk to the Shropshire Lieutenancy. They were later joined by Lord Bradford who remained until he resigned in 1999, later becoming the founder patron of the charity which was to preserve and protect his family's ancestral home.[2]

The handing over from family to foundation was facilitated by the Bradford estates' land agent David Weston, and his successor Piers Clerk, continued to ensure cordial relations existed between the neighbouring property owners. For the trustees, an appointment of Michael Evans of Balfour & Cooke (now Balfours) was made to provide land agency services to the foundation. In addition to the usual management of buildings and land, Michael's role also came to encompass a care and understanding for the collections within the house and their presentation. This work was delivered quietly over many years by Keith Verrell who had been the house carpenter and came to be a curator and custodian until his retirement in 2008.

The task of the initial trustees was, in many ways a daunting one, with initial trustee meetings tabled to face the challenges of two unavoidable reports. One of these was an architect's report that had originally been commissioned in 1982 for the National Trust who were then considering the property. It was produced by S.T. Walker of Wolverhampton which conservatively estimated that the then colossal sum of £900,000 was required for urgent property repairs at the house and on a number of listed structures that were located within the crumbling seven-mile long park wall. This document was accompanied by a straight-faced report of 24 June 1986, by Smiths Gore, which assessed the property management accounts and concluded that there was an annual deficit which considerably exceeded the income or, indeed, the likely income from the endowment, much of which was generated from investments.[3] Where public opening alone was concerned, this figure had grown from £37,000 to be a deficit of £47,000 in 1985. Means of generating income in a way that did not harm the heritage assets, had to be found whilst at the same time coping with a historic building which was in a condition that left a great deal to be desired. The roof was a particular problem and sections of balustrading along the Victorian Wing became detached, within a short period of the foundation's establishment, crashing to the carriage ring below and making manifest the urgency of repairs to the house's structure. Although Smiths Gore noted that repairs had been made that diminished the full financial suggestion of the architect's report, they did see fit to comment that 'the Trustees [of the Weston Park Foundation] could be forgiven for supposing that they had been offered the keys of Dresden in 1945' since building costs and VAT had increased the liability. The report made a number of frank suggestions, which included the wholesale demolition of Victorian additions to the house and the possibility of the freehold disposal of some of the park structures, by way of avoiding in-perpetuity maintenance costs. The Jacob and Hebridean sheep might, similarly, be culled. There can be little doubt that the founder trustees were well aware of the responsibilities and the liabilities that they had inherited, although the report is a sobering document and one which highlights the challenges that were then evident.

The one great asset that the trustees did inherit, though, was a number of key members of staff with a strong working knowledge of the house and its setting, which would prove invaluable in future years. One of these was Martin Gee, whose forebear John Gee had first arrived in Staffordshire from Weeting in Norfolk in 1803 as ploughman to the 1st Bridgeman Earl of Bradford, and who was the latest in the line to devote themselves to Weston. Martin, at the time of writing, remains the head gardener to the Foundation.

As the Foundation's new trustees got to grips with their responsibilities, the executors of the 6th Earl of Bradford held a sale, run by Christie's South Kensington, on 13 and 14 May 1986, to sell surplus contents. Much was secondary in nature to the core collections, although there were some escapees that were to be regretted, such as a desk stand that had probably been supplied by Lignereux, a pair from a suite of pollard oak bookcases supplied to the 3rd Earl and Countess and also the busts of Fox and Pitt that had sat in the Library and which Christie's catalogued as a 'marble bust of a portly gentleman' and 'marble bust of a gentleman'. As a record of the losses, the sale catalogue is not its best memorial.

In tandem with the dispersal, a mammoth cataloguing and photographing exercise took place for the foundation. All of its chattels – totalling some 30,000 objects – had to be catalogued following the Christie's schedules that had accompanied the establishment of the foundation. This remarkable work was overseen by Alice Dugdale, the Chairman's daughter, and it still forms the cornerstone of the present inventory of collections.

Giving the property a firm financial footing became an imperative for the trustees and it became increasingly apparent that the large-scale public opening of the house – as with all historic houses – did not, on its own, bring in the level of income that Weston Park required. The complexities of the Victorian roof structures, superimposed on Georgian and Restoration fabric, had led to a maintenance nightmare that required significant, sustained and strategically planned investment if the place was going to remain a viable heritage site. What had been established by Lord Bradford as Bradford Enterprises was renamed Weston Park Enterprises and this became the charity's wholly owned subsidiary that was able to generate income that could then be Gift Aided back to the charity for its core purposes. Weston Park Enterprises forged ahead with the use of the house as an exclusive-use venue and the use of the park for large-scale events, although these purposes, of course, required an infrastructure that was safe, presentable and, at the same time, true to the history of the place.

For the house, repairs and the long-term planning of the site was entrusted to the architects Arrol & Snell of Shrewsbury. Andrew Arrol oversaw the creation of a new space that might be used for conferences on the ground floor of Burn and MacVicar Anderson's east wing, where Lord Bradford's room and the former housekeeper's room were united by the removal of the party wall. Mouldings in Lord Bradford's room were replicated into the housekeeper's room and the chimneypiece was moved from the west to the east wall. Further bedrooms and either en-suite or private bathrooms were created within the body of the house and these were decorated by Caroline Lawson of Chelsea Decorators in an elegant and handsome style appropriate to the house.

Yet there was still a monumental backlog of major repairs that the trustees had inherited and difficult decisions had to be made. Recognising the challenges, some additional funding was made available by the NHMF and, at the same time, a new adviser came to support the trustees. Sir Francis Pemberton had developed his family land agency Bidwells to be a highly regarded business, adept at developing productive business plans in a no-nonsense manner. He applied himself to Weston Park in helping the trustees to take cost-cutting decisions and also to seeing the possibility and viability of the assets that they had within Weston's park wall, remaining as a highly respected and commercially astute adviser until well into the new millennium.

Around the park, the buildings that had given so much pleasure to previous Earls of Bradford and their family had been identified as being of national heritage importance. Their heritage importance, though, did not of course arrest their decay and with English Heritage (now Historic England) grants being at an all-time low, the trustees offered the Grade I listed Temple of Diana, Grade II listed Pink Cottage, Grade II listed Knoll Tower and Grade II listed Boathouse at Park Pool on long leases. Although there was interest, no one was prepared to commit and so, ultimately, it fell back on the Foundation to resolve the problem. Fortunately, in the case of the Temple of Diana, saviours were waiting in the wings in the form of Peter and Susan Janney who had been declined when they had asked the 6th Earl in the 1970s if they might rent the Temple from him. Taking a lease from 1995, they proved to be the perfect custodians who dedicated time, money and effort to coaxing the building back to life as their home and undertaking much of the work themselves.

As time went by and Weston Park Enterprises started to bring in income, the other park follies began to find tenants. Where the Knoll Tower was concerned, the revival of the structure – which is essentially one room on each of its three floors – owes to a single-storey stone ashlar extension containing a kitchen and a bathroom. This, resplendent with battlements, was carefully added to the designs of David Buckle who had initially gone to work as clerk of works to the Bradford Estate before joining the Balfours team. He oversaw the restoration of the other follies at Weston Park to a meticulously high standard and played an important role in the long-term maintenance of the house and other Foundation-owned structures.

The park and gardens became a particular focus of the trustees. In 1989, Elizabeth Banks had produced designs for the restoration of the Italian Garden and Broderie and initial researches to fully understand the historical progression

FIGURE 183 The Teardrop Garden, created for the Trustees of the Weston Park Foundation with advice from Fred and Nada Jennett in the 1990s. Located at the end of the Rose Walk, the garden links with Capability Brown's Shrewsbury Walk to the north-west of the house. (Copyright Trustees of the Weston Park Foundation.)

of the designed landscape were undertaken by Todd Longstaffe-Gowan. This eventually led on to the drafting of a rolling twenty-five-year Landscape Management Plan by Patrick James and his colleagues at the Landscape Agency, which remains a core document for the development and the use of the park.

By 1991–8 the restoration of the formal gardens became an especial focus. This was led by the then chairman Philip Trevor-Jones who, with his wife Ann, had been responsible for the creation of exceptional gardens at their Shropshire home of Preen Manor. Philip wanted the gardens to reflect the history of the site, providing an appropriate setting for the house, whilst at the same time requiring as little maintenance as possible. This was achieved with design assistance from Nada and Fred Jennett, who focused their attentions on the Italian garden in the angle of the Orangery and west front, and also in the recreation of a Broderie garden on the south front. In the Italian garden, the restoration of a complex parterre was achieved by using box hedges combined with purple sage, blue rue and other plants that would subtly achieve the effect of bedding without the labour that would have been required in the Victorian original. Around the Poultry House, the rose walk – with yew buttresses punctuating the roses along the boundary wall – and a new 'Teardrop Garden' – so called from its ground plan and from the statue of a weeping woman at its centre – was created with paths defined by weeping pears.

Following the arrival of a new chief executive, Colin Sweeney, in 1997, a series of new business opportunities presented themselves which were to define Weston Park in the media and in the perceptions of the wider world. The first of these was the selection of Weston Park as the venue for the retreat days of the G8 summit of world leaders in 1998. Weston Park's location close to Birmingham, where the main summit was based, its secure environment – without any public rights of way across the park – plus its incomparable accommodation and service, made the estate a natural choice. Britain's Prime Minister and European Union President Tony Blair, together with Bill Clinton, Helmut Kohl, Boris Yeltsin, Romano Prodi, Jacques Chirac, Jean Chrétien, Ryutaro Hashimoto and Jacques Santer were therefore duly welcomed to the house with their retinues.

Three years later, Tony Blair was to return to Weston, this time with Irish premier Bertie Ahern, the Ulster Unionist Party leader David Trimble, the

FIGURE 184 World leaders gathered at the G8 Summit at Weston Park in 1998. Weston Park's Orangery forms the backdrop. Left to right: Bill Clinton, Ryutaro Hashimoto, Jacques Santer, Jacques Chirac, Romano Prodi, Tony Blair, Boris Yeltsin and Chancellor Kohl. (Image copyright *Shropshire Star/Express and Star*.)

FIGURE 185 The Northern Ireland Peace Talks in the Orangery at Weston Park in 2001. Sinn Fein President Gerry Adams (left) holds a bottle of water, before British Prime Minister Tony Blair, Irish Prime Minister Bertie Ahern and other Ulster politicians start talks to advance the Northern Ireland peace process at Weston Park, Shropshire, Monday 9 July 2001. (Image PA photo: David Jones/WPA/PA.)

Northern Ireland secretary John Reid, and Sinn Fein president Gerry Adams, when the house was the setting for the Northern Ireland Peace talks from 9 until 14 July. Although no agreement was reached, a rescue package was drawn up at Weston Park which was presented to all the parties on 1 August and which was referred to as the Weston Park Agreement.

In 1999 an event of a very different and more public kind had found its home within the thousand acres of Weston Park, bringing in its wake massive economic benefits to the entire region annually until 2017. This was the V Festival, a huge music festival which each year brought 60,000–80,000 people within the park wall, giving a wholly new meaning to entertainment within Capability Brown's landscape. Whilst Sir Henry Bridgeman's theatre had brought audiences from Shrewsbury and Birmingham to see the family and their friends performing, the V Festival brought globally acclaimed artists to perform at Weston Park and its sister site at Hylands Park in Essex. Lady Gaga, The Killers, Oasis, Amy Winehouse … – the wider visitor book of Weston was enriched in a totally new manner that showed how relevant and responsive the Weston Park Foundation could be to audiences and to business opportunities.

In tandem with the V Festival's annual appearance, monumental works took place within the park itself to restore the land to its naturalistic parkland appearance. Although many of the 6th Earl's plantations had, in their time, represented experimental forestry, their trees were approaching maturity and, in many instances, comprised species such as leylandii which were alien

FIGURE 186 The bright lights and crowds of the V Festival at Weston Park – Calvin Harris performs in 2015.
(Sam Neill/Trustees of the Weston Park Foundation.)

to the Brownian landscape. The Landscape Agency's team oversaw a mass felling operation at the Knoll and in the southern part of the park, which not only enabled the varied character of the landscape to be appreciated but also liberated the King and Queen veteran oaks which had become engulfed by a softwood plantation.

In the meantime, however, the foundation itself had seen great changes to the very form of its board. Sadly, in 2000, the chairman Philip Trevor-Jones died suddenly and was succeeded by William Montgomery. Lord Scarbrough had also departed and his place as a trustee was taken by his niece, the Hon. Rose Paterson. By this date, other new trustees had also joined the board including Catherine, Lady Forester, William Mostyn-Owen and Jonathan Asquith.

The income brought by the V Festival generated not only opportunities for the wider regional economy but, for Weston Park, aided a revival in the property's fortunes – sustaining improvements to the heritage and the business fabric of the property over the next eighteen years of its existence at Weston Park.

In the house, the trustees decided to enable public access to the large collections of historic silver that had been amassed by successive generations of Newports and Bridgemans. On the ground floor, a cloakroom that had been created by MacVicar Anderson in 1899 was selected as a suitably secure space on the visitor route, and with further defences installed, this was reinvented as a treasury. The cases, created from materials with a low VOC content, were designed by Charles Manners in 2000 and based upon the cabinets in the house's Victorian plate room yet here fitted with fibre optic lighting to enable clear visibility of the individual pieces.

A re-presentation of the Tapestry Room, with advice from James Finlay, including new curtains by Ann Lister, and conservation of the tapestries by May Berkouwer, was undertaken at this time. Within the collection, an outstanding George II gesso pier table, bearing the apparent monogram of

Richard Newport, 2nd Earl of Bradford and attributed to James Moore was conserved under the aegis of the trustee's then-adviser Michael Thompson, whilst new carpets were commissioned for the library and dining room from David and Sara Bamford. The former carpet was a replica Feraghan, whilst the latter was a reinvention of a classically inspired carpet that had been supplied for the 1st Bridgeman Earl and Countess's daughter Lady Lucy Whitmore for the library of Dudmaston.

As the house developed a new life of being a place of hospitality for groups using it exclusively, the decoratively segregated arrangement of the rooms, which had worked well since the 1960 opening, when the house had a stratified form of open, public areas and private family spaces, was found to be visually unsatisfactory. The salons at the heart of the house, in particular, although functional as galleries for the house's indigenous treasures, did not connect aesthetically with the other principal rooms. William Mostyn-Owen, who had begun his career as Bernard Berenson's secretary and gone on to serve as a Christie's director prior to becoming a foundation trustee, devised a new hang of works in tandem with a general representation of these spaces and the Marble Hall and Staircase in 2005–6. This was formulated by Janie Money of Sibyl Colefax & John Fowler, a company which had first come to be involved at Weston in the 1930s and whose design ethic of country house excellence was *sympathique* in its timelessness. With the encouragement of the trustees, Janie ingeniously reinvented the salons as what might have been Victorian living-halls. Rugs were introduced to calm the endless expanses of terrazzo chequerboard flooring, with central groups of furniture to give human scale and to encourage use of the spaces, whilst the walls were calmed with eucalyptus green, and woodwork and ceilings yielded to a cleverly conceived range of soft whites. The result gave the spaces a patina that had been lacking and enabled them to function, variously, as dining and sitting rooms which could, with little

FIGURE 187 A part of the silver display commissioned by the Trustees of the Weston Park Foundation in 2000. The cases were ingeniously designed by Charles Manners to reflect the design of the 3rd Earl's plate room cases whilst, simultaneously offering state-of-the-art conservation protection and lighting. (Copyright Trustees of the Weston Park Foundation.)

fuss, be transformed from rooms of public parade for visitors keen to see the artworks into rooms where a reception might be held.

In 2006 a new post was created of curator and head of learning, tying together the charity's core objectives and challenged with responsibility for developing life-long learning and cultural tours, together with the long-term conservation of the heritage assets. The curator and head of learning also led on interpretation for the opening of Weston to general public visitors. A public access season had, by this time, developed which was threaded between the income-generating private events. Most of the days were in school holidays, when the majority of general public visits would be likely to take place, and in many instances with engaging holiday activities prepared, most recently by the former education manager Claire Cumming. In all of the public access, though, Weston Park could not function without its enthusiastic team of volunteers. Some of the volunteers first came as school visitors or on work experience, others have taken retirement, although for all of them there is a great sense of fellowship to be gained, which now sees volunteers actively involved not only in room stewarding and guiding, but in gardening, helping with educational delivery, in conservation, and in archival research.

One of the biggest projects to be undertaken in the first decade of the millennium, and which confirmed a commitment to public access, was the restoration and conversion of James Paine's model Home Farm – or the Granary, as it had become known. This great brick Palladian structure, with its pair of flanking towers and giant pedimented threshing portals, had largely lain empty since it had ceased to be used for farming purposes in the later twentieth century. Its upper floors had latterly been used for rearing pheasants, taken up there in bread-crates, but otherwise its ground floor merely offered a useful workshop to the park team, a place to store events peripherals and as a dry-store for lesser items from the indigenous collection. With designs obtained from the architect Graham Wright, an approach was successfully made to the Heritage Lottery Fund (now National Lottery Heritage Fund) for £1 million of funding, which enabled the building's reinvention as a main entrance to the estate for general public visitors. On the ground floor of the northern range a farm shop

FIGURE 189 The Marble Staircase following Janie Money's redecoration in 2005–6. The eucalyptus green forms a unifying element for the decoration of the main circulation spaces. (Photographer: Simon Upton; Credit: Sibyl Colefax & John Fowler/Janie Money, associate design director.)

FIGURE 190 The new forest school at Weston Park, developed from 2021 by Educating Kids Outdoors (EKO), is the latest offer for curricular-based studies, building on the achievements of former education manager Claire Cumming who, with a volunteer team, annually welcomed up to 7,000 children to Weston Park. (Photo: Karen Hartnell-Beavis/EKO.)

FIGURE 191 The Granary Art Gallery, a part of the National Lottery Heritage Fund supported development of the Granary building at Weston Park. Exhibitions have included the 2018 showing of Daimler Art Collection's Dieter Blum photography: *Cowboys: The First Shooting*, shown here. (Copyright Trustees of the Weston Park Foundation.)

was initially created, whilst on the second floor of the same wing an art gallery was formed, with assistance from architects Purcell, to create an adaptable pace for exhibitions that is open freely year round. In the following year, Colin Sweeney was able to secure further funding in the form of a grant from the Regional Development Agency which enabled the west wing to be converted into a restaurant, the Granary Brasserie, which, like the gallery, would be a year-round public offering. In the years following, further works were done to the upper floors of the west wing and these spaces were converted to tenanted office space.

For the house, too, significant ongoing works to conserve the fabric of the building have continued to be a part of life at Weston Park. Major building projects never sit happily alongside events which require immaculate presentation, and so many of the most significant works to the house's Grade I listed structure have to take place in the winter months. This, of course, then places the work at the mercy of, at times, less-than-clement British weather. Nevertheless, in the last ten years, the trustees have been able to undertake a major reroofing of the Orangery, where the leaking roof's cast-iron framing was fully refurbished and then re-glazed with double glazed units that help the house to be more environmentally conscious. In the last twelve months, at the time of writing, the cellar of the house has been reinvented as a space for more informal parties, with a new bar installed and new seating and dining spaces created, whilst the central roofs over the First and Second Salons are currently being prepared for major works funded by Historic England at the time of writing.

When Lady Anne, Viscountess Cowdray died in 2009, her family made a generous gift to the foundation in her memory. Lady Anne had been a devoted plant collector and gardener, creating a ten-acre garden at Broadleas, her Wiltshire home near Devizes. Here, she grew over forty different magnolias

FIGURE 192 In the Walled Garden, in tandem with the Granary Art Gallery, Meadow Arts worked with the Weston Park team in 2017 to create a response to the Capability Brown 300 celebrations in the previous year. The exhibition was called Synthetic Landscapes and amongst the highlights were works by Pablo Bronstein, including his *Chinese Bridges*, shown here. (Photo: Stefan Handy.)

FIGURE 193 Following the death of Lady Anne Cowdray, her family gave a generous gift which was used to develop the gardens, including the restoration of an eastern garden which became known as the Lady Anne Garden. The garden was formally opened in 2014 by HRH the Duke of Gloucester, photographed here with Lady Anne's son and daughter, Viscount Cowdray and the Hon. Mrs Teresa Stopford-Sackville, and (second from left) the then chairman of the Weston Park Foundation, William Montgomery. (Copyright Trustees of the Weston Park Foundation.)

FIGURE 194 In Temple Wood, the Lady Anne bequest was also employed in restoring the Garden of Memory, a rock garden laid out in memory of Lady Anne's sister Lady Joan Bridgeman. As a part of the works a new Chinese Bridge of oak was installed to link the garden to Temple Wood, replacing a twentieth-century bridge which was in disrepair and non-compliant for visitors with disabilities. (Copyright Trustees of the Weston Park Foundation.)

and her planting choices informed the restoration of the south-eastern garden
at Weston Park, which her family's gift funded and which became known as
the Lady Anne Garden. So generous was the funding that the foundation was
also able to commission a new oak Chinese Bridge across the western arm of
Temple Pool and to restore the Garden of Memory, the garden that had been
created in the memory of Lady Anne's sister Lady Joan.

The Victorian terraces have since had further works to improve their
design and planting, with the Italian garden reworked by Martin Gee and his
team with advice from Simon Gulliver. This has taken the garden closer to its
Victorian origins, with coloured gravel used in the central parterre and the
paths restored to their original widths, thus helping with the aesthetic of the
garden as a whole. On the south front, below the upper terrace, a rose garden
has been restored in 2018–19, following assistance from the rosarian Michael
Marriott, with roses supplied from the internationally celebrated David Austin
Roses which is within five miles of Weston.

The twenty-fifth anniversary of the Weston Park Foundation's establishment was marked by a redecoration of the entrance hall in 2011. This
followed paint analysis by Catherine Hassall and a competition for interior
decorators to pitch their schemes, the most sympathetic to the brief being that
put forward by John Fullick, which witnessed a mushroom damask wallpaper
being introduced, the return of pendant lighting and also the reintroduction
of an upholstered ottoman in the centre of the room, made for the space by
the Shropshire upholsterer John Allen.

FIGURE 195 In 2018–19 the lower south terrace rose garden was restored. Here head gardener Martin Gee is seen with rosarian
Michael Marriott who advised the trustees on planting. Roses were supplied by nearby David Austin Roses. (Copyright Trustees
of the Weston Park Foundation.)

Three years later the drawing room was redecorated. This was a room that had suffered with some water damage to walls and ceiling in the 1980s and in which the 1960s decoration had served its time. Janie Money from Sibyl Colefax & John Fowler devised a scheme with dragged pink walls – harkening back to the colour used in the 3rd Earl and Countess's time. A full Victorian restoration would have been impracticable, in view of the removal of decorative elements in the time of the 5th and 6th Earls, but the new scheme introduced its own highly successful swagged curtains to give the room a sense of feminine charm appropriate to the solely female sitters of the portraits in the room.

Decoration has always been an important part of Weston Park's zeitgeist. The family's custodianship was delivered with style and efficiency; each generation brought to the house the finest talent and craftsmanship of its day. It is, therefore, wholly correct that the foundation's trustees should also seek to bestow this upon the house, keeping the place relevant and comfortable for the guests who chose to stay at Weston Park and who, in turn, sustain the very fabric of the place. This has led to the house's twenty-eight bedrooms being decorated by a range of interior decorators who have each brought their own taste to the house to create rooms of individuality and yet which still, through their indigenous contents, embrace the history of the place. In recent years rooms have been decorated by Shirley Guy, Rita Konig and Lucinda Griffith – the variety of their schemes adding to the sense of continuity that Weston Park still conveys to its guests. This is true not only in the house but also in the follies

FIGURE 196 The entrance hall as redecorated to the design of John Fullick to mark the twenty-fifth anniversary of the Weston Park Foundation. (Paul Highnam/Copyright Trustees of the Weston Park Foundation.)

FIGURE 197 The drawing room following redecoration by Janie Money of Sibyl Colefax & John Fowler in 2014. The handsome swagged curtains formed a part of the redesign of the room. (Photographer: Simon Upton; Credit: Sibyl Colefax & John Fowler/Janie Money, associate design director.)

FIGURE 198 Selina Bedroom at Weston Park, redecorated by Rita Konig. (Copyright Trustees of the Weston Park Foundation.)

around the park. These, the buildings that caused so much concern to the early generation of trustees, have since become the satellite stars in Weston's galaxy, converted in the second decade of the new century to be holiday cottages and thus enabling a new level of access and enjoyment whilst, at the same time, helping to sustain their historic fabric from the income that they generate. In addition to the Temple of Diana, Knoll Tower and the Pink Cottage, two further buildings were created at the west side of the walled garden, with a lean-to structure cleverly reinvented at The Potting Shed and The Bothy by the architects Purcell.

Weston's role as a place of cultural excellence and, in many ways the ultimate art-hotel, has been defined by the property becoming an Arts Council accredited museum, whilst at the same time being a vibrant place of hospitality for visitors from around the globe. To some it is the place where they married, where they celebrated a key anniversary, or a place of happy memory. For others it is the place of solitude that enabled their conference or meeting to be a success. In the case of many global travellers, it has been their place to call home, surrounded by masterpieces, whilst enjoying a cultural tour of Shropshire. And, at the same time, it is a place of learning and discovery for all visitors from school age to retirees.

FIGURE 199 The greenhouse of the Temple of Diana as redecorated by Janie Money of Sibyl Colefax & John Fowler as a part of the reinvention of the building. A masterpiece of neo-classical architecture and a globally important garden building, the Temple is now available for guests to enjoy as a holiday cottage. (Photographer: Dylan Thomas; Credit: Sibyl Colefax & John Fowler/Janie Money, associate design director.)

FIGURE 200 Weston Park has welcomed cultural tour groups from around the globe, drawn by the attraction of staying amidst an important indigenous art collection in one of Britain's most significant country houses, and with notable private houses available in the locality for visiting itineraries. Here the patrons of WGBH Masterpiece – makers of television programmes that include *Downton Abbey* – are joined by members of the Albrighton Hunt who especially exercised their hounds for the entertainment of the guests. (Copyright Trustees of the Weston Park Foundation.)

Rose Paterson succeeded William Montgomery as chairman and, after a distinguished tenure in which she and the board not only witnessed significant growth of visitors and income but sought to protect the heritage assets from unsuitable development close to Weston Park, she retired from the role in 2019. She handed on the mantle to Christina Kenyon-Slaney, who had previously joined the board as a trustee. With Selina Graham, Mark Bridgeman, Andrew Kenyon, Charles Moyle and Nicholas Crawley, the trustees of the Weston Park Foundation and their team of staff have since faced the unprecedented challenge of the coronavirus pandemic. A period of uncertainty, where prediction has been all but useless, proved a unique challenge and one which, as with so many historic houses, has been supported by external agencies. Yet it has also enabled the charity to show a resilience and an ability to nimbly change and to adapt. Never before has the motto of Weston Park's donor family, the Earls of Bradford, ever been so apt: *Nec Temere Nec Timide* – neither rashly nor timidly.

Notes

CHAPTER ONE *Dramatis Personae*

1. Restoration of the church in 1877, however, did find fragments of Norman mouldings, now reset in the west tower's fabric. See Bridgeman, Rev. Ernest R.O. & Bridgeman, Charles G.O. (eds), 'History of the Manor and Parish of Weston-under-Lizard, in the County of Stafford compiled from the MSS. Of the Late Rev. The Hon. George T.O. Bridgeman Rector of Wigan', in *Collections for a History of Staffordshire*, Vol. XX (Vol. II New Series), London, 1899, pp. 310–11.
2. At Domesday, Weston had a population of ten villeins (tenants who held land in return for labour services) and two serfs. There was sufficient land for six plough teams and the manor was worth 40 shillings annually.
3. Bridgeman & Bridgeman (eds), op. cit., pp. 11–12.
4. Ibid., p. 13.
5. It was recorded by Garter King of Arms William Segar in 1632 when illustrated with the family's illuminated pedigree (BL Add MS 74251A).
6. The dates appear to stem from the 1632 pedigree by Segar and Lilly, although even in the late nineteenth century the authority of the monument was doubted. Bridgeman & Bridgeman (eds), op. cit., p. 14, wrote: 'These monuments are unfortunately of no great authority, as they were only put up by Dame Elizabeth Wilbraham when she restored the church … The effigies are apparently referenced in Lady Wilbraham's Palladio notes where she mentioned painting of "figures".'
7. Bridgeman & Bridgeman (eds), op. cit., p. 29.
8. Ibid., pp. 32–3.
9. Ibid., pp. 50–2.
10. Ibid., pp. 53–5, 330.
11. Ibid., p. 60.
12. Isabella now has a nineteenth-century head as a result of restoration by Hardman in 1876 – see Bridgeman & Bridgeman (eds), op. cit., pp. 310–11.
13. Ibid., p. 96.
14. BL Add MS 74251A The de Weston Illuminated Genealogy
15. Bridgeman & Bridgeman (eds), op. cit., pp. 330–1.

CHAPTER TWO *Powerful Patronage in the Provinces*

1. Plot, Robert, *The Natural History of Stafford-shire …*, Oxford, 1686, p. 359.
2. A portrait of the 4th Earl of Meath, attributed to Mary Beale, was recorded on the staircase at Castle Bromwich in an inventory of that house: SA D1287/4/1 (R/901).
3. See Hawkins, Edward (ed.), 'Travels in Holland the United Provinces England Scotland and Ireland …', in *Remains Historical & Literary Connected with the Palatine Counties of Lancaster and Chester Published by the Chetham Society, Vol. 1, 1844*.
4. Frederick William Willmore, *A History of Walsall and Its Neighbourhood*, Walsall & London, 1887, pp. 95–6.
5. It is possible that this was a posthumous gift since Pevsner records the church's flagon as hallmarked 1707–8.
6. Inventory number 118.0539.
7. See Smith, Peter, 'West Dean House, Wiltshire', *Georgian Group Journal*, Vol. IX (1999), pp. 86–106.
8. Morris, Christopher (ed.), *The Illustrated Journals of Celia Fiennes 1685–c.1712*, Stroud, 1995, p. 188. Fiennes also noted passing 'Mr Peirpoynts', i.e. Tong Castle.
9. Ibid.
10. Osborn fb214, Beinecke Rare Books Library, Yale University, New Haven, CT.
11. See Clarke, Bridget, 'William Taylor: New Discoveries', *Georgian Group Journal*, Vol. VIII (1998), pp. 1–11, and Harris, John, 'William Taylor: Further Attributions', *Georgian Group Journal*, Vol. VIII (1998), pp. 12–18; Hewlings, Richard, 'Achitapel's Architect', *Georgian Group Journal*, Vol. XVI (2008), pp. 3–4; and, most notably, Hewlings, Richard, 'The Architect of Weston Park', *Georgian Group Journal*, Vol. XIX (2012), pp. 22–32.
12. Myddelton, W.M. (ed.), *Chirk Castle Accounts AD 1666–1753*, Horncastle, 1931, pp. 100, 102, cited in Richard Hewlings, 'The Contriver of Chirk', in *National Trust Historic Houses and Collections Annual, Apollo*, June 2012.
13. Cited by Richard Hewlings in op. cit., June 2012.
14. Sir Christopher Wren was to propose a pair of giant flanking segmental pediments in his design of a stable for Charles II of the 1670s: collection of All Souls College, Oxford accession number 402 – AS II.100.
15. Smith, Peter, 'Rufford Abbey and its Gardens in the 17th and 18th Centuries', *English Heritage Historical Review*, Vol. 4 (2009), pp. 122–53.
16. SA D1287/4/1 (R/89).

17. William Salt Library Stafford SMS 454/33, John 2nd Viscount Masserene to John Swynfen, 16 April 1678.

18. Bridgeman, Rev. Ernest R.O. & Bridgeman, Charles G.O. (eds), 'History of the Manor and Parish of Weston-under-Lizard, in the County of Stafford compiled from the MSS. Of the Late Rev. The Hon. George T.O. Bridgeman Rector of Wigan', in *Collections for a History of Staffordshire*, Vol. XX (Vol. II New Series), London, 1899, p. 144.

19. J.M. Wright's letter to Sir Walter Bagot of Blithfield of 27 July 1676, cited by Smith, William James, 'Letters from Michael Wright', p. 234, *The Burlington Magazine*, Vol. 95, No. 604 (July 1953), p. 234.

20. SA D1287/18/4 (P/2002).

21. SA D1287/18/4 (P/2003).

22. See Rowell, Christopher (ed.), *Ham House: 400 Years of Collecting and Patronage*, New Haven, CT & London, 2013, pp. 280, 360.

23. SA D1287/19/3(P/1318), Commonplace book of Thomas Wilbraham of Woodhey 1640s, 'Sr Richard Wilbrahams Will'.

24. Bridgeman & Bridgeman, 1899, op. cit., p. 141.

25. The inner projections of Woodhey's entrance front and the *oeil-de-boeuf* windows recall similar features on the north and south fronts, respectively, of Ham House, Surrey, suggesting influence from Lord Huntingtower, later Earl of Dysart who in 1680 had married the Wilbraham's daughter Grace.

26. Bridgeman & Bridgeman, 1899, op. cit., p. 142.

27. SA D1287/8/5 (M/645).

28. See Whitehead, David, 'Job Marston's Chapel', *Georgian Group Journal*, Vol. II (1992), pp. 79–81.

29. Geoffrey Fisher, formerly on the staff of the Conway Library, Courtauld Institute of Art, has attributed both of the large east end monuments to Joshua Marshall (1628–1678) since the escutcheons and the lettering style of the Mytton monument corresponds to Marshall's oeuvre, and he suggests a date from the mid-1660s – pre-dating the rebuilding of the church itself. Joshua Marshall's father Edward (1597/8–1675) is credited with the family monument of Lady Wilbraham's father-in-law Sir Thomas Wilbraham, 2nd Bt (1601–1660) at St Mary's Church, Acton, Cheshire.

CHAPTER THREE *Civil War and Restoration*

1. J.M. Shuttleworth (ed.), *The Life of Edward, First Lord Herbert of Cherbury Written by Himself*, London, New York & Toronto, 1976, p. 8.

2. Georgiana Blakiston, *Woburn and the Russells*, London, 2000, p. 64.

3. Richard Gough, *Human Nature Displayed in the History of Myddle*, New York, 1968, p. 40.

4. See W. Phillips (ed.), 'Sequestration Papers of Sir Richard, First Baron Newport and Francis, his Son', *TSANHS*, 2nd Series, XII (1900), pp. 1–38. The fine was reduced by the House of Commons from £16,687.

5. PRO, L.C. 5/139, p. 368.

6. PRO, L.C. 5/140, p. 203 – 28 February, 1672–3.

7. G.C. Baugh (ed.), *Victoria County of Shropshire*, Vol. XI, Oxford, 1985, pp. 98–9. This was located just south of High Ercall.

8. Created for the Shrewsbury ironmaster William Hazledine, during his tenure at the house. Ex inf. Andrew Arrol.

9. John Macky, *Memoirs of the Secret Services of John Macky, Esq., During the Reigns of King William, Queen Anne, and King George I*, London, 1733, p. 58. Both Francis and his wife were immensely cultured people. Lady Newport became, as Pepys's diary 11 June 1679 reveals, a godparent to 'Poor Billy', Sir Christopher Wren's son, in 1679.

10. Vertue Note Books Vol. V, *Walpole Society* (26th Vol.), Oxford, 1938, p. 55. Vertue lists van Dyck's 'Tho Killigrew and a Mastiff – 83' as amongst the notable works and this was a Newport purchase which is currently hanging at Weston Park.

11. Graham sold the work on in 1712 through Peletier London, 6 March 1712, lot 41, and it was acquired by the Child family, descendants of whom sold the picture at Sotheby's on 9 December 2009, lot 8, whereafter it was acquired for the British nation with assistance from Art Fund.

12. Oliver Millar, 'Van Dyck and Thomas Killigrew', *The Burlington Magazine*, Vol. 105, No. 726 (Sept. 1963), p. 409.

13. Diana Dethloff, 'The Dispersal of Sir Peter Lely's Collection', *Journal of the History of Collections*, Vol. 8, no. 1 (1996), p. 18.

14. Milo Keynes, 'The Portrait of Dr William Harvey in the Royal Society Since 1683', *Notes & Records of the Royal Society*, Vol. 60, No. 3 (22 Sept. 2006), p. 251.

15. Mary Beal, 'The Royalist Richard Symonds and an Unclaimed Portrait by Sir Peter Lely', *The British Art Journal*, Vol. XVII, No. 1 (Spring 2016), pp. 16–21.

16. See Vertue Note Books Vol. IV, *Walpole Society* (24th Vol.), Oxford, 1936, p. 69: 'Lord Bradford bought several good pictures out of Holland house.'

17. Ashmolean accession WA1938.43.

18. www.gutenberg.org/files/42081/42081-h/42081-h.htm.

19. Referenced in a codicil of Francis Newport, 1st Earl of Bradford's will, inserted in 1705: NA PROB 11/569 sig.116.

20. Accession number 1952.5.39.

21. Accession number F.1969.18.P. The work had a brief return to Shropshire in the nineteenth century when it was in the collection of the Heywood-Lonsdale family of Shavington Hall.

22. Respectively, National Gallery of Scotland NG2281; Staedel 2024: 2054: 2118: 2119: 2131: 2140: 2142; Fitzwilliam 532 and 539.

23. Edward Ironside, *History and Antiquities of Twickenham ...*, London, 1797, p. 78.

24. Vertue Note Books Vol. I, *Walpole Society* (18th Vol.), Oxford, 1930, p. 31.

25. Churchill was probably known to Bradford; he had other Shropshire links in being a friend of Richard Hill of Hawkstone and his portrait can still be found in the saloon of that north Shropshire house.

26. Sue Hamilton-Miller, *Richmond House and its Inhabitants*, Richmond, n.d., p. 10.

27. G.C. Baugh (ed.), *A History of Shropshire*, vol. XI, Oxford, 1985, p. 183.
28. NA PROB 11/569 sig.116.
29. www.pepysdiary.com/diary/1668/05/30/.
30. Sharp Brown, Ralph and Sheldon Lewis, Wilmarth (eds), *Horace Walpole's Correspondence with George Montagu*, New Haven, CT, 1941, p. 135.
31. These comprised: 'General Monk, in armour to the knees ... by Sir Peter Lely. General Lambert, in armour to the knees; by Walker. Lord Falkland ... by Vandyke. Sir George Byng; Lord Viscount Torrington; Admiral Russell; Earl of Orford; and a son of Lord Torrington examining a globe; view of the sea and ships at a distance by Sir Peter Lely. Queen Mary, when princess, full length; by Sir Godfrey Kneller. A picture representing the departure of Cleopatra from Mark Anthony; by Lorenzo de Castro ... Charles II. James II. Princess Mary, when children; copy from Vandyke. Representation of a bull fight at Madrid in Spain, with the king, queen, and court, viewing it. The four seasons, representing four satyrs, composed of various fruits and flowers, so judiciously blended together as to resemble a human figure ... Several small portraits of the ladies of the court of Charles II. drawings in crayons, with this mark, B; by Sir Peter Lely. Queen Mary I. small. A pope. Two pictures of boys. Marquis of Graham, when young. Lot and his daughters. A landscape, figures, and cattle.' Edward Ironside, op cit., pp. 76–7. The portrait of Byng, Torrington and Russell, given in the inventories as by 'Baker' (i.e. John James Baker) is conceivably the painting in the Government Art Collection GAC 6436 which is currently said to depict Orford, Benbow and Delavall.
32. Horace Walpole, *Anecdotes of Painting in England in 4 Volumes*, Vol. II, New York, 1969, p. 71, fn. 2, 72; Vertue had also observed this picture – see Vertue Note Books Vol. II, *Walpole Society* (20th Vol.), Oxford, 1932, p. 142.
33. Ibid., p. 72, fn. 1.

CHAPTER FOUR *The Early Bridgemans*

1. Bridgeman, The Hon. & Rev. George T.O., *The History of the Church and Manor of Wigan in the County of Lancaster*, Vols 15, 16, 17, 18, Chetham Society, Manchester, 1888, p. 183.
2. Ibid., p. 184.
3. Farrer, William and Brownbill, J. (eds), *A History of the County of Lancaster: Volume 4*, London, 1911, pp. 68–78.
4. Ibid., pp. 57–68.
5. This picture, painted as a pendant to that of his wife Elizabeth Helyar, appears to date from 1616, when he became Rector of Wigan, and noted 'for my wife's picture drawing & my own 55s 11'. See Bridgeman, The Hon. & Rev. George T.O., op. cit., p. 201 and fn. 11. A further portrait was recorded by him as being painted in 1619, for which he paid 35 shillings and this is probably the painting in the present Bishop's Palace at Chester. See Canon Bridgeman, op cit., p. 237 and fn. 1.
6. His ledgers are located in SA D1287/3/1 (F/632) and BA ZBR/3/1, with a further eighteenth-century copy to be found at Wigan Archives.
7. Bridgeman, The Hon. & Rev. George T.O., op. cit., p. 724.
8. Ibid., p. 305.
9. Ibid., p. 455.
10. Cited in ibid., p. 331 and www.pepysdiary.com/diary/1662/11/10/. Swinfen in fact mistook Bishop John for his son Bishop Henry Bridgeman.
11. Bridgeman, The Hon. & Rev. George T.O., op. cit., p. 337.
12. For instance, BA ZBR/5/1 Agreements for working the coal at Farnworth 13 Feb 1636/7.
13. Bridgeman, The Hon. & Rev. George T.O., op. cit., p. 387.
14. Ibid., p. 394.
15. Dr William Harvey's portrait hangs in the collection at Weston Park; it was acquired by Francis Newport, 1st Earl of Bradford of the first creation (see Chapter 4).
16. Bridgeman, Rev. Ernest R.O. & Bridgeman, Charles G.O. (eds), 'History of the Manor and Parish of Weston-under-Lizard, in the County of Stafford compiled from the MSS. Of the Late Rev. The Hon. George T.O. Bridgeman Rector of Wigan', in *Collections for a History of Staffordshire*, Vol. XX (Vol. II New Series), London, 1899, p. 225.
17. Bridgeman, The Hon. & Rev. George T.O., op cit., pp. 436–7.
18. Ibid., p. 477.
19. Ibid., p. 493.
20. 31 August 1667: www.pepysdiary.com/diary/1667/08/31/.
21. 4 September 1667: www.pepysdiary.com/diary/1667/09/04/.
22. The burse seems to have passed to a younger son of the second baronet, Orlando Bridgeman of Clifton, since it was amongst the effects of his widow Catherine at her house in Cavendish Square in 1742. See SA D1287/4/1(R/77) 'An old purse for the Great Seal'.
23. PROB 11/345/321 Will of Sir Orlando Bridgeman, 4 July 1674.
24. Bridgeman House, Teddington, where Sir Orlando is thought to have lived, was demolished in 1911.
25. Dugdale cited in Anon., 'Castle Bromwich Hall', *Country Life*, 17 August 1921, p. 228.
26. Ibid.
27. See Beard, Geoffrey, 'William Winde and Interior Design', in *Architectural History*, vol. 27, *Design and Practice in British Architecture: Studies in Architectural History Presented to Howard Colvin* (1984), pp. 150–62; Barre, D.C. and Chaplin, R.A. (eds), 'William Winde: Advice on Fashionable Interior Decoration: Winde–Bridgeman Correspondence for Castle Bromwich Hall 1685–1703', typescript, 1983. The original correspondence is in SA D1287/18/4 (P/1083).
28. Lady Bridgeman to Winde, late June/July 1688.
29. The statues were supplied in 1697 at a cost of 12 guineas.

30. Friedman, Terry, *James Gibbs*, New Haven, CT & London, 1984, p. 324.

31. Stamper, Dr Paul, 'Blodwell Hall', Report for Shropshire Sites and Monuments Record, 1994.

32. The greenhouse has Sir John's marital arms whilst the summer house has the arms of Sir Orlando Bridgeman,

CHAPTER FIVE *Georgian Weston*

1. www.british-history.ac.uk/survey-london/vols29-30/pt1/pp154-159 accessed 27 June 2021.

2. Bridgeman, The Hon. and Rev. G.T.O., *Genealogical Account of the Family of Newport of High Ercall, in the County of Salop, afterwards Earls of Bradford*, printed by W.J. Rowley, High Street, Bridgnorth, nd (1851), p. 34.

3. Ingamells, John, *A Dictionary of British and Irish Travellers in Italy 1701–1800*, New Haven, CT and London, 1997, p. 705.

4. Garbet, Samuel, *The History of Wem*, Shrewsbury, 1982, p. 106.

5. NA SP 36/48/170 Folio 170 Memorial from Ann Smyth to the Duke of Newcastle.

6. Garbet, op. cit., p. 107.

7. SA D1287/5/3(P/371) Copy will of Mary Newport, Countess of Bradford 8 Oct 1737.

8. Bridgeman, The Hon. and Rev. G.T.O., op cit., p. 34.

9. Garbet, op. cit., pp. 107–8.

10. SA D1287/4/1 (R/89) 1762 Inventory.

11. SA 5735/5/1/2/21 Letter from Hutton Perkins to Sir Hugh Brigges, 21 April 1748.

12. The Bridgeman's Soho Square house collapsed in 1725 whilst Lady Ann 'great with child' was resident. She – and the future 5th baronet – escaped although her housekeeper was killed. *Whitehall Evening Post*, 7 August 1725.

13. SA D1287/5/3(P/371) Copy will of Mary Newport, Countess of Bradford 8 Oct 1737.

14. Ibid.

15. Bridgeman, Rev. Ernest R.O. & Bridgeman, Charles G.O. (eds), 'History of the Manor and Parish of Weston-under-Lizard, in the County of Stafford compiled from the MSS. Of the Late Rev. The Hon. George T.O. Bridgeman Rector of Wigan', in *Collections for a History of Staffordshire*, Vol. XX (Vol. II New Series), London, 1899, p. 267. Sir Henry went on to add to the Weston estate with acquisitions of property at Blymhill (including the advowson) and also land at Brockhurst (see p. 271).

16. SA D1287/6/64/7 and 8 Leases relating to Sir Henry Bridgeman's Ham house, plus advertisement for sale of garden paraphernalia by Mr Willock, on Sir Henry's behalf at 'his late Mansion-house, the Entrance of Clapham Common', in *Public Advertiser*, 28 July 1775.

17. John Bridgeman Simpson also became the heir to Bilton Hall, Warwickshire on the death of Miss Simpson in 1797. She was the daughter of Addison – who bought Bilton in 1711 – and his wife, Charlotte, Countess of Warwick and Holland (a daughter of Sir Thomas Middleton and Charlotte daughter of Sir Orlando Bridgeman, 1st Bt). Orlando, 1st Earl of Bradford, John Bridgeman Simpson's brother, was also a personal representative of Miss Simpson and was instrumental

4th Bt and his wife Lady Anne Newport, whom he had married in 1719.

33. Lines, Charles, *Weston Park and the Earls of Bradford*, Leamington Spa, 1972, pp. 22–3.

in commissioning Westmacott's monument to Joseph Addison for Poet's Corner, Westminster Abbey. See SA D1287/18/8 (P/277) Correspondence of 1806–8.

18. Markham, Sarah, *John Loveday of Caversham 1711–1789*, pp. 490–1, 444–5.

19. Beard, Geoffrey W., 'Weston Hall: Staffordshire Home of the Earl of Bradford', in *The Connoisseur Year Book, 1955*, London, 1955, p. 25.

20. SA D1287/19/1(P/1211) Journal of Lady Elizabeth Bridgeman 1787–8 – 4 August 1788 'began a letter to Ganny abt the Pine apples sent to B'.

21. Bridgeman, Rev. Ernest R.O. & Bridgeman Charles G.O. (eds), op. cit., p. 335.

22. SA D1287/3/50(F/163) John Heaton's accounts. A Coadestone vase costing £48 18s was also paid for in 1777 but this can no longer be traced at Weston (F/162).

23. The date appears on rainwater heads at the house.

24. Lady Bridgeman notes his work at both Ham and Weston, including 'Papier Mashier ornament for the top of the dining room' in her 1766 diary SA D1287/19/2A(P/1159). Paine also surveyed the house of Sir Henry Bridgeman's brother George Bridgeman (1727–1767) in South Street in 1776, the house having passed to Sir Henry on his brother's death (SA D1287/4/1 (R/92)). In the 1780s, the family turned to John Carr of York for advice. See SA D1287/2/1(E/80) John Carr Report on roof and chimneys 8 Nov. 1784.

25. V & A accession 3310.

26. SA D1287/3/50(F/161) includes a payment of a gratuity to 'Mrs Yeats' in July 1775. Another lady who received benefits from the family was Catherine Hughes, who lived in the Cave at Nesscliffe in the 1780s. See SA D1287/1/28 G/90 Henry Bowman's Estate Accounts 1782. The cave, even in 1828 (SA D1287/1/31 G/129), was listed in the estate accounts as being assigned to the 'overseers of the poor'.

27. SA D1287/4/1/R71, R72, R73.

28. Leach, Peter, *James Paine*, London, 1988, pp. 215, 219.

29. Exhibited at the Society of Artists 1772. Waterhouse, E.K., *Painting in Britain 1530–1790*, London, 1994, p. 242, illustrated in *Country Life*, 26 April 1946, p. 760.

30. Robinson, John Martin, *Georgian Model Farms*, Oxford, 1983, p. 79 saw similarities with William Kent's Horse Guards, Whitehall.

31. Hussey, Christopher, 'Weston Park, Staffordshire I', *Country Life*, 9 November 1945, p. 821.

32. These were probably works undertaken in 1777; see Robinson, op. cit., p. 143.

33. www.search.staffspasttrack.org.uk/details.aspx?ResourceID=24666&ExhibitionPage=2&PageIndex=6&SearchType=2&ThemeID=750.

34. Bell, Mrs G.H. (ed.), *The Hamswood Papers of the Ladies of Llangollen and Caroline Hamilton*, London, 1930, p. 62.

35. Letter from Miss Katharine M.R. Kenyon, The Drove, Twyford, Winchester, published in *Country Life* – from a cutting at Weston Park and Mavor, Elizabeth, *A Year with the Ladies of Llangollen*, Harmondsworth, 1984, p. 181. The friendship with the Ladies continued into the next generation, evidenced by a letter thanking the 2nd Lord and Lady Bradford in 1825 for a hare and brace of pheasants at Christmas: SA D1287/18/18(P/1029) 4 Letters from Ladies of Llangollen.

36. Chappelow was the great uncle and encourager of Rev. Leonard Jenyns (later Blomefield) who was the intended naturalist on HMS *Beagle*.

37. Ingamells, John, *A Dictionary of British and Irish Travellers in Italy, 1701–1800*, New Haven, CT and London, 1997, p. 196.

38. Bloom, Edward A. & Bloom, Lillian D., *The Piozzi Letters Vol. 3 1799–1804*, Newark, DE, London and Toronto, 1993, p. 267.

39. A painting of Lichfield Cathedral in the collection has Anna Seward provenance and she also wrote lines on the death of John Bridgeman Simpson's first wife; see Scott, Walter (ed.), *The Poetical Works of Anna Seward*, Vol. II, Edinburgh, 1810, p. 190.

40. Bridgeman & Bridgeman, 1899, op. cit., p. 278.

41. SA D1287/4/1/R71, R72, R73.

42. See Goodison, Nicholas, *Matthew Boulton: Ormolu*, London, 2002, p. 191.

43. Ibid., p. 407.

44. Beard, Geoffrey W., 'Weston Hall, Staffordshire', in L.G.G. Ramsey (ed.), *The Connoisseur Year Book 1955*, p. 27.

45. Dr Kenneth Quickenden has also noted references to the purchase of a silver coffee pot and stand in October 1774 and also the supply of silver prongs for fork handles supplied by Lady Bridgeman in December 1774; Matthew Boulton Papers, Central Library, Birmingham (MS3782/1/10 pp. 166–7 and pp. 208–9).

46. SA D1287/19/1(P/1215).

47. Sold, respectively, Christie's King Street, London, 15 November 1978, lot 66 and 25 October, lot 283.

48. SA D1287/4/1/R71 1777 Inventory of Weston Hall 'Two Favourite Horses painted on Canvas' in the dining room.

49. The Greek key carved waists also appear on documented hall chairs supplied by Chippendale to Nostell and Harewood.

50. SA D1287/3/50(F/164) Gillow and Co., 22 Sept. 1786 £36–4–6 and 30 Sept. £37–18.

51. Sir Henry set out for Paris, 4 May 1766; SA D1287/19/2A(P/1159). He also undertook a tour of the Low Countries and France from August to October 1784; his journal is at SA D1287/19/1(P/1212).

52. Adam's bill was settled by John Heaton, 21 August 1777 (SA D1287/3/50(F/161), whilst John Wright 'Plaisterer' was paid for work at Weston on 18 Sept 1778 (F/163). SA D1287/3/11A(R/301) George Halley's Painting at Weston Hall 1767–1775.

53. Hussey, Christopher, 'Weston Park Staffordshire II', *Country Life*, 16 November 1945, p. 865 erroneously suggests that they were in a first-floor bedroom when first installed.

54. SA D1287/4/1 (R/71) Inventory of Weston Hall 22 May 1771.

55. Andrews, C. Bruyn (ed.), *The Torrington Diaries*, vol. 3, New York and London, 1970, p. 303.

56. The Hamilton Kerr Institute's in situ cleaning of the painting in 2014 enabled identification by Dr Martin Perkins of the Royal Birmingham Conservatoire.

57. The scores in the collection at Weston date back to 1685. For a full discussion of Sir Henry and his family's music-making, see Fleming, Simon D.I. and Perkins, Martin (eds), *Music by Subscription: Composers and their Networks in the British Music-Publishing Trade, 1676–1820*, Oxford and London, 2022 (forthcoming), chapter 8.

58. BL g.192.a.(22).

59. Ibid.

60. WRO CR 1291/437 Memoranda book Henry Greswold Lewis.

61. Leslie, C.R., *Memoirs of the Life of John Constable*, London, 1937.

62. See Pritchard, T.W., *Wynnstay and the Wynns*, Caerwys, 1982, p. 114.

63. *Derby Mercury*, Friday 15 September 1775.

64. SA D1287/3/50 (F/161) 1776 'July 22 paid a subscription towards building a Bridge across the Severn £50'.

65. The family also took friends to see the Ironbridge Gorge, Lady Bridgeman noting on 2 July 1789 'went with George Mr Gregory & Fisher to ye Ironbridge saw with them the Iron works'; Diary – SA D1287/19/1(P/1216).

66. Bridgeman, The Hon. & Rev. G.T.O, *The History of the Church and Manor of Wigan in the County of Lancaster*, Vols 15, 16, 17, 18, Chetham Society, Manchester, 1888, p. 395, citing Dorning Rowbotham's comments in 1788.

67. Aiken, John, *A Description of the Country from Thirty to Forty Miles Round Manchester*, London, 1792, pp. 261–2.

68. He shared the seat with George Byng until September 1780 when Hon. Horatio Walpole, later 2nd Earl of Orford, was elected.

69. Bridgeman, The Hon. and Rev. G.T.O., op. cit., p. 644.

70. Boyle, K.C.B., Sir Courtenay, *Mary Boyle: Her Book*, London, 1902, p. 56.

71. www.british-history.ac.uk/survey-london/vols29-30/pt1/pp154-159, accessed 27 June 2021.

72. SA D1287/19/2A(P/1159) 1766 Diary.

73. SA D1287/19/1(P/1199) Pocket Companion & Almanack.

74. SA D1287/19/1/1214.

75. SA D1287/19/1(P/1216) – second booklet.

76. SA D1287/19/1(P/1216).

77. SA D1287/3/50(F166) A payment 'for your newly furnished house in New Burlington street' was made to Mr Squibb in July 1795.

78. 10 July 1789: 'the India paper in my bed chamber takd down' D1287/19/1(P/1216).

79. Bloom, Edward A. & Bloom, Lillian D., *The Piozzi Letters, Vol. 1 1784–1791*, Newark, DE, London & Toronto, 1989, p. 252, LC to HLP 19 March 1795.

80. Bloom, Edward A. & Bloom, Lillian D., *The Piozzi Letters Vol. 4 1805–1810*, Newark, DE, London and Toronto, 1996, p. 85, n. 10.

CHAPTER SIX *The Early Nineteenth Century*

1. SA D1287/19/1(P/1215).
2. Ibid.
3. Ibid.
4. SA D1287/19/1(P/1199) Pocket Companion & Almanack.
5. Wilkins, W.H., *Mrs Fitzherbert & George IV*, Vol. I, London, 1905, p. 97.
6. Bloom, Edward A. and Bloom, Lillian D., *The Piozzi Letters Vol. 3 1799–1804*, Newark, DE, London and Toronto, 1993, p. 350, HLP to LC 1 May 1802.
7. Linnell 'extremely gladly accepted the order of sending down his people to finish the Great House', cited in Moore, Gerry and Twist, Anthony, *Weeting Worthies*, Weeting History Group, 2004, pp. 39–40.
8. SA D1287/18/20 P/887h. Lady Bradford to the Hon. George Bridgeman 25 March 1802.
9. SA D1287/18/13 P/869p, Charles Bridgeman to Lady Bradford dated 17 October 1807 from the 'Repulse, off Sicily'.
10. Ingamells, John, *A Dictionary of British and Irish Travellers in Italy 1701–1800*, New Haven, CT and London 1997, p. 215.
11. Colvin, Howard, *A Biographical Dictionary of British Architects 1600–1840*, New Haven, CT and London, 2008, p. 1110.
12. Building accounts that also reference Richard Westmacott, Francesco Bernasconi, Thomas Papworth and Joseph Bramah are at SA D1287/R/313.
13. SA D1287/18/20 P/887a. Lady Bradford to the Hon. George Bridgeman 2 Feb. 1802. The painter mentioned was Thomas Weaver.
14. SA D1287/18/20 P/887i. Lady Bradford to the Hon. George Bridgeman 31 March 1802.
15. SA D1287/3 (P/100) Account Book of Lady Bradford. The Apollo clock garniture is almost identical to another, also with movement by Charles-Guillaume Manière, in the collection at Uppark, West Sussex supplied in 1803, whilst two further examples – one of sienna rather than griotte marble – are owned by the Royal Collection Trust. An ink stand, sold as lot 188, at Christie's South Kensington's on the premises sale at Weston Park on 13/14 May 1986 was also probably supplied by Lignereux.
16. A related pair can be found in the Wallace Collection, whilst a further pair was sold by Sotheby's New York, 21 May 2004 as lot 102.
17. A similar circular table, based upon a design by Charles Percier (1764–1838), is in the collection of the Victoria and Albert Museum, London W.13–1939. The family were also making acquisitions of silver to add to the plate collection, including items from the Royal silversmiths Rundells and pieces by Paul Storr. Pre-eminent amongst items that have comparable related pieces in the royal collection is a set of three sideboard chargers by William Pitts, hallmarked 1821. These depict the *Rape of Europa* and a *Meeting of the Gods: Jupiter, Juno, Diana, Neptune and Venus holding Cupid*.
18. SA D1287/3/37 (P/134) Lord Bradford's misc. vouchers for personal and household expenditure 1803–23.
19. SA D1287/3/13 R/316 Furnishing supplied by Morel & Hughes for Weston Hall, 4 June 1805.
20. These, and the Weston Morel & Hughes commission, are described by Rogers, Phillis, 'A Regency Interior: The Remodelling of Weston Park', *Furniture History*, Vol. XXIII (1987), pp. 11–34.
21. SA D1287/3/413 (R/320).
22. SA D1287/18/13 P/869p, Charles Bridgeman to Lady Bradford dated 17th October 1807 from the 'Repulse, off Sicily'.
23. SA D1287/3/13/11A (R/300) Joshua Jowett Bill Jan–June 1806.
24. SA D1287/18/8(P/867) Letter to Sir Henry Bridgeman addressed 'My Lord' – therefore post-1794 when the barony of Bradford was created
25. SA D1287/18/20 P/890d. Lady Bradford to the Hon. George Bridgeman 20 January 1813.
26. Southall, Mark & Maddocks, Robert (eds), *Extracts from the Personal Diary between the Years 1817–1862 of Edward Walhouse Littleton afterwards The First Lord Hatherton 1791–1863*, nd, entry for 13 February 1840, where Littleton notes Webb's involvement twenty years earlier and how the trees had grown poorly due to bad soil.
27. *Red Book* for Babworth in a private collection. The 'Swiss Cottage' added by John Bridgeman Simpson is referenced in Piercy, John S., *The History of Retford*, Retford, 1828, p. 201.
28. Leighton, Rachel (ed.), *Correspondence of Charlotte Grenville, Lady Williams-Wynn and Her Three Sons*, London, 1920, p. 232.
29. Pitt, William, *A Topographical History of Staffordshire ...*, Newcastle-under-Lyme, 1817, p. 94.
30. SA D1287/18/24 (Q/25).
31. William Pitt, op. cit., 1817, p. 94.
32. See McGuffie, T.H., 'The Lord Bradford Militia Documents in the Shire Hall, Shrewsbury, Salop', *Journal of the Society for Army Historical Research*, Vol. XLIV, No. 179 (September 1966), pp. 135–146.
33. Bloom, Edward A. and Bloom, Lillian D., *The Piozzi Letters Vol. 4 1805–1810*, Newark, DE, London and Toronto, 1996, p. 239, n. 5.
34. His letters have been edited and published: Glover, Gareth, *A Young Gentleman at War: The Letters of Captain Orlando Bridgeman 1st Foot Guards in the Peninsula and at Waterloo*, Ken Trotman Publishing, 2008.
35. Bloom, Edward A. and Bloom, Lillian D., *The Piozzi Letters Vol. 4 1805–1810*, Newark, DE, London and Toronto, 1996, p. 256, n. 8.
36. Bloom, Edward A. and Bloom, Lillian D., *The Piozzi Letters Vol. 5 1811–1816*, Newark, DE & London, 1999, p. 425.
37. BA ZBR/5/2/1 Copy of Letter to Ed Charlton, 29 Oct 1804.
38. SA D1287/3/21 R/399 Continental Trip expenses.
39. Bloom, Edward A. and Bloom, Lillian D., *The Piozzi Letters Vol. 5 1811–1816*, Newark, DE and London, 1999, p. 255 n. 7. LC letter to HLP of 29 April 1814. Mrs Piozzi also commented in the following month: 'Lord Bradford makes himself amends in his gay Moments for the Depression he feels in the melancholy ones.' Bloom, Edward A. and Bloom, Lillian D., *The Piozzi Letters Vol. 5 1811–1816*, Newark, DE and London, 1999, p. 254, HLP to LC 2 May 1814.

40. SA D1287/3/21 R/399 Continental Trip expenses.

41. SA D1287/18/11 P/837c. Part 1 of 4. George, Viscount Newport to Lady Bradford in Brussels, 5 March 1817.

42. Southall, Mark & Maddocks, Robert (eds), *Extracts from the Personal Diary between the Years 1817–1862 of Edward Walhouse Littleton afterwards The First Lord Hatherton 1791–1863*, Trowbridge, nd, entry for 28 December 1818 notes that the Bradfords had been abroad for four years.

43. SA D1287/3/37 (P/134) Lord Bradford's misc. vouchers for personal and household expenditure 1803–23. Fogg's bill also included '2 Japan figures with Gourds' which remain in the collection at Weston Park.

44. SA D1287/18/12 P/936c Chappelow to Piozzi, London, 12 June 1820.

CHAPTER SEVEN *A Changing World*

1. SA D1287/18/11 P/836y. Viscount Newport to Countess of Bradford, 22 November 1816: 'I cannot say I am glad my Father has got a picture of the Desolater of Europe; since when has he become Napoleon's advocate? I wish every image of that enemy of mankind were burnt and destroyed with every memento of him, but all people do not agree in this opinion with me.'

2. George Gybbon Potter, Edward Gybbon Potter and Charles Potter followed in succession. See Rogers, Cathal, 'Land Agents and Urban Aristocratic Estates in Nineteenth Century Staffordshire: a Comparison of Longton and Walsall', PhD thesis, University of Keele, 2018, p. 43.

3. SA D1287/18/K75 Bill of sale for 2/3 January 1826.

4. SA D1287/18/11 P/836w, Viscount Newport to Lord Bradford, 13.11.1816.

5. SA D1287/18/11 P/836o, Viscount Newport to Countess Bradford, 4.9.1816.

6. Rogers, Cathal, 2018, op. cit., pp. 268–9.

7. Ibid, p. 68.

8. See Potter's intent in a letter of April 1826: SA D1287/12/1/K/227 Letter Peter Potter to Lord Bradford, 25 April 1826.

9. These villas included the birthplace of the writer Jerome K. Jerome (1859–1927). They originally had uninterrupted views over the former racecourse prior to its destruction when the railways were later built.

10. SA D1287/18/24 K/79 59/21 Letter No: 1966 and BA ZBR/5/2/19 Letter from Peter Potter to Earl of Bradford, 19 December 1830.

11. Collection of BA.

12. WLHC 59/21 Letter Potter to Cory, 11 Feb 1831.

13. Ex inf Bolton Museums. It was enlarged in 1838 and 1864.

14. Here the family contributed £500 to building costs.

15. St Stephens & All Martyrs site was donated plus £500 in 1845; St Simon & St Jude's site was gifted in 1898; St Michael's church site and £1,000 was gifted by the family and the church consecrated in 1851. The church now has a bell cast for Ralph Assheton to go in Great Lever Hall Chapel in the sixteenth century, which was gifted to the church by the 6th Earl of Bradford.

16. Lewis, Samuel, *A Topographical Dictionary of England*, London, 1848, pp. 74–8. Bridgeman, The Hon. & Rev. George T.O., *The History of the Church and Manor of Wigan in the County of Lancaster*, Vols 15, 16, 17, 18, Chetham Society, Manchester, 1888, p. 395 suggested that the conversion took place in 1852 and that it remained until 1862 when the new school opened.

17. Later renamed St Mark's.

18. Ex inf Bolton Documentary Photography.

19. BA ZBR/5/5/14 Letter Lord Bradford to George Pigott, 2 September 1844.

20. BA ZBR/5/8/10 Memo of George Pigott relating to mines, 22 July 1847.

21. BA ZBR/5/2/35 Memo of agreement by Peter Potter for Bradford with Andrew Knowles, 7 November 1833 leasing Three Yards, Three Feet, and Six Feet Coalmines in Darcy Lever; agreement with Mr Smith to use the waterfall and waterwheel at Great Lever Works to pump out mines.

22. BA ZBR/5/7/2 George Pigott letter to Bailey, Shaw & Smith, 31 January 1846.

23. Ex inf. Bolton Documentary Photography.

24. Various studies have been undertaken into the importance of the Bradford estate in Walsall. See, for instance, Tucker, Alan, 'The Economic Exploitation of the Earl of Bradford's Walsall Estate (1802–1865)', MA thesis, Wolverhampton Polytechnic, 1983, and Rogers, Cathal, op. cit.

25. Glew, Edward Lees, *History of the Borough and Foreign of Walsall*, Walsall, 1856, p. 25.

26. SA D1287/M/686 Plan, elevation and section of a hothouse at Castle Bromwich by Jones & Clark.

27. SA D1287/M/385 Elevation of West front of Weston Park, Rickman and Hutchinson; SA D1287/3/38 (R/616) Letters from Rickman re Weston 1834; SA D1287/18/25 (Q/57) Letters to 2nd Earl from Rickman repointing of Weston 1832; SA D1287/3/38 (R/3602) Rickman's Account for repairs and alterations at Weston 1830–33; SA D1287/3/32 (R/538) Corresp with Rickman re Weston 1831–33.

28. WLHC Accession 59/21 Letter No: 1915 Potter to Rickman & Hutchinson, 10 November 1830.

29. The carpet remains at Weston Park and is now in store. The desk is now in the collection at Waddesdon Manor, Bucks, and is used in the academic library of that house.

45. SA D1287/4/2 (R/127) Import details of items October 1821 to October 1823; D1287/4/2 (R/144) list of prints from Geneva; D1287/4/4 (R/274) alabasters 1822; D1287/4/4 (R/741) list of pictures 1822; D1287/4/1 (R/104) pictures bought at Genoa from Madame Costa.

46. Since retained by the Bradford family and sold; Bernardo Strozzi, *The Crucifixion: Christ on the Cross with Saints Mary Magdalene, Nicholas of Tolentino and Peter* (lot 49, Sotheby's London, 12 December 2002).

47. The Weston Park modello was exhibited at the Iveagh Bequest, Kenwood, 1993, no. 26.

48. SA D1287/4/4 (R/288).

49. *The Sporting Magazine*, Vol. 12 (1823), p. 264.

50. *Gentleman's Magazine* (1825), p. 371.

30. Bradford, Lady Ida, Countess of, 'Castle Bromwich Hall, Warwickshire: A Property of the Earl of Bradford', reprinted from an article published in the *Pall Mall Magazine*, 1898, General Electric Company Birmingham circa 1950, p. 10.

31. SA D1287/18/26 (Q/78) Business Correspondence of 2nd Earl inc. Rickman & Hussey; D1287/18/34 (F/791) receipts inc Rickman & Hussey; SA D1287/M/97 Plans for alterations at Castle Bromwich inc screen in hall, hall ceiling and hall fireplace 1837–8.

32. SA D1287/add 2011/1.

33. www.ladycharlottesdiaries.co.uk.

34. Close to Weston he acquired land at Blymhill; Bridgeman, Rev. Ernest R.O. & Bridgeman, Charles G.O. (eds), 'History of the Manor and Parish of Weston-under-Lizard, in the County of Stafford compiled from the MSS. Of the Late Rev. The Hon. George T.O. Bridgeman Rector of Wigan', in *Collections for a History of Staffordshire*, Vol. XX (Vol. II New Series), London, 1899, p. 285.

35. Taylor, Angus (ed. by Janet Martin), *The Websters of Kendal: A North-Western Architectural Dynasty*, Kendal, 2004, pp. 129–30.

36. Oxford Archaeology North, *Historic Landscape Survey: St Catherine's Windermere, Cumbria*, February 2005, p. 31.

37. The travelling coach commissioned by the 2nd Earl from Thrupp in 1842, and which has recently been restored by the Weston Park Foundation, has a drop brake which would have been helpful to the horses in hill country like that around Windermere.

38. SA D1287/18/26 K/101/1 and 24 June 1840 Potter to Lord Bradford containing Durant's letter.

39. www.ladycharlottesdiaries.co.uk.

40. Much of his patronage has been examined and discussed by Davis, Diana, *The Tastemaker: British Dealers and the Anglo-Gallic Interior, 1785–1865*, Los Angeles, CA, 2020, pp. 254–6.

41. SA D1287/4/2 (R/121) Receipted bills for Belgrave Square.

42. Ibid.

43. SA D1287/4/2/7.

44. Ibid.

45. http://ladycharlottesdiaries.co.uk/Search/ShowFound Entry.php?Entry=1846-08-21&Key=Hollins.

46. http://ladycharlottesdiaries.co.uk/Search/ShowFound Entry.php?Entry=1850-11-12&Key=Hollins.

47. BA ZBR/5/9 1848.

48. *Walsall Free Press*, Saturday 1 April 1865, 'LATE EARL OF BRADFORD'.

49. He was son of Sir George Gunning, 2nd Bt (MP for Wigan 1800–2), and the Hon. Elizabeth Bridgeman, daughter of Sir Henry Bridgeman, 5th Bt and 1st Baron Bradford.

50. BA ZBR/5/2/44 Gunning to Lord Bradford letter re lease of mines and application of £2,000 towards repair of rectory.

51. Bridgeman & Bridgeman, op. cit., 1899, p. 285, fn. 3.

52. Farrer, William and Brownbill, J (eds), *A History of the County of Lancaster: Volume 4*, London, 1911, pp. 57–68.

53. This, however, was demolished in 1956 and a date-stone that it supported was reset into a new north gable at the point of truncation.

54. Bridgeman, The Hon. & Rev. George T.O., *The History of the Church and Manor of Wigan in the County of Lancaster*, Vols 15, 16, 17, 18, Chetham Society, Manchester, 1888, p. 678.

55. Bridgeman & Bridgeman, op. cit., 1899, p. 286.

56. 'Memories of the Sisters', typescript, nd.

CHAPTER EIGHT *The Reign of Victoria*

1. Harwood, Helen, *Staffordshire Coal Mines*, Stafford, 2018.

2. Pennant was also a hunting companion of the Ladies' brother Orlando. See Bridgeman, Orlando George C., Viscount Newport, *Hunting Journal Kept By Viscount Newport at Newport Lodge, Melton Mowbray …*, London, 1889, p. 104 for 2 February 1852.

3. V & A accession number 3817–1953.

4. *Annual Register* 1859, pp. 452/3 and *The Gentleman's Magazine*, Vol. 206 (1859), p. 04. Both publications give the place of the accident as the Drawing Room which is the room now known as the Tapestry Room.

5. During his lifetime, he also extended the Weston Park estate with purchases of property at Blymhill, Church Eaton, Sheriffhales, and Shifnal, including the Lizard Hill. See Bridgeman & Bridgeman, op. cit., 1899, p. 290.

6. Brownlow, Jack, *Melton Mowbray: Queen of the Shires*, Sycamore Press, 1980, pp. 184–8. The house was sold by the Bradfords soon after 1900 and was demolished in the 1930s.

7. Ibid.

8. These include Rowton, Teddy the Tiler, The Engineer and Tom of Lincoln. Another of the hunters, Planet, is also represented and the diary relates that this horse – 'perhaps the best horse I ever had' – was miraculously saved from a pitchfork injury by the Whatton vet, Mr Talbot. See Bridgeman, Orlando George C., Viscount Newport, op. cit., p. 176 fn.

9. Bridgeman, Orlando George C., Viscount Newport, op. cit., p. 112 for 3 February 1853.

10. Noted as such in Weston Park MS 'Inventory of Furniture, China, Etc. At Weston, 1910', when displayed in the Family Staircase.

11. Hussey's plans are signed and dated May 1862 SA D1287/M/664, 665, and 666. The building accounts for the new wing are SA D1287/3/39/R643 (part).

12. Building accounts SA D1287/3/39 R/643.

13. SA D1287/R/617 R.C. Hussey letter to Lord Bradford, 29 August 1865, including Forsyth's bill dated London, 25 August 1865.

14. SHA 818/49 Weston Park 1866 Ground Plan.

15. SA D1287 add 2011–5.

16. The additional plasterwork was added in 1870: SA D1287/R/633 May 16 1870 MacVicar Anderson Sketches.

17. SA D1287/R/621 George Trollope 1868 bill.

18. SA 818/63 and SA D1287 add 2011–10 and 11.

19. SA D1287 add 2011–12.

20. SA D1287/R/620 Turner & Co Bill.

21. SA D1287/R/625 William Burn, Stratton Street, letter to Lord Bradford, 24 May 1869.

22. Bridgeman, Rev. Ernest R.O. & Bridgeman, Charles G.O. (eds), 'History of the Manor and Parish of Weston-under-Lizard, in the County of Stafford compiled from the MSS. Of the Late Rev. The Hon. George T.O. Bridgeman Rector of Wigan', in *Collections for a History of Staffordshire*, Vol. XX (Vol. II New Series), London, 1899, p. 290.

23. SA D1287/R/624 J. Burch, Clerk of Works' Account.

24. SA D1287/M/306 1878 Plans by Edward Kemp.

25. SA D1287/19/8(R/692) Weston Park Visitor Book 1873–189.8

26. See Murphy, N.T.P., *In Search of Blandings*, London, 1981, pp. 213–31.

27. Zetland, The Marquis of (ed.), *The Letters of Disraeli to Lady Bradford and Lady Chesterfield Vol. I*, London, 1929, p. 75, Disraeli to Selina, Countess of Bradford, 20 April 1874.

28. Ibid., *Vol. I*, p. 81, Disraeli to Selina, Countess of Bradford, 5 May 1874.

29. Ibid., p. 177 6 December 1874 Disraeli to Selina, Countess of Bradford concerning muffetees knitted by Lady Bradford.

30. Ibid., p. 75 Disraeli to Anne, Countess of Chesterfield, 27 August 1874. Later in his letters, Disraeli noted that in 1877 Princess Christian, Queen Victoria and Prince Albert's third daughter, visited the family at St Catherine's.

31. Ibid., p. 145, Disraeli to Selina Countess of Bradford, 7 September 1874.

32. Bridgeman, John, *I Remember it Well: The Diaries, Recollections and Art of Three Generations over Three Centuries*, Washington, DC, 2015, p. 63.

33. Zetland, The Marquis of (ed.), *The Letters of Disraeli to Lady Bradford and Lady Chesterfield Vol. II*, London, 1929, p. 169, Disraeli to Selina, Countess of Bradford, 8 June 1876.

34. *Bye-Gones* 6 July 1910, p. 232, where the writer, J.H.C., noted that a part of the park was still known as 'Charcoal Hearth'.

35. SA D1287/9/11 K/109 Potter to Lord Bradford, 9 November 1844. Peter Potter had written to Lord Bradford whilst Durant was on his death bed that: 'He [Durant's son Ernest] spoke (rather heartlessly, I am compelled to say) of his father's decease as being hourly expected, two physicians from Birmingham being constantly in attendance upon him, and that Your Lordship upon your next visit to Weston would perceive that the Tong monument was no longer standing, as he (Mr. E. Durant) was taking present steps to blow it up with gunpowder! I hardly know what he meant but certainly there was nothing like intoxication apparent. I am inclined to think in the event of Mr. Durant's death some extra-ordinary attempts will be made.'

36. Rough, John R.C., 'The Black Sheep of the Family', typescript at Weston Park (nd) and Francis Leach (ed.), *The County Seats of Shropshire*, Shrewsbury, 1891, p. 350.

37. Bridgeman & Bridgeman, op. cit., 1899, pp. 310–11.

38. Ibid., p. 335 and SA D1287/M/447 Elevations and sections of Weston-under-Lizard almshouses.

39. SA D1287/R/633 John MacVicar Anderson Mausoleum plan 1867.

40. Drawings for the alternatives in SHA 818/66 and /62.

41. Correspondence in SA inc. D1287/R/642 Completion certificate for the Mortuary Chapel, 6 July 1872 by MacVicar Anderson, R. Yates as builder. Total cost £1194-10-10. Bridgeman & Bridgeman, op. cit., 1899, p. 335 note that it was begun in 1870 in memory of the Bradford's third son, the Hon. Gerald Bridgeman, who died that year.

42. Disraeli wrote to Lord Bradford, 7 January 1875, to ask him to permit his name being put forward. See Zetland, op cit., vol. I, p. 190.

43. This same subject was painted by Lutyens for the Duke of Westminster in 1880, exhibited with an 1884 painting of the Royal Mews by the Trustees of the Grosvenor Estate in the exhibition *C.H.A. Lutyens*, at The Towner Art Gallery, Eastbourne and The Guildhall, Winchester, 1971 as Nos. 47 & 48 respectively. I am grateful to Mark Lutyens for drawing this to my attention.

44. Zetland (ed.), op. cit., Vol. I, London, 1929, p. 269, Disraeli to Selina, Countess of Bradford, 29 July 1875.

45. Ibid., Vol. II, p. 84, Disraeli to Selina, Countess of Bradford, 24 October 1876.

46. Ibid., Vol. II, p. 243, Disraeli to the Countess of Bradford, October 1879.

47. Ibid., Vol. II, p. 81, Disraeli to Selina, Countess of Bradford.

48. Rogers, Cathal, 'Land Agents and Urban Aristocratic Estates in Nineteenth Century Staffordshire: a Comparison of Longton and Walsall', PhD thesis, University of Keele, 2018, pp. 132, 175–7.

49. Ibid., p. 196.

50. Ex inf. Bolton Documentary Photography.

51. SA D1287/8/6 (M635A-B) Tapestry Room Jan. 1882.

52. SHA 818/71 Dining Room and Housekeeper's Room alterations 1893.

53. *The Newport & Market Drayton Advertiser*, 'Coming of Age of the Honourable Orlando Bridgeman'.

54. *The Parish Almanack for Weston-under-Lyziard*, Newport, 1895, p. 40.

55. Ibid., pp. 35–6.

56. Ibid., p. 33.

57. Weston Park MS 'Inventory of Furniture, China, Etc. At Weston, 1910'.

58. Ex inf. Eaton Hall Estate Office.

59. *The Parish Almanack for Weston-under-Lyziard*, Newport, 1895, p. 44.

60. Bridgeman, John, op cit., 2015, p. 22.

CHAPTER NINE   *Edwardian Weston*

1. Lady Beatrice Bridgeman (1870–1952) married on 28 June 1894 to Colonel Rt Hon. Ernest George Pretyman (1859–1931); Lady Margaret Alice Bridgeman (1872–1954) married John Montagu Douglas Scott, 7th Duke of Buccleuch, on 30 January 1893 and had issue, one being Princess Alice, Duchess of Gloucester; Orlando Bridgeman, 5th Earl of Bradford (1873–1957); Lady Helena Mary Bridgeman (1875–1947) married

Osbert Molyneux, 6th Earl of Sefton, on 8 January 1898; Lady Florence Sibell Bridgeman (1877–1936) married Ronald Collet Norman, on 10 February 1904; Commander The Hon. Richard Orlando Beaconsfield Bridgeman (28 February 1879–9 January 1917); Lieutenant-Colonel The Hon. Henry Bridgeman (1882–1972) married on 30 December 1930 to Joan Constable-Maxwell (1901–1991).

2. Bridgeman, John, *I Remember it Well: The Diaries, Recollections and Art of Three Generations over Three Centuries*, Washington, DC, 2015, p. 10.

3. Zetland, The Marquis of (ed.), *The Letters of Disraeli to Lady Bradford and Lady Chesterfield Vol. I*, London, 1929, p. 74, Disraeli to Selina, Countess of Bradford, 20 April 1874.

4. Some of the spoils of his travels were noted by his wife Lady Ida in her Weston Park MS Inventory of Furniture, China, Etc. at Weston, 1910, including '2 carved wood Pedestals with Boys holding Shells' that had come from Rome and '1 Persian Rug 15 ft x 6 ft' which had come from Tangiers and were to be found in the Marble Hall.

5. Included in Bridgeman, John, op. cit., as pp. 69–110.

6. Weston Park Collection MS Inventory of Furniture, China, Etc. at Weston, 1910, '1 oil Painting Fire Screen in Gilt Frame', and '1 Red plush painted & gilt 3 fold Screen' – both in the Tapestry Room.

7. Zetland, The Marquis of (ed.), *The Letters of Disraeli to Lady Bradford and Lady Chesterfield Vol. II*, London, 1929, p. 53, Disraeli to Lady Chesterfield, 11 June 1876.

8. A chimneypiece of similar design is shown in the drawing room of Tong Castle in family photographs of the Hartley family taken in circa 1890.

9. SHA 818/73 & 75 1899 plans.

10. Bridgeman, John, op. cit., p. 22.

11. *Oswestry & Border Counties Advertiser*, 13 May 1896, 'Discovery of a Valuable Mineral Spring at Knockin'.

12. SA D1287 Box 38: Weston Hall 1.

13. Bridgeman, John, op. cit., p. 27.

14. Ibid., p. 19.

15. Ibid., p. 24.

16. Ibid., p. 68.

17. Lees-Milne, James, *Prophesying Peace*, London, 1986, p. 62.

18. Bridgeman, John, op. cit., p. 52.

19. Ex inf. Bolton Documentary Photography.

20. Ibid.

21. Weston Park Collection MS Inventory of Furniture, China, Etc. at Weston, 1910, 'One long old Oak Dresser brought about 1900 from Great Lever Hall – Date Carved on 1649', when in the Front Hall.

22. D1287/1995/W7/8/8 Scrapbook – *Bolton Chronicle* Cutting, p. 43.

23. Ex inf. Bolton Documentary Photography.

24. Bridgeman, John, op. cit., p. 27.

25. Weston Park MS Inventory of Furniture, China, Etc. at Weston, 1910, in Lord Bradford's sitting room '2 Ivory Statuettes of Popes (?)' from Corsica and in Marble Hall '1 'Coffere de Marriage' Florentine' from Lugano, and '2 Greek Cups' from Athens.

26. SA D1287/5/5(P/456) Memo by 4th Earl for his executors re his wishes to be carried out after his death including Disraeli's letters.

27. SA D1287/18/1(P/611) Letter to 5th Earl from Lady Ida, 18 June 1936.

28. Weston Park MS Inventory of Furniture, China, Etc. at Weston, 1910.

29. The Burton provenance pieces are: Henry Clay Frick Bequest 1915.8.51 and 1915.8.52.

30. Weston Park MS Inventory of Furniture, China, Etc. at Weston, 1910.

31. The correspondence including designs is in SA D1287 R/729 Armorial Dessert Service. Coalport wrote on 5 March 1908 to confirm that the identities of the artists and gilders would be marked on the pieces.

32. Bridgeman, John, op. cit., p. 30.

33. SA D1287/5/5 (P/446) Epitome of 4th Earl's Will 1911.

34. SA D1287/Add11/58/1–30 Diary of 5th Earl of Bradford 1917.

35. Mentioned in The Countess of Bradford, 'Oriental China', unpublished MS, 1912, accession number 111.2555.

36. Bridgeman, John, op. cit., pp. 36 and 43.

37. V & A accession number T.134–1928.

38. Cited in Bridgeman, John, op. cit., p. 45.

39. Cited in Bridgeman, John, op. cit., p. 51.

CHAPTER TEN *The Reality of the Twentieth Century*

1. Bridgeman, John, *I Remember it Well: The Diaries, Recollections and Art of Three Generations over Three Centuries*, Washington, DC, 2015, p. 24.

2. SA D1287/1997/13/14.

3. SA D1287/ADD/1986(C/309/26) Letter to Lord Bradford from Godfrey Kopp asking to buy Gobelin tapestries, 13 January 1915.

4. SA D1287/Add11/58/1–30 5th Earl's diary – 1919.

5. Sale particulars in Historic England NMR Collection SC00889, 14 June 1913.

6. The Bradfords were presented by the Princess with a gold snuff box decorated with enamel landscapes.

7. SA D1287 Weston Hall: Redecoration Pre WW2 Box 38: Weston Hall 1.

8. SA D1287/Add11/58/1–30.

9. SA D1287/Add11/58/1–30 Pocket diary of Orlando 5th Earl of Bradford 1925 'Mr Blomfield (architect) came from London to discuss Squash Court' – presumably Sir Reginald Blomfield (1856–1942, in fact Kt. 1919).

10. SA D1287/M/361–366 14 November 1929 Bayliss, Jones and Bayliss Ltd., Victoria Works, Wolverhampton. Letter and drawings.

11. These alterations and dates detailed in Weston Park MS, 'Record of Some Alterations at Weston Park Since 1918'.

12. SA 1921 Diary of 5th Earl of Bradford 25 November 1921 ref to Mr Tindel [sic] coming to estimate for the drawing room and 1 December when the Bradfords visit Tilden at his London house. D1287/Add11/58/1–30 Pocket diary of Orlando 5th Earl of Bradford 1925.

13. Father of Zita and Teresa 'Baby', two of the 'Bright Young Things'.

14. SA D1287/5/5(P/456) Memo by 4th Earl for his executors re his wishes to be carried out after his death including Disraeli's letters.

15. SA D1287/2004/5/1/2/34 Wilson Lovatt & Sons Ltd to Messrs. Gerald Wellesley and Trenwith Wells.

16. Heffer, Simon (ed.), *Henry 'Chips' Channon: The Diaries 1918–1938*, London, 2021, p. 235, 11 August 1926.

17. Ibid., pp. 243–4, 24 November 1926.

18. Beaton, Cecil, *The Book of Beauty*, London, 1933, p. 32.

19. Lees-Milne, James, *Midway on the Waves*, London 1985, p. 201

20. Weston Park MS, 'Record of Some Alterations at Weston Park Since 1918'. Bakers had exhibited at Chelsea in 1934. Elliott, B., 'The British Rock Garden in the Twentieth Century', in *Occasional Papers from The RHS Lindley Library*, Volume Six (May 2011), p. 36.

21. Lees-Milne, James, *Prophesying Peace*, London, 1986, p. 236.

22. Ibid., pp. 236–7.

23. Sales took place on 19, 20 Sept and 14/15 Dec 1944, and also 6, 7 March 1945 – ex inf. June Ellis.

24. Neal, Toby, *Shropshire Airfields*, Telford, 2005, pp. 134–8.

25. Weston Park MS, 'Record of Some Alterations at Weston Park Since 1918'.

26. Lees-Milne, op cit., 1986, p. 62.

27. Ibid.

28. Parrish, Heather, *Knockin: A Brief History*, 1995, p. 22.

29. This did not include the ducal residence of Endsleigh Cottage which was initially acquired by a fishing club.

30. SA D1287/2004/5/5/1 Leaton Knolls Papers. The house was also considered for a school, married army officers' accommodation or as a hotel.

31. Ex inf. Bolton Documentary Photography.

32. Sotheby's, lots 77–80, 16 November 1962.

33. SA D1287/2004/5/1/1/6 Weston Hall papers 1952–1965 Includes redecoration 1959–63.

34. Ibid. Originally the intention was to leave the oak boards in the smoking room.

35. Probably by Perry & Co. and which had originally been from Lanrick Castle, Perthshire.

36. SA D1287/M/5000 Design for No. 2 Bedroom by Charles Hammond Ltd, nd.

37. SA D1287/M/5001 Alternative design for the Tapestry Room ceiling 1966 & Jacksons' correspondence SA

D1287/1997/18/10 Plans & letter re re-arrangement of Tapestry Room.

38. *The Wellington Journal and Shrewsbury News*, 15 November 1963, 'Salop Stately Home to Be Open'.

39. *Express & Star*, 29 April 1964, 'Praise from the Earl for Mr. T. after the "Dress Rehearsal"'.

40. *Express & Star*, 22 May 1964, 'Bumper Figures'.

41. *Telegraph*, 28 October 1964, 'Stately Homes Record Bumper Season: Best Year Since the War'.

42. Millar, Oliver, 'Van Dyck and Sir Thomas Hanmer', *The Burlington Magazine*, Vol. 100, No. 664 (July 1958), pp. 247–9. The Barton Hall Hanmer, by then in the Cleveland Museum, Ohio, was subsequently deaccessioned and was with the London dealer Leger in 1960.

43. Millar, Oliver, 'Van Dyck and Thomas Killigrew', *The Burlington Magazine*, Vol. 105, No. 726 (Sept. 1963), p. 409 revealed that it was the 'Mr *Tho. Killigrew*, with a Mastiff' of 41 by 3 in. that had been recorded as sold from Lely's collection.

44. Strutt & Parker: Weston Park: Feasibility Study – Stage 1, October 1971. Farming changes were also implemented in the years following the report and there was a dispersal sale of the Home Farm at Weston Park on Lord Bradford's instructions, which included the sale of 177 Hereford-cross nurse cows and Charolaise heifers in November 1977 – see SA SC/43/4.

45. The books were at Sotheby's on 18 July 1967, lots 401–424, with the plays forming lot 407; the prints were sold at the same house on 25 July 1967, lots 135–157.

46. British Museum 1975, 0621.22.

47. The 1978 Christie's library sales also included 8 November lots 118, 122, 178, 181; 25 October lots 283, 284, 309, 311, 316, 320, 380, 385, 402; 15 November lots 55–66.

48. Christie's, 21 November 1980, lot 38 was Thomas Weaver's *Spaniel with Jacobe a German Servant*, lot 39 a pair of Marmaduke Craddocks; 18 December lot 68 nine works by Frans Francken the younger; lot 69 Venetian school *Portrait of a Gentleman*; 23 January 1981 comprised lots 156–160. Some items which remained in the family's ownership after 1986 have also since been sold including: Paul Bril, *Cadmus and the Dragon* (lot 2, Sotheby's London, 12 December 2002; Giovanni de Momper, *A Landscape With Classical Ruins, Horses and Peasants* (lot 202, Sotheby's London, 12 December 2002; Filippo Lauri, *Glaucus and Scylla* (lot 192, Sotheby's London, 12 December 2002).

CHAPTER ELEVEN   *The Weston Park Foundation*

1. Auction by Bidwells at Pack Horse Hotel, Nelson Square, Bolton on 16 June 1983. The estate retained the freehold ownership of sportsgrounds and of Bolton railway station.

2. Full details of the establishment of the charity and ongoing references for the facts contained in this

chapter are to be found in the minutes of Trustees' Meetings of the Weston Park Foundation 1986–2022, archived at Weston Park.

3. Byrne, N., for Smiths Gore, 'Weston Park, Staffordshire: Preliminary Review', 24 June 1986.

Bibliography

Archives

Beinecke Rare Books Library, Yale University, New Haven, CT
    Osborn fb214
Bolton Archives, Bolton
    ZBR/3/1
Public Records Office
    PROB 11/345/321
Shropshire Archives
    SHA 818/73 & 75 John MacVicar Anderson plans
Staffordshire Archives, Stafford
    D1287 – Bradford MS

Weston Park Collection
    Byrne, N., for Smiths Gore, 'Weston Park, Staffordshire:
        Preliminary Review', 24 June 1986
    Inventory of Furniture at Weston, MS 1910
    'Record of Some Alterations at Weston Park Since
        1918', MS 1918
    Strutt & Parker: 'Weston Park: Feasibility Study – Stage
        1', October 1971
    The Countess of Bradford, 'Oriental China', MS, 1912,
        accession number 111.2555

Other sources

Aiken, John, *A Description of the Country from Thirty to
    Forty Miles Round Manchester*, London, 1792
Andrews, C. Bruyn (ed.), *The Torrington Diaries*, vol. 3,
    New York and London, 1970
Barre, D.C. and Chaplin, R.A. (eds), 'William Winde: Advice
    on Fashionable Interior Decoration: Winde–Bridgeman
    Correspondence for Castle Bromwich Hall 1685–1703',
    typescript, 1983
Baugh, G.C. (ed.), *Victoria County of Shropshire*, Vol. XI,
    Oxford, 1985
Beal, Mary, 'The Royalist Richard Symonds and an
    Unclaimed Portrait by Sir Peter Lely', *The British Art
    Journal*, Vol. XVII, No. 1 (Spring 2016), pp. 16–21
Beard, Geoffrey W., 'Weston Hall: Staffordshire Home of the
    Earl of Bradford', in *The Connoisseur Year Book, 1955*,
    London, 1955, pp. 22–32
———, 'William Winde and Interior Design', in
    *Architectural History, vol. 27, Design and Practice in
    British Architecture: Studies in Architectural History
    Presented to Howard Colvin* (1984), pp. 150–62
Beaton, Cecil, *The Book of Beauty*, London, 1933
Bell, Mrs G.H. (ed), *The Hamswood Papers of the Ladies of
    Llangollen and Caroline Hamilton*, London, 1930
Blakiston, Georgiana, *Woburn and the Russells*, London,
    2000
Bloom Edward A. & Bloom, Lillian D., *The Piozzi Letters,
    Vol. I 1784–1791*, Newark, DE, London & Toronto,
    1989
———, *The Piozzi Letters Vol. 3 1799–1804*, Newark, DE,
    London and Toronto, 1993
———, *The Piozzi Letters Vol. 4 1805–1810*, Newark, DE,
    London and Toronto, 1996
Boyle, K.C.B, Sir Courtenay, *Mary Boyle: Her Book*,
    London, 1902

Bradford, Lady Ida, Countess of, 'Castle Bromwich Hall,
    Warwickshire: A Property of the Earl of Bradford',
    reprinted from an article published in the *Pall
    Mall Magazine*, 1898, General Electric Company,
    Birmingham, circa 1950
Bridgeman, Rev. Ernest R.O. & Bridgeman, Charles G.O.
    (eds), 'History of the Manor and Parish of Weston-
    under-Lizard, in the County of Stafford compiled
    from the MSS. Of the Late Rev. The Hon. George
    T.O. Bridgeman Rector of Wigan', in *Collections for a
    History of Staffordshire*, Vol. XX (Vol. II New Series),
    London, 1899
Bridgeman, The Hon. & Rev. George T.O., *The History
    of the Church and Manor of Wigan in the County
    of Lancaster*, Vols 15, 16, 17, 18, Chetham Society,
    Manchester, 1888
———, *Genealogical Account of the Family of Newport
    of High Ercall, in the County of Salop, afterwards
    Earls of Bradford*, printed by W.J. Rowley, High Street,
    Bridgnorth, nd (1851)
Bridgeman, John, *I Remember it Well: The Diaries,
    Recollections and Art of Three Generations over Three
    Centuries*, Washington, DC, 2015
Bridgeman, Orlando George C., Viscount Newport,
    *Hunting Journal Kept By Viscount Newport at
    Newport Lodge, Melton Mowbray …*, London, 1889,
    p. 112, for 3 February 1853
Brown, Ralph Sharp and Lewis, Wilmarth Sheldon (eds),
    *Horace Walpole's Correspondence with George
    Montagu*, New Haven, CT, 1941
Brownlow, Jack, *Melton Mowbray: Queen of the Shires*,
    Sycamore Press, 1980
Clarke, Bridget, 'William Taylor: New Discoveries',
    Georgian Group Journal, Vol. VIII (1998), pp. 1–11

Colvin, Howard, *A Biographical Dictionary of British Architects 1600–1840*, New Haven, CT and London, 2008

Davis, Diana, *The Tastemaker: British Dealers and the Anglo-Gallic Interior, 1785–1865*, Los Angeles, CA, 2020

Dethloff, Diana, 'The Dispersal of Sir Peter Lely's Collection', *Journal of the History of Collections*, Vol. 8, No. 1 (1996), p. 18

Elliott, B., 'The British Rock Garden in the Twentieth Century', *Occasional Papers from The RHS Lindley Library*, Vol. 6 (May 2011), p. 36

Everard, Judith, Bowen, James P. and Horton, Wendy, *The Victoria County History of Shropshire: Wem*, London, 2019

Farrer, William and Brownbill, J. (eds), *A History of the County of Lancaster: Volume 4*, London, 1911

Fleming, Simon D.I. and Perkins, Martin (eds), *Music by Subscription: Composers and their Networks in the British Music-Publishing Trade 1676–1820*, Oxford and London, 2022 (forthcoming), chapter 8

Friedman, Terry, *James Gibbs*, New Haven, CT & London, 1984

Garbet, Samuel, *The History of Wem*, Shrewsbury, 1982

Glew, Edward Lees, *History of the Borough and Foreign of Walsall*, Walsall, 1856

Glover, Gareth (ed.), *A Young Gentleman at War: The Letters of Captain Orlando Bridgeman, 1st Foot Guards, in the Peninsula and at Waterloo 1812–15*, Ken Trotman Publishing, 2008

Goodison, Nicholas, *Matthew Boulton: Ormolu*, London, 2002

Gough, Richard, *Human Nature Displayed in the History of Myddle*, New York, 1968

Hamilton-Miller, Sue, *Richmond House and its Inhabitants*, Richmond, nd

Harris, John, 'William Taylor: Further Attributions', *Georgian Group Journal*, Vol. VIII (1998), pp. 12–18

Harwood, Helen, *Staffordshire Coal Mines*, Stafford, 2018

Hawkins, Edward (ed.), 'Travels in Holland the United Provinces England Scotland and Ireland …', in *Remains Historical & Literary Connected with the Palatine Counties of Lancaster and Chester Published by the Chetham Society*, Vol. 1, 1844

Heffer, Simon (ed.), *Henry 'Chips' Channon: The Diaries 1918–1938*, London, 2021

Hewlings, Richard, 'Achitaphel's Architect', *Georgian Group Journal*, Vol. XVI (2008), pp. 3–4

———, 'The Architect of Weston Park, *Georgian Group Journal*, Vol. XIX (2012), pp. 22–32

———, 'The Contriver of Chirk', in *National Trust Historic Houses and Collections Annual, Apollo*, June 2012

Hussey, Christopher, 'Weston Park, Staffordshire I', *Country Life*, 9 November 1945, pp. 818, 865

———, 'Weston Park, Staffordshire II, *Country Life*, 16 November 1945

Ingamells, John, *A Dictionary of British and Irish Travellers in Italy 1701–1800*, New Haven, CT & London

Ironside, Edward, *History and Antiquities of Twickenham …*, London, 1797

Keynes, Milo, 'The Portrait of Dr William Harvey in the Royal Society Since 1683', *Notes & Records of the Royal Society*, Vol. 60, No. 3 (22 Sept. 2006), p. 251

Leach, Francis (ed.), *The County Seats of Shropshire*, Shrewsbury, 1891

Leach, Peter, *James Paine*, London, 1988

Lees-Milne, James, *Midway on the Waves*, London, 1985

———, *Prophesying Peace*, London, 1986

Leighton, Rachel (ed.), *Correspondence of Charlotte Grenville, Lady Williams-Wynn and Her Three Sons*, London, 1920

Leslie, C.R. (ed.), *Memoirs of the Life of John Constable*, London, 1937

Lewis, Samuel, *A Topographical Dictionary of England*, London, 1848

Lines, Charles, *Weston Park and the Earls of Bradford*, Leamington Spa, 1972

Macky, John, *Memoirs of the Secret Services of John Macky, Esq., During the Reigns of King William, Queen Anne, and King George I*, London, 1733

Markham, Sarah, *John Loveday of Caversham 1711–1789*, Norwich, 1984

Mavor, Elizabeth, *A Year with the Ladies of Llangollen*, Harmondsworth, 1984

McGuffie, T.H., 'The Lord Bradford Militia Documents in the Shire Hall, Shrewsbury, Salop', *Journal of the Society for Army Historical Research*, Vol. XLIV, No. 179 (September 1966), pp. 135–46

Midgley, M. (ed.), *Victoria County History of Staffordshire, Volume IV: Staffordshire Doomsday and West Cuttleston Hundred*, Oxford, 1958

Millar, Oliver, 'Van Dyck and Sir Thomas Hanmer', *The Burlington Magazine*, Vol. 100, No. 664 (July 1958), pp. 247–9

Millar, Oliver, 'Van Dyck and Thomas Killigrew', *The Burlington Magazine*, Vol. 105, No. 726 (Sept. 1963), p. 409

Moore, Gerry & Twist, Anthony, *Weeting Worthies*, Weeting History Group, 2004

Morris, Christopher (ed.), *The Illustrated Journals of Celia Fiennes 1685–c.1712*, Stroud, 1995

Mostyn-Owen, William & Sawtell, Richard, *Weston Park guidebook*, 2004

Murphy, N.T.P., *In Search of Blandings*, London, 1981

Myddelton, W.M. (ed.), *Chirk Castle Accounts AD 1666–1753*, Horncastle, 1931, pp. 100, 102 cited in Richard Hewlings, 'The Contriver of Chirk' in *National Trust Historic Houses and Collections Annual, Apollo*, June 2012

Neal, Toby, *Shropshire Airfields*, Telford, 2005

Paine, James, *Plans, elevations and sections of Noblemen and Gentlemen's Houses* (1767 and 1783)

Parrish, Heather, *Knockin: A Brief History*, 1995

Phillips, W. (ed.), 'Sequestration Papers of Sir Richard, First Baron Newport and Francis, his son', *TSANHS*, 2nd Series, Vol. XII (1900), pp. 1–38

Piercy, John S., *The History of Retford*, Retford, 1828

Pitt, William, *A Topographical History of Staffordshire …*, Newcastle-under-Lyme, 1817

Plot, Robert, *The Natural History of Stafford-shire …*, Oxford, 1686

Pritchard, T.W., *Wynnstay and the Wynns*, Caerwys, 1982

Robinson, John Martin, *Georgian Model Farms*, Oxford, 1983

Rogers, Phillis, 'A Regency Interior: The Remodelling of Weston Park', *Furniture History Society* (1987), pp. 11–34

Rogers, Cathal, 'Land Agents and Urban Aristocratic Estates in Nineteenth Century Staffordshire: a Comparison of Longton and Walsall', PhD thesis, University of Keele, 2018

Rough, John R.C., 'The Black Sheep of the Family', typescript at Weston

Rowell, Christopher (ed.), *Ham House: 400 Years of Collecting and Patronage*, New Haven, CT & London, 2013

Scott, Walter (ed.), *The Poetical Works of Anna Seward*, Vol. II, Edinburgh, 1810

Shuttleworth, J.M. (ed.), *The Life of Edward, First Lord Herbert of Cherbury Written by Himself*, London, New York & Toronto, 1976

Smith, William James, 'Letters from Michael Wright', *The Burlington Magazine*, Vol. 95, No. 604 (July 1953), p. 234

Smith, Peter, 'Rufford Abbey and its Gardens in the 17th and 18th Centuries', *English Heritage Historical Review*, Volume 4 (2009), pp. 122–53

———, 'West Dean House, Wiltshire', *Georgian Group Journal*, Vol. IX (1999), pp. 86–106

Southall, Mark & Maddocks, Robert (eds), *Extracts from the Personal Diary between the Years 1817–1862 of Edward Walhouse Littleton afterwards The First Lord Littleton 1791–1863*, ND

Stamper, Dr Paul, 'Blodwell Hall: Report for Shropshire Sites and Monuments Record', 1994

Taylor, Angus, *The Websters of Kendal: A North-Western Architectural Dynasty*, ed. Janet Martin, Kendal, 2004

Tucker, Alan, 'The Economic Exploitation of the Earl of Bradford's Walsall Estate (1802–1865)', MA thesis, Wolverhampton Polytechnic, 1983

Vertue Note Books Vol. I, *Walpole Society* (18th Vol.), Oxford, 1930

Vertue Note Books Vol. II, *Walpole Society* (20th Vol.), Oxford, 1932

Vertue Note Books Vol. IV, *Walpole Society* (24th Vol.), Oxford, 1936

Vertue Note Books Vol. V, *Walpole Society* (26th Vol.), Oxford, 1938

Walpole, Horace, *Anecdotes of Painting in England in 4 Volumes*, Vol. II, New York, 1969

Waterhouse, E.K., *Painting in Britain 1530–1790*, London, 1994

Whitehead, David, 'Job Marston's Chapel', *Georgian Group Journal*, Vol. II (1992), pp. 79–81

Wilkins, W.H., *Mrs Fitzherbert & George IV*, London, 1905

Willmore, Frederick William, *A History of Walsall and Its Neighbourhood*, Walsall & London, 1887

Zetland, The Marquis of (ed.), *The Letters of Disraeli to Lady Bradford and Lady Chesterfield Vol. I & Vol. II*, London, 1929

Index

Page numbers in **bold** type refer to illustrations and their captions

NEC · TEMERE   NEC · TIMIDE ·